AF814415

All in One

Recommended by Teachers
Trusted by Toppers

SOCIOLOGY
Class 11

EVERYTHING YOU NEED TO SCORE

- Simplified Theory
- NCERT & Other Important Questions
- CBQs, MCQs, A-R, Case Based
- Sample Question Papers

CBSE Exams 2026

All in one

Recommended by **Teachers**
Trusted by **Toppers**

SOCIOLOGY
Class 11

EVERYTHING YOU NEED TO SCORE

- Simplified Theory
- NCERT & Other Important Questions
- CBQs, MCQs, A-R, Case Based
- Sample Question Papers

CBSE Exams 2026

Author
Saumya Aggarwal

arihant
SUCCESS AND NOTHING LESS

arihant
SUCCESS AND NOTHING LESS

ARIHANT PRAKASHAN
(School Division Series)

卐 *ADMINISTRATIVE & PRODUCTION OFFICES*

Regd. Office
'Ramchhaya' 4577/15, Agarwal Road, Darya Ganj, New Delhi -110002
Tele: 011- 47630600, 43518550; Fax: 011- 23280316

卐 *Head Office*
Kalindi, TP Nagar, Meerut (UP) - 250002, Tel: 0121-7156203, 7156204

卐 *SALES & SUPPORT OFFICES*
Agra, Ahmedabad, Bengaluru, Bareilly, Chennai, Delhi, Guwahati, Hyderabad, Jaipur, Jhansi, Kolkata, Lucknow, Nagpur & Pune.

PO No : TXT-XX-XXXXXXX-X-XX

Published By Arihant Publications (India) Ltd.

For further information about the books published by Arihant, log on to www.arihantbooks.com or e-mail at info@arihantbooks.com

Follow us on

卐 *PRICE* ₹225.00

PRODUCTION TEAM

Publishing Managers
Mahendra Singh Rawat & Keshav Mohan

Cover Designer
Rakesh Rawat

Inner Designer
Ankit Tyagi

Project Head
Manju

Page Layouting
Lalit Chaprana

Proof Reader
Harsh Agarwal

Index *cum* Study Planner

		Studied	Revised	Exam ready
PART A Introducing Sociology				
1. Sociology and Society				
Chapter Theory	3-10	☐	☐	☐
NCERT Folder	11	☐	☐	☐
Exam Pattern Questions	12-19	☐	☐	☐
Self Assessment Test Test	19-20	☐	☐	☐
2. Terms, Concepts and Their Use in Sociology				
Chapter Theory	21-27	☐	☐	☐
NCERT Folder	28	☐	☐	☐
Exam Pattern Questions	29-36	☐	☐	☐
Self Assessment Test	37-38	☐	☐	☐
3. Understanding Social Institutions				
Chapter Theory	39-46	☐	☐	☐
NCERT Folder	46-48	☐	☐	☐
Exam Pattern Questions	48-56	☐	☐	☐
Self Assessment Test	56-57	☐	☐	☐
4. Culture and Socialisation				
Chapter Theory	58-64	☐	☐	☐
NCERT Folder	64-66	☐	☐	☐
Exam Pattern Questions	66-72	☐	☐	☐
Self Assessment Test	72-73	☐	☐	☐
PART B Understanding Society				
1. Social Change and Social Order in Rural and Urban Society				
Chapter Theory	77-85	☐	☐	☐
NCERT Folder	86-88	☐	☐	☐
Exam Pattern Questions	88-93	☐	☐	☐
Self Assessment Test	94-95	☐	☐	☐
2. Introducing Western Sociologists				
Chapter Theory	96-102	☐	☐	☐
NCERT Folder	103-105	☐	☐	☐
Exam Pattern Questions	106-112	☐	☐	☐
Self Assessment Test	113-114	☐	☐	☐
3. Indian Sociologists				
Chapter Theory	115-121	☐	☐	☐
NCERT Folder	122-124	☐	☐	☐
Exam Pattern Questions	125-129	☐	☐	☐
Self Assessment Test	130	☐	☐	☐
Project Work	**133-148**			
Sample Question Papers (1-3)	**151-165**			

One Book- Endless Features

to Help you Succeed

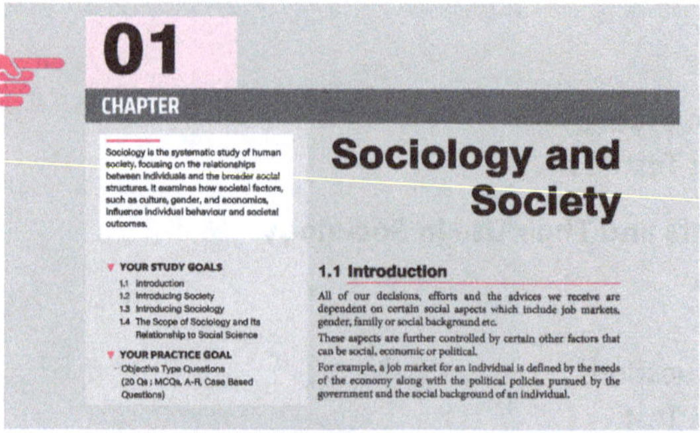
01

CHAPTER

Sociology is the systematic study of human society, focusing on the relationships between individuals and the broader social structures. It examines how societal factors, such as culture, gender, and economics, influence individual behaviour and societal outcomes.

Sociology and Society

YOUR STUDY GOALS
1.1 Introduction
1.2 Introducing Society
1.3 Introducing Sociology
1.4 The Scope of Sociology and its Relationship to Social Science

YOUR PRACTICE GOAL
- Objective Type Questions (20 Qs ; MCQs, A-R, Case Based Questions)

1.1 Introduction

All of our decisions, efforts and the advices we receive are dependent on certain social aspects which include job markets, gender, family or social background etc.

These aspects are further controlled by certain other factors that can be social, economic or political.

For example, a job market for an individual is defined by the needs of the economy along with the political policies pursued by the government and the social background of an individual.

Complete Theory in Each Chapter

Each chapter has Complete, Easy to Understand and Simplified theory covering latest syllabus and rationalised NCERT Textbook. Theory is developed in such a way that it is suitable for all types of learners.

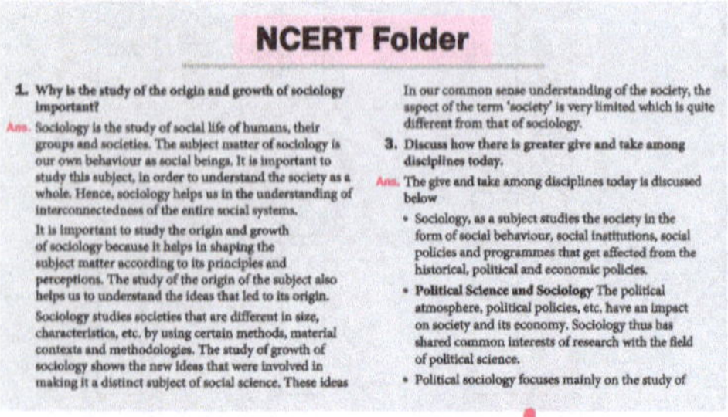
NCERT Folder

1. **Why is the study of the origin and growth of sociology important?**

Ans. Sociology is the study of social life of humans, their groups and societies. The subject matter of sociology is our own behaviour as social beings. It is important to study this subject, in order to understand the society as a whole. Hence, sociology helps us in the understanding of interconnectedness of the entire social systems.

It is important to study the origin and growth of sociology because it helps in shaping the subject matter according to its principles and perceptions. The study of the origin of the subject also helps us to understand the ideas that led to its origin.

Sociology studies societies that are different in size, characteristics, etc. by using certain methods, material contexts and methodologies. The study of growth of sociology shows the new ideas that were involved in making it a distinct subject of social science. These ideas

In our common sense understanding of the society, the aspect of the term 'society' is very limited which is quite different from that of sociology.

3. **Discuss how there is greater give and take among disciplines today.**

Ans. The give and take among disciplines today is discussed below

- Sociology, as a subject studies the society in the form of social behaviour, social institutions, social policies and programmes that get affected from the historical, political and economic policies.
- **Political Science and Sociology** The political atmosphere, political policies, etc. have an impact on society and its economy. Sociology thus has shared common interests of research with the field of political science.
- Political sociology focuses mainly on the study of

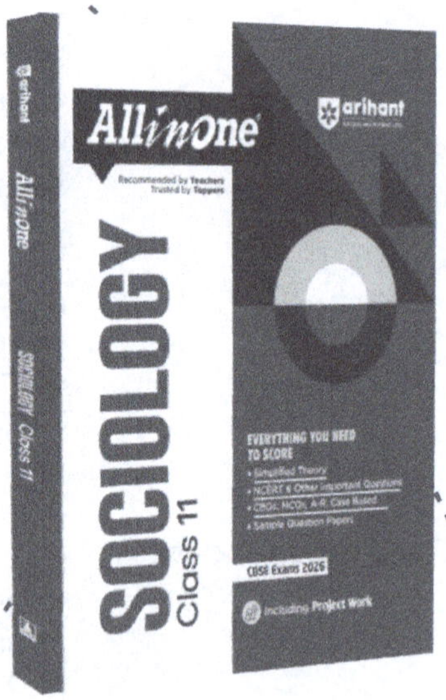

NCERT Folder

Complete explanations of all the questions of NCERT Exercises.

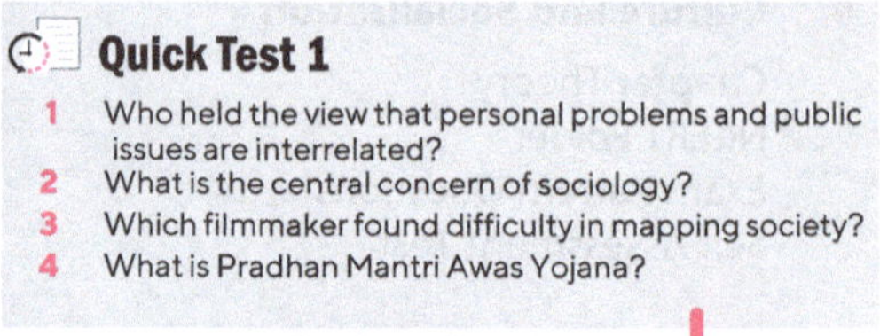
Quick Test 1

1. Who held the view that personal problems and public issues are interrelated?
2. What is the central concern of sociology?
3. Which filmmaker found difficulty in mapping society?
4. What is Pradhan Mantri Awas Yojana?

Quick Test

A set of 4-6 Questions given in between the text, helps students to remain connected with the text while studying. They can instantly assess themselves for their understanding.

One Book- Endless Features

to Help you Succeed

Exam Pattern Questions

Exam Pattern Questions have all types of questions; Objective Type Questions, VSA, SA & LA Type Questions

Exam Pattern Questions

Objective Type Questions

Multiple Choice Questions (MCQs)

1. .... makes an unusual but effective comparison to make the point. In any political or military conflict, it is of advantage to capture the information used by the intelligence organs of the opposing side. But this is so only because good intelligence consists of information free of bias.
(a) M.N. Srinivas (b) Peter Berger
(c) R.K. Lakshman (d) Herbert Spencer

2. The social survey that was based on the belief that human phenomena can be classified and measured. Thinkers of the early modern era were convinced that progress in knowledge promised the solution to all social ills. .... , the French scholar (1789–1857), considered to be the founder of sociology, believed that sociology would contribute to the welfare of humanity. Competency Based Que.
(a) C. Wright Mills (b) Peter Berger
(c) Auguste Comte (d) R.K. Lakshman

(c) The Enlightenment, an European intellectual movement of the late 15th and 16th centuries, emphasised reason and individualism.
(d) Sociology aimed to address social problems such as poverty, inequality and urbanisation.

6. Colonialism was an essential part of modern Capitalism and Industrialisation. The writings of Western sociologists on capitalism and other aspects of modern society are therefore relevant for understanding social change in India. Competency Based Que.
Which of the following is true in the given context?
I. Colonialism is always important to be a capital state.
II. One can get an understanding of society with the help of Western writings.
III. Modern society welcomes the idea of social change.
IV. Modern capitalism and industrialisaton are influenced by colonialism.

SELF ASSESSMENT TEST

Objective Type Questions

1. When of the following has influenced Indian Sociology?
(a) Slavery (b) Capitalism (c) British Colonialism (d) French Revolution

2. Whose study of suicide established a clear scope and method for sociology?
(a) Emile Durkheim (b) Karl Marx (c) Auguste Comte (d) Max Weber

3. Which among the following sociologist is known for his work in political sociology?
(a) Emile Durkheim (b) Auguste Comte (c) Herbert Spencer (d) Max Weber

4. **Assertion** (A) Colonialism was an essential part of modern capitalism and industrialisation.
Reason (R) Sociology in India also had to deal with western writing and ideas about Indian society correct.
(a) Both A and R are true and R is the correct explanation of A.
(b) Both A and R are true but R is not the correct explanation of A.
(c) A is true, but R is false.
(d) A is false, but R is true.

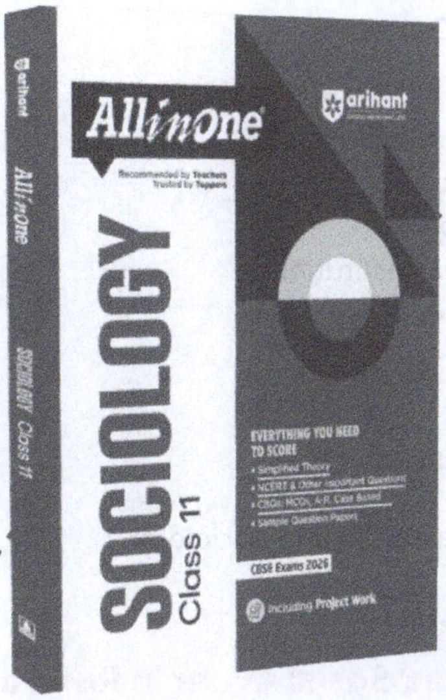

Self Assessment Test

Complete Test of chapter in Exam format.

Sample Question Papers

To make students practice of examination in real sense, there are 3 Sample Question Papers at the end. All these Sample Questions Papers are exactly prepared on the latest syllabus & pattern of examination.

SAMPLE QUESTION PAPER 1

A Highly Simulated Sample Question Paper for CBSE Class XI

SOCIOLOGY

General Instructions

- The question paper is divided into four sections.
- There are 35 questions in all. All questions are compulsory.
- Section A includes question No. 1-16. These are MCQ type questions. As per the question, there can be one answer.
- Section B includes questions 17-25. These are very short answer type questions carrying 2 marks each. Answer to each question should not exceed 30 words.
- Section C includes question No. 26-32. These are short answer type questions carrying 4 marks each. Answer to each question should not exceed 80 words.
- Section D includes question No. 33-35. They are long answer type questions carrying 6 marks each. Answer to each question should not exceed 200 words.

Time : 3 hours **Max. Marks : 80**

Section-A

1 In everyday language, the word .... means unbiased, neutral, or based on facts alone. In order to be neutral about something, we must ignore our own feelings or attitudes about that thing. On the other hand, the word .... means something that is based on individual values and preferences. As you will have learnt already, every science is expected to be neutral, to produce unbiased knowledge based solely on facts. (1)
(a) objective, subjective
(b) subjective, objective
(c) qualitative, quantitative
(d) quantitative, qualitative

3 The human relationships that are highly personal, intimate and enduring, those where a person's involvement is considerable if not total, as in the family, with real friends or a close-knit group. The phenomenon is known as .... (1)
(a) Association
(b) Community
(c) Society
(d) Agreement

4 **Assertion** (A) Women have started doing jobs and have become self sufficient that led to women empowerment.
Reason (R) They live in Patriarchal society. (1)
(a) Both A and R are true and R is the correct explanation of A.
(b) Both A and R are true, but R is not the correct

Latest Course Structure

A INTRODUCING SOCIOLOGY — 44 Marks

UNIT 1 **Sociology, Society and its Relationship with other Social Sciences Disciplines** — **18 Periods**

- Introducing Society: Individuals and collectivities. Pluralities and Inequalities among societies.
- Introducing Sociology: Emergence. Nature and Scope.
- Relationship with other Social Science disciplines

UNIT 2 **Terms, Concepts and their use in Sociology** — **16 Periods**

- Social Groups and Society
- Social Stratification
- Status and Role
- Society & Social Control

UNIT 3 **Understanding Social Institutions** — **20 Periods**

- Family, Marriage and Kinship
- Work & Economic Life
- Political Institutions
- Religion as a Social Institution
- Education as a Social Institution

UNIT 4 **Culture and Socialisation** — **16 Periods**

- Defining Culture
- Dimensions of Culture
- Socialisation
- Agencies of Socialisation and Sociology

B UNDERSTANDING SOCIETY — 36 Marks

UNIT 7 **Social Change and Social Order in Rural and Urban Society** — **20 Periods**

- Social Change: Types, Causes and Consequences
- Social Order: Domination, Authority and Law; Contestation, Crime and Violence
- Concepts: Village, Town and City
- Social Order and Social Change in Rural and Urban Areas

UNIT 9 **Introducing Western Sociologists** — **20 Periods**

- The Context of Sociology
- Karl Marx on Class Conflict
- Emile Durkheim : Division of Labour in Society
- Max Weber: Interpretive Sociology, Ideal Type and Bureaucracy

UNIT 10 Indian Sociologists — 20 Periods

- G.S. Ghurye on Caste and Race
- D.P. Mukherjee on Tradition and Change
- A.R. Desai on the State
- M.N. Srinivas on the Village

Project Work

40 Periods

Max. Marks 20		**Time allotted : 3hrs**
A.	Project undertaken during the academic year at school level	15 Marks
	1. Introduction	2 Marks
	2. Statement of Purpose	2 Marks
	3. Research Question	2 Marks
	4. Methodology	3 Marks
	5. Data Analysis	4 Marks
	6. Conclusion	2 Marks
B.	Viva - based on the project work	5 Marks

PART A
INTRODUCING SOCIOLOGY

01 CHAPTER

Sociology is the systematic study of human society, focusing on the relationships between individuals and the broader social structures. It examines how societal factors, such as culture, gender, and economics, influence individual behaviour and societal outcomes.

YOUR STUDY GOALS

1.1 Introduction
1.2 Introducing Society
1.3 Introducing Sociology
1.4 The Scope of Sociology and its Relationship to Social Science

YOUR PRACTICE GOAL

- Objective Type Questions (20 Qs ; MCQs, A-R, Case Based Questions)
- Subjective Questions (12 VSAs, 10 SAs, 5 LAs)

Sociology and Society

1.1 Introduction

All of our decisions, efforts and the advices we receive are dependent on certain social aspects which include job markets, gender, family or social background etc.

These aspects are further controlled by certain other factors that can be social, economic or political.

For example, a job market for an individual is defined by the needs of the economy along with the political policies pursued by the government and the social background of an individual.

1.2 Introducing Society

- Society is a group of people that shares a common culture, occupies a territorial area and is bound to each other by a common history.
- According to some sociologists, society is a system of relations in which humans live with each other by making relations.
- Society can thus be defined as an organisation of human relations which is formed, regulated and changed by humans.

Characteristics of Society

The important characteristics of society are as follows

- **It is based on relationships** Society is the web of social relationships in one family more than 15 types of relations exist.

- **It has similarities and dissimilarities** Social relations can be established if similarity among society exists.
- **It is based on interdependence** It is necessary for humans to keep relations with other persons to fulfill their needs.
- **It is abstract** We cannot see relations or touch them. We can only feel them.

Individual and Collective Perspective in Society

- Individuals and society are directly related to each other. The individuals are involved in collective activities due to necessity not compulsion.
- Human beings and their societies are closely connected. People can be compliant or rebellious, conventional or unorthodox, submissive or aggressive, showing a mix of different traits.
- In addition to personal effort, many factors influence us, including biological, ecological, psychological, and social aspects.
- The individual's collective personality development is also affected by political and economic measures as well as by the social background of their family. Sociology, thus, studies human society as an interconnected entity.

The Sociological Imagination : The Personal Problem and the Public Issue

- Individuals and society are deeply interconnected. This concept was highlighted by sociologist C. Wright Mills through the sociological imagination.
- This framework helps us understand how personal experiences relate to broader public issues.
- It distinguishes between 'personal troubles', which are individual experiences and small social circles and 'public issues', which involve larger social structures.
- The events in history also reflect the successes and failures of individuals. For example, when a society becomes industrialised, a peasant might become a factory worker and a feudal lord may either lose their status or turn into a businessman.
- When social classes change, some people find jobs while others lose them. Changes in investment rates can bring hope to some or lead others to financial ruin. In times of war, people's lives can change dramatically.

Pluralities and Inequalities Among Societies

- When amidst foreigners, the reference to 'our society' means 'Indian society', but amongst fellow Indians, the term 'our society' might refer to a specific linguistic or ethnic group, a religion or a caste.
- Amartya Sen highlights how inequality plays a big role in the differences within societies. Inequalities in wealth, education, opportunity and treatment in India highlight a critical need for serious attention and action.

Pradhan Mantri Awas Yojana

The Pradhan Mantri Awas Yojna-Gramin, launched in 2016 by the Ministry of Rural Development, supports homeless families and those in kutcha houses by providing financial and labour assistance to build pucca homes. This programme highlights the link between personal challenges and broader social issues.

Quick Test 1

1. Who held the view that personal problems and public issues are interrelated?
2. What is the central concern of sociology?
3. Which filmmaker found difficulty in mapping society?
4. What is Pradhan Mantri Awas Yojana?

1.3 Introducing Sociology

- Sociology studies human social life, groups and societies, focusing on our behaviour as social beings.
- We all have our own ideas about daily life and about other's lives, as well as our own 'society' and other's 'societies.' These ideas form our common sense, guiding how we live.

Origin of Sociology

- The word 'sociology' comes from the Latin word *socius* (meaning companion) and the Greek word *ology* (meaning study of). It means 'the science of society'. Sociology studies the relationships and structures within human societies.
- Sociology provides a systematic and analytical view of society.

Sociology vs Philosophical Reflections

- Philosophical and religious thinkers often explore what is moral and what a good society should look like. In contrast, sociology focuses on how norms and values operate in real societies, rather than prescribing ideals for people to pursue.
- Sociologists conduct **empirical studies**[1] to gather facts about societies. They aim for unbiased observation, even if they don't personally agree with the findings.
- *Peter Berger* compares sociologists to spies, emphasising the importance of unbiased reporting to provide accurate information about social issues.
- Sociology is a science that follows specific methods of evidence, ensuring conclusions are verifiable and repeatable. This distinguishes it from everyday observations and philosophical reflections.

Sociology and Common Sense Knowledge

- Common sense explanations are usually based on individual experiences or what seems 'natural' to people.
- Sociology differs from theology and common sense by using systematic analysis rather than relying on personal experiences or intuitive beliefs.
- Sociologists use specific concepts and methods that prioritise evidence and critical questioning, challenging even widely accepted beliefs.
- Sociological knowledge evolves gradually through careful research, rather than through sudden revolutionary discoveries.
- The development of sociology as a discipline is closely tied to advancements in modern science, which informs its emphasis on scientific methods and inquiry.

Unsuspected Connections

- In many societies, including parts of India, inheritance typically passes from father to son. This is known as a patrilineal system.
- After the Kargil War, the Indian government decided that financial compensation for soldiers who died, should go to their widows to support them.
- The government didn't expect that this decision would lead to many widows being forced to marry their brother-in-law (the deceased husband's brother).
- In some cases, the brother-in-law was a young child and the widow was a young woman. This was done to keep the compensation within the deceased man's family.

1 **Empirical Studies** A factual enquiry carried out in any given area of sociological study.

Emergence of Sociology

The Intellectual Ideas that went into the Making of Sociology

- Early sociology was shaped by scientific theories of natural evolution and observations of pre-modern societies made by early travellers and colonial administrators.
- Sociologists aimed to classify societies into types, including pre-modern societies (hunters and gatherers, pastoral, agrarian) and modern industrialised societies.
- This approach often viewed Western societies as the most advanced, while non-Western societies were seen as barbaric and less developed.
- Indian sociology reflects tensions from British colonialism, leading to a thoughtful and reflective approach in its development.
- Darwin's ideas on organic evolution influenced sociological thought. Society was compared to living organisms.
- The Enlightenment movement which started in Europe during the late 17th and 18th centuries emphasised reason and individualism.
- Poverty, previously seen as a 'natural phenomenon', began to be viewed as a 'social problem' caused by human ignorance or exploitation. This made it a subject for study and intervention.
- Auguste Comte, the founder of sociology, believed that sociology could enhance human well-being by addressing social problems through empirical study.

The Material Issues that went into the Making of Sociology

- The Industrial Revolution was driven by a new and active economic system called **capitalism**[2]. This system led to the growth of industrial manufacturing and introduced new attitudes and institutions.
- Entrepreneurs began to focus on making profits systematically. Markets became the main part of production. Goods, services and labour became commodities and their use was determined by rational calculations.
- Before industrialisation, most people in England worked in agriculture and textiles and lived in small villages. Society was hierarchical, with clear status and class positions. This led to close community interactions.
- Industrialisation led to the decline of labour status as work shifted from guilds and families to factories.
- Urban centers expanded and grew during this time. While there were cities before, they were very different from the industrial cities that emerged.
- According to Desai, many Indian artisans who lost their livelihoods because of the arrival of machine-made goods from British industries. As a result, most of these ruined handicrafts men turned to agriculture to survive.
- Factories and their mechanical division of labour were often viewed as a way to destroy the roles of peasants, artisans, families and local communities.
- Karl Marx described the factory as both oppressive and potentially liberating. In factories, workers learned to work together and push for better conditions.
- In the 18th and 19th centuries, clock time became crucial for organising daily life.
- However, factory production required **synchronised**[3] labour, with strict start times, **steady**[4] pace and set hours. The clock introduced a sense of urgency to work.

---

2 **Capitalism** A system of economic enterprise based on market exchange. 'Capital' refers to any asset, including money, property and machines, which can be used to produce commodities for sale or invested in a market with the hope of achieving a profit. This system rests on the private ownership of assests and the means of production.

3 **Synchronised** Coordinated to occur at the same time or rhythmically.

4 **Steady** Constant and unchanging; not fluctuating or irregular in pace.

The Importance of Studying the Growth of Sociology in Europe

- Studying the beginning and growth of sociology in Europe is important. This is because many of the issues and concerns of sociology emerged during a time of significant changes in European society in the 18th and 19th centuries, driven by capitalism and industrialisation.
- Urbanisation and factory production from that era remain relevant to modern societies, though they differ in context.
- Indian society, with its colonial history and diversity, is unique. Indian sociology reflects this uniqueness. Focusing on Europe is relevant because India's past is linked to British capitalism and colonialism.
- R.K. Laxman's travelogue of Mauritius points out the presence of its colonial and global past. He highlights that in this European land, many cultures-like Africans, Chinese, Biharis, Dutch, Persians, Tamils, Arabs, French and English-mingle with each other.

Capitalism and its Global but Uneven Transformation of Societies

- Between the 17th and 19th centuries, about 24 million Africans were enslaved, with 11 million surviving the journey to the Americas.
- These individuals were taken from their homes and cultures, transported under terrible conditions and forced to work for capitalist interests.
- Enslavement shows how people were caught up in the rise of modern society without their consent.
- Although slavery began to decline in the 1800s, this period also saw the rise of indentured labour.
- The British used indentured workers from India for their cotton and sugar plantations in faraway places like Surinam, the West Indies and Fiji.
- Notable writer V.S. Naipaul, who won the Nobel Prize, is a descendant of these indentured workers[5] who were taken to unfamiliar lands and who died without being able to return.

The Growth of Sociology in India

- Colonialism played a key role in modern capitalism and industrialisation. Western sociologists' writings help understand social change in India.
- The effects of industrialisation in India differed from those in the West.
- Karl Marx highlighted that India, with its cotton production history, was flooded with English cotton products. Indian cotton goods faced bans or harsh conditions in England, while British cotton items were sold in India with low taxes, thus harming local industries.
- Indian sociology confronted inaccurate Western views that often compared Indian society unfavourably to Western society. Colonial officials and scholars portrayed Indian villages as unchanging and as remnants from the **Infancy of society.**
- Another aspect of colonial influence is the distinction often made between sociology and social anthropology. In Western textbooks, sociology studies industrialised societies, while social anthropology focuses on simple societies and non-Western cultures.
- There is no strict division between sociology and social anthropology in India. This reflects the country's rich diversity in traditional and modern life across rural and urban settings.
- In India, social anthropology shifted from studying 'primitive' people to examining peasants, ethnic groups, social classes, ancient civilisations and modern industrial societies.
- M.N. Srinivas noted that India's diversity includes many groups based on region, language, religion, ethnicity (including caste) and urban-rural differences. This creates a wide range of 'others' in society. In India's culture, one can find these 'others' right next door.

---

5 **Indentured Workers** Labourers bound by a contract for work.

Quick Test 2

1 According to Peter Berger, how is a sociologist similar to a spy?
2 What was Auguste Comte's belief about the purpose of sociology?
3 How did the Enlightenment influence the study of society?
4 How did industrial cities differ from pre-industrial cities?
5 Why is sociology referred to as a science?

1.4 Scope of Sociology and its Relation to Social Science

- Sociology examines interactions between individuals, such as shopkeepers and customers, teachers and students or friends and family.
- It addresses larger issues like unemployment, caste conflicts, state policies on tribal rights and rural debt.
- Sociology also looks at global social processes, including the impact of labour regulations, electronic media on youth and foreign universities on education.
- What distinguishes sociology is not just its topics (families, trade unions, villages) but its approach to these issues.
- Sociology is part of a group of social sciences, including anthropology, economics, political science and history.
- The distinctions between these disciplines are not clear-cut, with shared interests, concepts and methods.
- Feminist theories emphasise the need for an interdisciplinary approach, showing how political scientists or economists must consider sociology when analysing gender roles and their effects.

Sociology and Economics

- Economics studies the production and distribution of goods and services. Traditionally, it focused on specific factors like prices, supply, demand and money flow.
- Sociology examines economic behaviour within a wider social context, considering norms, values and interests. For example, corporate managers recognise that advertising shapes lifestyles and consumption patterns.
- Trends like feminist economics expand the focus by considering gender, exploring how household work relates to productivity outside the home.
- Economics is seen as a precise discipline, admired for its clear terminology and practical applications that influence public policy.
- However, economists sometimes struggle to make accurate predictions because they overlook individual behaviours, cultural norms and institutional challenges which sociologists study.
- Pierre Bourdieu argued that true economic science should consider all economic costs, not just those relevant to corporations. This includes costs related to crimes, suicides and other social issues.
- He emphasised the 'economics of happiness', examining both individual and collective benefits, as well as material and symbolic aspects. It also includes considering costs related to inactivity or unstable jobs, such as high anxiety medication use in France.
- Unlike economics, sociology doesn't usually provide technical solutions. It promotes critical thinking and questions basic assumptions.
- Recently, economic sociology has gained popularity for its broader, critical perspective. Sociology helps in understanding social situations through factual knowledge and theoretical insights. It also considers the social desirability of goals.

Sociology and Political Science

- Political theory often looks at ideas about government from thinkers like Plato to Marx, while administration courses focus on the formal structure of government rather than how it actually works.
- Sociology studies all aspects of society, while traditional political science mainly studies power in formal organisations.
- Sociology emphasises the connections between different institutions, including government, while political science often focuses on processes within the government itself.
- Despite these differences, sociology and political science have long shared research interests.
- Sociologists like Max Weber contributed to political sociology, which studies political behaviour.
- Studies have also been conducted in membership of political organisations, process of decision making in organisations, sociological reasons for support of political parties, the role of gender in politics, etc.

Sociology and History

- Historians typically study the past, while sociologists focus more on the contemporary or recent past. Traditionally, historians were mainly concerned with detailing actual events and explaining how things happened. In contrast, sociologists aim to establish causal relationships.
- Historians look at specific details, whereas sociologists tend to abstract from these details to categorise and generalise.
- Nowadays, many historians are using sociological methods and concepts in their analyses.
- Traditional history often focused on kings and wars, while sociologists have been more interested in less glamorous topics, like changes in land relations or family gender roles.
- However, modern history has become more sociological, with social history becoming a major focus. This includes studying social patterns, gender relations, customs and important institutions, rather than just the actions of rulers or wars.

Sociology and Psychology

- Psychology is often described as the science of behaviour, primarily focusing on individuals. It focuses on aspects like intelligence, learning, motivation, memory, the nervous system and people's hopes and fears.
- Social psychology serves as a link between psychology and sociology. It focuses on individuals but studies how they act within social groups.
- In contrast, sociology seeks to understand behaviour within the broader context of society. It looks at how various social factors shape personality, such as economic and political systems, family structures, culture, norms and values.
- For example, Durkheim, in his well-known study of suicide, aimed to establish a clear scope and method for sociology. He focused on statistical data about the social characteristics of individuals, rather than their personal intentions.

Sociology and Social Anthropology

- Anthropology includes archaeology, physical anthropology, cultural history, linguistics and the study of life in 'simple societies'.
- Sociology studies modern, complex societies, while social anthropology focuses on simpler societies.
- Social anthropology developed in the West when researchers studied non-European societies, often seen as **exotic**[6], **barbaric**[7] and uncivilised. This created an unequal relationship between the researchers and the societies they studied.

---

6 **Exotic** Unusual or strikingly different, often from a foreign culture.

7 **Barbaric** Primitive or uncivilised; lacking refinement or culture in behaviour.

- However, times have changed, and many people from these societies, like Indians or Sudanese, now share their own perspectives in writing and research.
- Past anthropologists documented simple societies neutrally but often compared them to Western societies.
- Modern changes have redefined sociology and social anthropology. For instance, modernity led to a process whereby the smallest village was impacted by global processes like colonialism.
- Under British rule, the most remote villages in India experienced changes in land laws, revenue collection and the collapse of local industries. Modern global processes have made the world feel even smaller leading to the notion that 'Globe is shrinking'.
- The study of simple, non-literate societies has significantly shaped social anthropology. Social anthropology examines all aspects of these communities, often focusing on regions like the Andaman Islands, the Nuers or Melanesia.
- In contrast, sociologists study complex societies, analysing specific elements such as bureaucracy, religion, caste and social mobility.
- Social anthropology involves long fieldwork, where researchers live in the communities they study. They use ethnographic methods. In contrast, sociologists mainly use surveys and statistics.
- Indian sociology combines elements from both sociology and social anthropology. Sociologists study their own cultures and others, looking at both urban and tribal societies.
- Concerns existed that social anthropology might merge with sociology with the decline of simple societies. However, both fields have exchanged methods. Today, anthropological studies explore state and globalisation, while sociology uses both quantitative and qualitative techniques to understand modern complexities.

Quick Test 3

1. What is the primary focus of economics?
2. What does a true economic science consider?
3. Sociology and psychology deals with which studies?

NCERT Folder

1. Why is the study of the origin and growth of sociology important?

Ans. Sociology is the study of social life of humans, their groups and societies. The subject matter of sociology is our own behaviour as social beings. It is important to study this subject, in order to understand the society as a whole. Hence, sociology helps us in the understanding of interconnectedness of the entire social systems.

It is important to study the origin and growth of sociology because it helps in shaping the subject matter according to its principles and perceptions. The study of the origin of the subject also helps us to understand the ideas that led to its origin.

Sociology studies societies that are different in size, characteristics, etc. by using certain methods, material contexts and methodologies. The study of growth of sociology shows the new ideas that were involved in making it a distinct subject of social science. These ideas which were gradually involved in bringing up this subject affect its subject-matter. Therefore, studying the origin and growth of sociology is important to understand the various institutions and their functions present in the society.

2. Discuss the different aspects of the term 'society'. How is it different from your common sense understanding?

Ans. The different aspects of the term 'society' have been studied by early sociologists like Auguste Comte, Karl Marx and Herbert Spencer. They classified the societies into two broad groups

(i) Types of Pre-modern societies such as, hunters and gatherers, pastoral and agrarian and non-industrial civilisations.

(ii) Types of Modern societies such as the industrial societies.

Sociology is different from common sense in the following ways

Sociology studies society on the basis of some rules and principles that depend on concepts, data and methods. On the other hand, our common sense understanding of the society depends on our naturalistic or individualistic understanding.

Common sense knowledge does not question its own origins but Sociology has both the systematic and questioning approach that is derived from a broader tradition of scientific investigation.

In our common sense understanding of the society, the aspect of the term 'society' is very limited which is quite different from that of sociology.

3. Discuss how there is greater give and take among disciplines today.

Ans. The give and take among disciplines today is discussed below

- Sociology, as a subject studies the society in the form of social behaviour, social institutions, social policies and programmes that get affected from the historical, political and economic policies.
- **Political Science and Sociology** The political atmosphere, political policies, etc. have an impact on society and its economy. Sociology thus has shared common interests of research with the field of political science.
- Political sociology focuses mainly on the study of political behaviour of the various institutions and their interactions. Studies have been conducted to understand sociological reasons for support of political parties, the role of gender in politics, the process of decision-making in organisations, etc.
- **Economics and Sociology** The economic behaviour and activities are looked upon through sociological approach in a broader context of social norms, practices, values and interests. Also, the subject of economic sociology has been introduced, because of the wide and critical perspective of both sociology and economics.
- **History and Sociology** History as a subject has been different from sociology. However, the historians nowadays have started using sociological methods and concepts to understand the social matters, gender relations, customs and other important institutions of the past.
- **Psychology and Sociology** Psychology is the science of behaviour. The fact that society gets affected from individual behaviour in collective form and vice versa makes sociology and psychology interrelated.
  This has introduced the subject of social psychology, which studies the primary interest in the individual by observing his/her behaviour in social groups.

Exam Pattern Questions

Objective Type Questions

Multiple Choice Questions (MCQs)

1. **......... makes an unusual but effective comparison to make the point. In any political or military conflict, it is of advantage to capture the information used by the intelligence organs of the opposing side. But this is so only because good intelligence consists of information free of bias.**

(a) M.N. Srinivas (b) Peter Berger
(c) R.K. Lakshman (d) Herbert Spencer

2. **The social survey that was based on the belief that human phenomena can be classified and measured. Thinkers of the early modern era were convinced that progress in knowledge promised the solution to all social ills. .... , the French scholar (1789–1857), considered to be the founder of sociology, believed that sociology would contribute to the welfare of humanity.** **Competency Based Que.**

(a) C. Wright Mills (b) Peter Berger
(c) Auguste Comte (d) R.K. Lakshman

3. **Who pointed out the presence of a colonial and global past?**

(a) M.N. Srinivas (b) Herbert Spencer
(c) R.K. Lakshman (d) C. Wright Mills

4. **Put the following statements in the correct order regarding the development of sociology in colonial India**

I. British colonial rule impacted Indian society, leading to a change in social structures.
II. Western scholars and colonial officials portrayed Indian society as stagnant and unchanging.
III. Indian sociology had to contend with misrepresentations of its social reality.
IV. The writings of Marx and other Western scholars influenced social change discussions in India.

Codes
(a) I, II, III and IV (b) II, I, IV and III
(c) III, I, II and IV (d) IV, III, II and I

5. **Which of the following statements is incorrect?**

(a) The sociological imagination enables us to grasp history and biography.
(b) The Industrial Revolution led to the development of capitalism and the factory system.
(c) The Enlightenment, an European intellectual movement of the late 15th and 16th centuries, emphasised reason and individualism.
(d) Sociology aimed to address social problems such as poverty, inequality and urbanisation.

6. **Colonialism was an essential part of modern Capitalism and Industrialisation. The writings of Western sociologists on capitalism and other aspects of modern society are therefore relevant for understanding social change in India.** **Competency Based Que.**

Which of the following is true in the given context?

I. Colonialism is always important to be a capital state.
II. One can get an understanding of society with the help of Western writings.
III. Modern society welcomes the idea of social change.
IV. Modern capitalism and industrialisaton are influenced by colonialism.

Codes
(a) I and III (b) II, III and IV
(c) III and IV (d) All of these

7. **The Psychology is associated with the Sociology in terms of** **Competency Based Que.**

I. Science of behaviour
II. Contemporary or recent past
III. Production and distribution of goods and services
IV. Intelligence, learning, motivation and memory

Codes
(a) I, II and III (b) II and IV
(c) I, III and IV (d) I and IV

8. **Which discipline focuses on both simple and complex societies and involve fieldworks using ethnographic methods?**

(a) Economics
(b) Social Anthropology
(c) Sociology
(d) Political Science

9. What does the term 'Sociology' mean?
(a) The science of philosophy and religion
(b) The science of society
(c) The analysis of economics and politics
(d) The study of natural sciences

10. Who among the following is regarded as the founder of Sociology?
(a) Karl Marx (b) Auguste Comte
(c) M.N. Srinivas (d) Peter Berger

Assertion-Reason Questions

Direction (Q. Nos. 11-15) Two statements are given in the question below as Assertion (A) and Reason (R). Read the statements and choose the appropriate option.
(a) Both A and R are true and R is the correct explanation of A.
(b) Both A and R are true, but R is not the correct explanation of A.
(c) A is true, but R is false.
(d) A is false, but R is true.

11. **Assertion** (A) The Industrial Revolution was based upon a new dynamic form of economic activity-capitalism.
Reason (R) Capitalism involved new attitudes and institutions.

12. **Assertion** (A) The writings of Western sociologists on capitalism and other aspects of modern society are therefore relevant for understanding social change in India.
Reason (R) Sociology in India also had to deal with Western writings and ideas about Indian society that were not always correct.

13. **Assertion** (A) The distinction between sociology and social anthropology reflects colonial influences in India.
Reason (R) In Western contexts, sociology focuses on industrialised societies, while social anthropology studies 'other' cultures.

14. **Assertion** (A) Sociology distinguishes itself from common sense by relying on systematic analysis and evidence based enquiry.
Reason (R) Common sense explanations are often based on individual experiences and maturalistic assumptions.

15. **Assertion** (A) Sociology and economics overlap because sociology examines economic behaviour within a broader social context.
Reason (R) Economists often overlook cultural norms and individual behaviours, which are critical to understanding economic activity.

Case Based Questions

Read the passage given below and answer the questions that follow by choosing the correct option.

16. Observations of philosophical and religious thinkers are often about what is moral or immoral in human behaviour, about the desirable way of living and about a good society. Sociology too concerns itself with norms and values. But its focus is not on norms and values as they ought to be, as goals that people should pursue.

(i) How does sociology differ from philosophical and religious studies?
(a) Sociology only studies religious communities.
(b) Sociology is concerned with empirical findings rather than ideals.
(c) Sociology focuses solely on individual behaviour.
(d) Sociology ignores cultural norms.

(ii) When sociologists study a society, how do they approach findings that conflict with their personal beliefs?
(a) They ignore them.
(b) They alter the findings to fit their views.
(c) They observe and collect findings regardless of personal preference.
(d) They prioritise personal beliefs over empirical evidence.

17. The Industrial Revolution was based upon a new, dynamic form of economic activity — capitalism. This system of capitalism became the driving force behind the growth of industrial manufacturing. Capitalism involved new attitudes and institutions. Entrepreneurs now engaged in the sustained, systematic pursuit of profit. The markets acted as the key instrument of productive life. And goods, services and labour became commodities whose use was determined by rational calculation. The new economy was completely different from what it replaced. England was the centre of the Industrial Revolution.

(i) Which of the following is regarded as a crucial component of modern capitalism and industrialisation.
(a) Colonialism (b) Regionalism
(c) Communalism (d) Urbanisation

(ii) What characterised the new economy during the Industrial Revolution?
(a) A focus on traditional methods
(b) Goods, services and labour became commodities
(c) Social interaction was prioritised
(d) The preservation of rural lifestyle

18. An indicator of the emergence of modern societies was the new significance of clock-time as a basis of social organisation. A crucial aspect of this was the way in which, in the 18th and 19th centuries, the tempo of agricultural and manufacturing labour increasingly came to be set by the clock and calendar in a way very different from pre-modern forms of work. For both employer and employee 'time is now money: it is not passed but spent'.

(i) Prior to industrial capitalism, which factors primarily influenced work rhythms?
(a) Clock time and factory schedules
(b) Social duties and deadlines
(c) Daylight and breaks between tasks
(d) Personal preferences of workers

(ii) What does the phrase 'time is now money' imply in the context of modern labour?
(a) Time should be enjoyed rather than measured
(b) Every moment of labour has economic value
(c) Workers should take breaks frequently
(d) Time management is irrelevant to productivity

19. Economics is the study of production and distribution of goods and services. The classical economic approach dealt almost exclusively with the inter - relations of pure economic variables–the relations of price, demand and supply; money flows; output and input ratios, and the like. The focus of traditional economics has been on a narrow understanding of 'economic activity', namely the allocation of scarce goods and services within a society. Economists who are influenced by a political economy approach seek to understand economic activity in a broader framework of ownership of and relationship to means of production.

(i) Which of the following sociologist worked in Political sociology?
(a) Karl Marx
(b) Woodrow Wilson
(c) Max Weber
(d) None of the above

(ii) Root of capitalism lies in the Industrial Revolution of which country?
(a) Germany (b) France
(c) India (d) England

20. Psychology is often defined as the science of behaviour. It involves itself primarily with the individual. It is interested in her/his intelligence and learning, motivations and memory, nervous system and reaction time, hopes and fears. Social psychology, which serves as a bridge between psychology and sociology, maintains a primary interest in the individual but concerns itself with the way in which the individual behaves in social groups, collectively with other individuals. Sociology attempts to understand behaviour as it is organised in society, that is the way in which personality is shaped by different aspects of society. For instance, economic and political system, their family and kinship structure, their culture, norms and values.

(i) Which subject maintains a primary interest in the individual but concerns itself with the way in which the individual behaves in social groups, collectively with other individuals.
(a) Social Anthropology
(b) Social Psychology
(c) Sociology
(d) Social Philosophy

(ii) What was Durkeim's approach to the study of suicide?
(a) He focused on individual intentions of those who commit suicide
(b) He studied suicide through personal stories and experiences
(c) He focused on statistical data concerning social characteristics of individuals
(d) He ignored the concept of suicide altogether

Answers

1. (b) Peter Berger
2. (c) Auguste Comte
3. (c) R.K. Lakshman
4. (a) I, II, III and IV
5. (c) The Enlightenment, an European intellectual movement of the late 15th and 16th centuries, emphasised reason and individualism.
6. (b) II, III and IV
7. (d) I and IV
8. (c) Social Anthropology
9. (b) The science of society
10. (b) Auguste Comte
11. (b) Both A and R are true, but R is not the correct explanation of A.
12. (b) Both A and R are true, but R is not the correct explanation of A.
13. (a) Both A and R are true and R is the correct explanation of A.
14. (a) Both A and R are true and R is the correct explanation of A.
15. (a) Both A and R are true and R is the correct explanation of A.
16. (i) (b) Sociology is concerned with empirical findings rather than ideals.
    (ii) (c) They observe and collect findings regardless of personal preference.
17. (i) (a) Colonialism
    (ii) (b) Goods, services and labour became commodities
18. (i) (c) Daylight and breaks between tasks
    (ii) (b) Every moment of labour has economic value
19. (i) (c) Max Weber
    (ii) (d) England
20. (i) (b) Social Psychology
    (ii) (c) He focused on statistical data concerning social characteristics of individuals

Subjective Questions

Very Short Answer Type Questions

1. The chances of the individual student are affected both by these broader political and economic measures as well as by the social background of her/his family. This gives us a preliminary sense of how sociology studies human society as an interconnected whole. How will you define society in sociology?

Ans. In sociology, society is a system of relations in which humans live with each other by making relations with them.

2. How is society interdependent?

Ans. For the existence of society, interdependence is an important element. It is necessary for humans to keep relations with other persons to fulfill their needs. The way in which a person grows, depends upon others also increases his/her, needs.

3. Can you justify that society is abstract?

Ans. The society is the web of relationships. We neither can see these relations nor can touch them. We can only feel them. Thus relations do not have any concrete form and are abstract. Since society is made by relations, it is considered abstract.

4. Wright Mills rest his vision of the sociological imagination precisely in the unravelling of how the personal and public related. Competency Based Que.
What is the view of Mills on sociological imagination in society?

Ans. C. Wright Mills in 1959 observed that the sociological imagination enables us to grasp the relations between individual and public within society. The sociological imagination works in between the personal troubles of the people and the public issues of social structure.

The Pradhanmantri Awas Yojna Gramin was a major scheme launched by Ministry of Rural Development (MORD).

5. What is the purpose of the Pradhan Mantri Awas Yojna-Gramin launched in 2016?

Ans. The scheme aims to provide financial and labour support to houseless families and those in dilapidated kutcha houses, enabling them to construct durable pucca homes, improving rural housing conditions.

6. State how sociology is a progressive science?

Ans. Sociology is a modern science which originated in recent times. Latest concepts are included in sociology which keeps the subject upto date. That is why it is known as Progressive science.

7. What is the view of Darwin about society?

Ans. Charles Darwin's ideas about organic evolution were a dominant influence on early sociological thought. Society was often compared with living organisms and efforts were made to trace its growth through stages comparable to those of organic life.

8. The Industrial revolution was based upon a new, dynamic form of economic activity capitalism. This system of capitalism became the driving force behind the grwoth of industrial manufacturing. Name two feature of English society which changed after the advent of Industrial Revolution. Competency Based Que.

Ans. Following are the two features of its society which changed after the advent of Industrial Revolution

(i) Population of England shifted from rural areas to urban areas to work in industries.

(ii) Capitalism led to degradation of labour and loss of work from the protective contexts of guild, village and family.

9. In a culture and society such as India's, 'the other' can be encountered literally next door. Explain. Competency Based Que.

Ans. In India's diverse society, 'the other' refers to people with different backgrounds, such as language, religion or caste. These differences are often found in close proximity, emphasising how various communities coexist and interact with each other every day.

10. State one relationship of sociology with psychology.

Ans. Psychology is often defined as the science of behaviour. It involves itself primarily with the individual. On contrary to it, sociology attempts to understand behaviour as it is organised in society of an individual.

11. What do you understand by Anthropology?

Ans. Anthropology is the study of a simple primitive society. It studies cultures which are small and static. It is the study of man and development of human race.

12. An evidence of the colonial heritage of countries like India is the distinction often made between sociology and social anthropology. Cite two difference between sociology and social anthropology. Competency Based Que.

Ans. The two difference between sociology and social anthropology is given below

(i) The scope of social anthropology is related to the study of simple and non-literate societies whereas sociologists study complex societies.

(ii) Social anthropology was characterised by long fieldwork tradition, living in the community being studied and using ethnographic research methods. Whereas, sociologists have often relied on survey method and quantitative data using statistics and questionnaire mode.

Short Answer Type Questions

1. Write a short note on society.

Ans. Society is a group of people who share a common culture, occupy a territorial area and are bound to each other by a common history. Society is mandatory not only for mere survival but also for a good life.

Society will be made only when the meaningful relations will be established among people of the society. These relations are abstract in nature.

In sociology, society is a system of relations in which humans live with each other by making relations with them. In this way, we can define society as an organisation of human relations which is formed, regulated and changed by humans.

2. Bring out four differences between sociological perspective and common sense knowledge.

Ans. The four differences between sociological perspective and common sense knowledge is given below

(i) Sociological perspective is a rational knowledge whereas common sense knowledge is based on general understanding.

(ii) Sociological perspective is objective in nature whereas common sense knowledge is subjective.

(iii) Sociological perspective has a body of concepts, methods whereas common sense knowledge is unreflective as it does not question its own origin.

(iv) Sociological knowledge arrives at conclusion by studying society from divergent perspective whereas common sense tends to limit itself to constraints of time, space gender, etc.

3. Critically, examine how sociology is concerned with norms and values?

Ans. Observation of philosophical and religious thinkers are often about what is moral or immoral in human behaviour, about the desirable way of living and about a good society. Sociology too concerns itself with norms and values. But its focus is not on norms and value as they ought to be, as goals that people should pursue. Its concern is the way in which they actually function in a real society.

Empirical study of society is an important part of sociology but it does not mean that sociologist or sociology does not concern with values. It only means that a sociologist is willing to observe and collect findings, even if they are not to his/her personal linking.

Thus, the above discussions indicate that the sociology is concern with the values and norms of the society as well as human behaviour.

4. What is sociology? Discuss sociology as a science.

Ans. Sociology is the study of human society as a whole which is interconnected to each other. In other sense, sociology is the study of human social life, groups and society.

Sociology is a science as it involves objectives and systematic methods of investigation and evaluation of social reality in the light of empirical evidence and interpretation. It studies the design and norms of the society. It provides understanding about groups, social actions, subject matter and structure.

Sociology presents general principles related to social interaction so it is a general science. In other words, it is science of society which studies human societies.

5. Colonialism implied that the impact of industrialisation in India was not necessarily the same as in the West. Karl Marx's comments on the impact of the East India Company bring out the contrast. Explain

Competency Based Que.

Ans. Colonialism changed how industrialisation affected India compared to the West. Karl Marx points out that India, once a leading producer of cotton, faced tough competition from British goods. The East India Company made it difficult for Indian cotton products to compete, as British textiles flooded the market with low taxes. This led to the decline of India's traditional cotton industry. While industrialisation in the West often led to growth and development, in India, it resulted in economic ruin and dependence on British imports, highlighting the negative effects of colonial exploitation.

6. The scope of sociological study is extremely wide. It can focus its analysis of meaningful interactions between individuals such as that of a shopkeeper with a customer, between teachers and students, between two friends or family members. Write down scope of sociology in detail.

Ans. The scope of sociological study is extremely wide. It offers a specific way of looking at society and help us to understand it in a comprehensive way. The scopes of sociology is given below

- Sociology focus its analysis of interaction between individuals or groups.
- Sociology can focus on national issues such as poverty, unemployment and global social issues such as migration and refugee crisis.
- Sociology is referred as sum total of all social sciences as it covers not only one or two aspects but studies the society in its totality.

7. List any four differences between sociology and economics.

Ans. The differences between sociology and economics are

	Sociology	Economics
(i)	It is concerned with social relations. So, it is general science.	It is concerned with economic relations. So, it is special science.
(ii)	Its nature of study is based on collectivism.	Its nature of study is individualistic.
(iii)	Quantitative and numeral methods are followed in sociology.	Inductive and deductive methods are followed in economics.
(iv)	It provides clearer or more adequate understanding of a social situation.	It provides basic assumption to economic related situation.

8. List any four points of relationship between sociology and political science.

Ans. The sociology is defined as science of society whereas political science is science of state and government.

The relationship between sociology and political science is given below

(i) Sociology has long shared similar interests of research with political science. Max Weber worked in what can be termed as political sociology which increases the study of political behaviour.

(ii) Both of these disciplines have studied the political system such as capitalism, communism and socialism and their impact on society.

(iii) Sociology stresses the inter-relationships between sets of institution including government and political science and also tends to turn attention towards the processes within the government.

(iv) Sociologist have turned their attention on different political processes such as study of political patterns of voting, membership of political organisations, process of decision-making etc.

9. What are the four main differences between sociology and psychology?

Ans. Four main differences between sociology and psychology are

	Sociology	Psychology
(i)	It focuses on the study of the society as a whole.	It focuses on the study of an individual's mind.
(ii)	It is the study of social behaviour of man in society.	It is the science of behaviour, attention memory, learning, etc.
(iii)	It studies social institutions in an organised way.	It studies hopes and fears of individual.
(iv)	It deals with social processes.	It deals with mental processes.

10. It had been feared that with the decline of simple societies, social anthropology would lose its specificity and merge with sociology. However, there have been fruitful interchanges between the two disciplines and today often methods and techniques are drawn from both. Explain. Competency Based Que.

Ans. There were concerns that social anthropology would lose its uniqueness as simple societies declined. Instead, both sociology and social anthropology have benefited from exchanging ideas. Anthropologists now study topics like the state and globalisation, moving beyond traditional focuses. On the other hand, sociology too has been using quantitative and qualitative techniques, macro and micro approaches for studying the complexities of modern societies. In India, the close relationship between these two fields enhances their research. This blending of techniques and topics allows both disciplines to grow and adapt to changing social realities.

Long Answer Type Questions

1. Explain the characteristics of the society.

Ans. Characteristics of society are as follows

- **Based on Relationships** Society is the web of social relationship. It means that society is based on social relationships. The web of social relationship indicates that in one family more than 15 types of relations exist. Society is not just a collection of humans but also a formation of many types of relationship.
- **Similarities and Dissimilarities** Society depends both upon similarities and dissimilarities society cannot exist without them. Without this people cannot attract each other and society can not be formed.
- **Interdependence** For the existence of society, interdependence is an important element. It is necessary for humans to keep relations with other persons to fulfill their needs. The way in which a person grows, his/her dependence upon others also increases and his/her needs also start to increase.
- **Society is Abstract** Society is abstract because it is the web of relationships. We neither can see these relations and nor can touch them. We can only feel them.

2. In what ways did the Industrial Revolution lead to the birth of sociology in Europe?

Ans. The Industrial Revolution began in Britain in the late 18th and early 19th centuries. It marked the beginning of scientific age and led to changes in social lives of people. Before industrialisation the rural sector was important.

The chief occupation was farming and weaving. Society was hierarchical in terms of status and class conscious. People worked according to their needs factors like daylight and deadlines.

New forms of economic activity gave rise to capitalism as the pursuit of profit was geared to markets in distant colonies. Huge factories were set up for large scale production of goods. There was dramatic change in social life as a new working class emerged. Farmers migrated to industrial cities which were characterised by overcrowded housing, poor sanitation and general squalor.

As indicator of this new society was the emergence of clock time. The tempo of work was set up by the clock and calendar. Factory production meant that work began punctually and people worked in shifts for set hours and were paid according to what they produced.

Karl Marx and Durkheim were appalled at the degradation of factory workers and became concerned with the scientific analysis of developments in industrial society. Sociology was born as a result of this and it was based on the understanding of science of new modern industrial world.

3. What were the key changes in social life brought about by the industrial revolution compared to pre-industrial society?

Ans. The key changes in social life brought about by the industrial revolution compared to pre-industrial society are as follows

- Before industrialisation, agriculture and textiles were the chief occupations of the British.
- Most people lived in villages. Like in our own Indian villages, there were peasants and landlords, the blacksmith and leather workers, the weavers and the potters, the shepherds and the brewers.
- Society was small. It was hierarchical in which status and class positions of different people were clearly defined. Like all traditional societies, it was also characterised by close interaction. With industrialisation, each of these features changed.
- One of the most fundamental aspects of the new order was the degradation of labour, the wrenching of work from the protective context of guild, village and family. Both the radical and conservative thinkers were shocked by the decline of the status of the common labourer, and the skilled craftsmen.
- Urban centres expanded and grew. It was not that there were no cities earlier. But their character prior to industrialisation was different.
- The industrial cities gave birth to a completely new kind of urban world.
  It was marked by overcrowded slums of the new industrial working class, bad sanitation and general squalor. It was also marked by new kinds of social interactions.

4. Discuss, how did slavery and indentured labour reflect the effects of capitalism on societies between the 17th and 19th centuries, particularly in the context of India?

Ans. Between the 17th and 19th centuries, capitalism had a profound impact on societies through the systems of slavery and indentured labour. An estimated 24 million Africans were enslaved, with 11 million surviving the brutal journey to the Americas. This forced removal from their homes demonstrated how capitalism exploited human lives for profit. Although slavery declined in the 1800s, the British turned to indentured labour, bringing many Indians to work on plantations in places like Surinam and the West Indies. This practice echoed the previous exploitation of enslaved Africans, as workers faced harsh conditions and limited rights. The story of V.S. Naipaul, a descendant of indentured labourers, highlights the long-lasting effects of these systems on individuals and cultures. Overall, both slavery and indentured labour showcase how capitalism reshaped lives and societies, often at great human cost.

5. Discuss the emergence and growth of sociology in India.

Ans. Following points discuss the emergence and growth of sociology in India

- During 18th and 19th century, many British civil servants, missionaries and Western scholars studied Indian society in order to provide more control on territories and people of India.
- They wanted to understand about Indian society and culture so that they could easily rule over the country.
- Many of the phenomena such as Industrial Revolution, capitalism, urbanisation etc. which influenced the emergence of sociology also is relevant to India. Hence, writing of Western sociologists and their works significantly contributed in growth of Indian sociology.
- The colonial scholar believed Indian 'villages as a past of Europe', they also criticised Indian society for their indifferent attitude and backward nature. This led to the comprehensive study of Indian society by Indian sociologist such as MN Srinivas and AR Desai. Hence, the detailed study of Indian society which began in it's colonial past has now turned into full fledged academic discipline which has significantly enriched our understan- ding of society and many social phenomena.

SELF ASSESSMENT TEST

Objective Type Questions

1. When of the following has influenced Indian Sociology?
(a) Slavery (b) Capitalism (c) British Colonialism (d) French Revolution

2. Whose study of suicide established a clear scope and method for sociology?
(a) Emile Durkheim (b) Karl Marx (c) Auguste Comte (d) Max Weber

3. Which among the following sociologist is known for his work in political sociology?
(a) Emile Durkheim (b) Auguste Comte (c) Herbert Spencer (d) Max Weber

4. **Assertion** (A) Colonialism was an essential part of modern capitalism and industrialisation.
Reason (R) Sociology in India also had to deal with western writing and ideas about Indian society that were not always correct.
(a) Both A and R are true and R is the correct explanation of A.
(b) Both A and R are true but R is not the correct explanation of A.
(c) A is true, but R is false.
(d) A is false, but R is true.

5. Which of the following is true for enlightenment?
I. An European intellectual movement of late 17th and 18th centuries
II. India was the main centre.
III. Emphasised reason and individualism.

Codes

(a) I is false (b) I, II are true (c) I, IV are true (d) I, II and III are ture

Case Based Questions

1. The advent of capitalism and industrialisation brought significant changes to European society, including urbanisation and factory production. Colonialism, as a part of modern capitalism, led to global population movements, such as slavery and indentured labour. In India, colonialism affected industrialisation differently compared to the West. Western sociologists often misrepresented Indian society as unchanging, contrasting it with Western societies.

(i) Which of the following was a global consequence of colonialism?

(a) Technological advancements in Europe
(b) Urbanisation in Indian villages
(c) Population movements through slavery and indentured labour
(d) Decline of Western capitalism

(ii) How did Western sociologists portray Indian society?

(a) As dynamic and evolving (b) As a remnant of an unchanging past
(c) As an industrialised society (d) As identical to Western societies

Very Short Answer Type Questions

1. The Industrial Revolution led to a drastic change in society, especially in England. While the country shifted from a predominantly rural society to an urban one, India experienced a different pattern due to colonialism and the influx of British manufactured goods. How did the process of industrialisation in India differ from that in Britain, especially in terms of its impact on urbanisation and agriculture?

2. The rise of capitalism during the Industrial Revolution played a key role in shaping the economy and society in the West. Entrepreneurs engaged in the systematic pursuit of profit and goods, services and labour became commodities, which were controlled by rational calculations. How did the new economic system of capitalism introduced during the Industrial Revolution change society in terms of labour and class structures?

Short Answer Type Questions

1. Sociology is termed as scientific knowledge. Explain.

2. Discuss nature and scope of sociology.

3. The factory system, a hallmark of the Industrial Revolution, was seen as oppressive yet potentially liberating. Karl Marx noted the collective nature of factory work and its ability to unite workers for better conditions, despite the oppressive work environment.

What role did factories play in reshaping social interactions and labour, according to Marx and how did this differ from pre-industrial work environments?

Long Answer Type Questions

1. There are pluralities and inequalities among societies. Explain?

2. Describe the material issues that contribute to the making of sociology.

3. Sociology and economics both study human behavior, but they approach it from different perspectives. Explain how sociology looks at economic behaviour in relation to social norms and values, and how this approach contrasts with traditional economic theories.

02

CHAPTER

Sociological concepts have deeper meanings and historical contexts. They help us understand significant social changes, particularly those from pre-modern to modern societies.

Terms, Concepts and Their Use in Sociology

▼ **YOUR STUDY GOALS**

2.1 Introduction
2.2 Social Groups and Society
2.3 Social Stratification
2.4 Status and Role
2.5 Society and Social Control

▼ **YOUR PRACTICE GOAL**

– Objective Type Questions (14 Qs ; MCQs, A-R, Case Based Questions)
– Subjective Questions (19 VSAs, 9 SAs, 7 LAs)

2.1 Introduction

Sociology relies heavily on terminology to clarify its subject matter. While people are familiar with social institutions, they often lack a precise understanding of these institutions. Sociologist Peter Berger warned that everyday experiences can confuse common sense with sociological insight. For instance, many believe they fully understand families just because they live in them. Early sociology saw conflicting views of society. For example, Karl Marx emphasised **class conflict** while Emile Durkheim focused on **social solidarity**[1]. In the post-World War II era, structural functionalism became influential.

It viewed society as harmonious, whereas, conflict theorists, influenced by Marxism, viewed society as fundamentally conflict-ridden. Key concepts in sociology, such as status and role, focus on individuals, while social control and stratification relate to broader contexts.

1 **Solidarity** It refers to unity and mutual support among individuals or groups.

These classifications serve as tools to understand reality and require ongoing modification.
The existence of different definitions and perspectives can create unease, as seen in the contrasts between conflict theory[2] and functionalism[3]. However, these diverse approaches enrich our understanding of society by highlighting various viewpoints.

2.2 Social Groups and Society

- Sociology is the study of human social life, focusing on how people interact, communicate and construct social collectivities i.e. form social groups.
- A key aspect of sociology is its comparative and historical perspective, which highlights two important facts as following
  - (i) First, that human groups exist in all societies, whether they are ancient, feudal or modern and regardless of whether they are in Asia, Europe or Africa.
  - (ii) Second, the types of groups and collectivities vary across different societies.
- Not every gathering of people forms a social group. An **aggregate** is simply a collection of individuals who happen to be in the same place at the same time but do not share any meaningful connections. Examples of aggregates include passengers waiting at a train station or an audience at a movie theater. Such groups are often called **quasi-groups.**
- A quasi-group lacks organisation or structure, and its members may not even be aware of their grouping. Examples include social classes, status groups, age groups, gender groups and crowds.
- Quasi-groups may become social groups in time and in specific circumstances. For instance, individuals from the same social class or caste may not initially feel a sense of unity, but over time, these identities can lead to the formation of political parties.
- Similarly, during India's anti-colonial struggle, people from different communities developed a collective identity as a nation with a shared history and future. The women's movement has also led to the creation of women's groups and organisations.
- A social group typically has several key characteristics as following
  - Persistent interaction to provide continuity
  - Stable patterns of interaction
  - Sense of belonging
  - Shared interests
  - Acceptance of common norms and values
  - Definable structure
- Social structure refers to the patterns of regular and repetitive interactions between individuals or groups. Therefore, a social group is a collection of people who continuously interact and share common interests, culture, values and norms within a given society.

2 **Conflict Theory** A sociological perspective emphasising tensions and competing interests in society. It argues that resource scarcity leads to conflict as group struggle for access and control over valuable resources.

3 **Functionalism** A theoretical perspective that explains social events by their functions and contributions to societal continuity. It views society as a complex system where various parts work together and need to be understood in relation to one another.

Types of Groups

- Sociologists and social anthropologists categorise groups in various ways. One common distinction is between traditional, small-scale societies and modern, large-scale societies.
- In traditional societies, interactions are close, intimate and face-to-face. On the other hand, modern societies are marked by interactions which are often impersonal, detached and distant. However, a complete contrast between the two is likely not an accurate reflection of reality.

Primary and Secondary Social Groups

- A primary group is used to refer to a small group of people connected by intimate and face-to-face association and co-operation.
- Members of primary groups feel a strong sense of belonging. Examples of primary groups include family, close friends and small communities.
- On the other hand, secondary groups are larger and have more formal, impersonal relationships.
- While primary groups are person oriented, secondary groups are more goal-oriented. Examples of secondary groups include schools, government offices, hospitals and student associations.

Community and Society or Association

- The comparison between traditional, agrarian ways of life and modern, urban lifestyles has been a topic of interest since the time of classical sociologists.
- The term community describes human relationships that are personal, intimate and lasting as seen in families, close friendships or close-knit groups.
- In contrast, society or association refers to the more impersonal , superficial and transitory relationships typical of modern urban life.
- In a society or organisation, commerce and industry emphasise a more calculative and rational approach, where people deal with one another based on self-interest.
- Community can be thought of as similar to a primary group, which focuses on close personal connections, while society or association resembles a secondary group, where interactions are more structured.

In-Groups and Out-Groups

- A sense of belonging is a key feature of an in-group. This feeling creates a separation between 'us' (the in-group) and 'them' (the out-group). For example, children in a particular school may see themselves as part of an in-group compared to those who are not a part of that school.
- On the other hand, an out-group consists of individuals who do not belong to the in-group. Members of the in-group may have negative feelings or hostile reactions toward the out-group.
- Migrants are often viewed as an out-group in many societies.
- Sociologist M.N. Srinivas, during a census in Rampura in 1948, noted how villagers distinguished between recent and older migrants.
- The recent arrivals were looked down upon and referred to as 'those who came yesterday or the day before', while older migrants were called 'those who came long ago' or 'old lineages'.

Reference Group

- For any group of people there are always other groups whom they look up to and aspire to be like.
- The groups whose lifestyles are emulated are known as Reference groups.
- Reference groups provide important information about culture, lifestyle, aspirations and goals.
- During the colonial period, many middle-class Indians wanted to behave like the Englishman. In this case, the English could be seen as a reference group for those looking to improve their status.

- However, this process was influenced by gender. Indian men often wanted to dress and act like British men but expected Indian women to maintain their traditional ways.

Peer Groups

- A peer group is a type of primary group made up of individuals who are usually of similar age or share a common profession.
- Peer pressure refers to the social influence that peers have on each other, affecting what one should or shouldn't do.

Quick Test 1

1. Who warned about the confusion between common sense and sociological insight?
2. Define social structure.
3. What does a reference group provide?
4. How do quasi groups transform into social groups over time?

2.3 Social Stratification

- Social stratification refers to the structured inequalities between different groups in society regarding their access to material or symbolic rewards.
- This concept is often compared to layers of rock in the Earth, with society resembling a hierarchy: the more privileged at the top and the less privileged at the bottom.
- Inequality of power and advantage is important for sociology because it shapes how society is organised. Stratification affects every aspect of life for individuals and households, including opportunities for health, longevity, security, education, job satisfaction and political influence, which are distributed unevenly.
- Historically, there have been four main systems of stratification in human societies are **slavery, caste, estate** and **class.**
- **Slavery** is an extreme form of inequality where some people are owned by others. It has appeared at various in ancient Greece and Rome and in the Southern States of the USA during the 18th and 19th centuries.
- **Estates** were common in feudal Europe, where social hierarchy was based on land ownership and noble titles.

Caste

- In a **caste stratification system**, a person's position is determined by the status attributes ascribed by birth.
- While class societies also have limitations based on factors like race and gender, in a caste society, the attributes given at birth define a person's status more completely.
- In traditional India, different castes created a hierarchy, where each caste's position was based on notions of purity and pollution.
- The belief was that the most pure caste, the Brahmins (priestly caste), was superior to all others, while the Panchamas, often called 'outcastes', were seen as inferior.
- Traditionally, the caste system is described through four main varnas are Brahmins, Kshatriyas, Vaishyas and Shudras. However, there are many specific occupational groups within these categories, known as jatis.

- Upper castes believed that practices like endogamy i.e. marrying within one's caste and avoiding contact with lower castes were essential to maintain purity. However, changes brought by urbanisation have challenged these beliefs and practices.
- Sociologist A.R. Desai noted the social effects of urbanisation in India. He observed that modern industries led to the growth of cities. Which attracted people from all castes and backgrounds. In trains and buses, it became common to sit next to lower caste members. However, Desai emphasised that caste has not disappeared.
- Franco noted that some refuse to drink water from lower-caste individuals and use abusive language, believing they are superior. This attitude has lasted for years, no matter how well lower-caste individuals dress.
- Even today, strong caste discrimination exists. However, the functioning of democracy has impacted the caste system. Caste groups have become more powerful as interest groups. Discriminated castes are often seen asserting their democratic rights in society.

Class

- In Marxist theory, social classes are defined by their relationship to the **means of production**[4].
- Weber introduced the concept of 'life chances', which refers to the opportunities and advantages people have based on their market situation. He argued that inequality can come from economic relationships, but also from prestige and political power.
- Functionalist theory, on the other hand, believes that no society is 'classless' or unstratified. It suggests that social stratification exists to place and motivate individuals within the social structure.
- In traditional caste systems, social hierarchy is fixed, rigid and passed down through generations.
- In contrast, modern class systems are more open and based on achievement.
- Sociological studies of social mobility, even in Western societies, reveal that perfect mobility is rarely achieved. Sociology must address both the challenges to the caste system and the ongoing discrimination. People placed at the lower levels of the system face not only social disadvantages but also economic hardships.

Quick Test 2

1. What are the four basic systems of stratification?
2. Who are the Panchamas in the caste hierarchy?
3. Mention one change brought by urbanisation that challenged the caste system.
4. According to Marx, how are social classes defined?
5. How is stratification explained by functionalist theory?

4 **Means of Production** It means whereby the production of material goods is carried on in a society, including not just technology but the social relations between producers.

2.4 Status and Role

- The concepts of 'status' and 'role' are closely related.
- Status refers to the social position with specific rights and duties. For example, being a mother comes with certain responsibilities.
- A role is the behavioural aspect of status. When you occupy a status, you 'play' a role. Status is an institutionalised role, meaning it is standardised and formalised in society.
- A status is a position someone holds in society or a group.
- In complex societies, individuals have many different status. For example, as a school student, you are a student to your teacher, a customer to a grocer, a sibling to your brother or sister and a patient to your doctor.
- In simpler societies, people usually have fewer statuses.
- In modern societies, individuals have a status set, which includes all the different status they hold.
- Over time, people go through a status sequence, gaining different status at various life stages, such as becoming a son and then a father.
- An ascribed status is assigned at birth based on factors like age, caste, race or family ties. Traditional societies often have ascribed status.

Nature of Roles and Status

- In contrast, an achieved status is gained through personal effort or choices, often based on education or professional skills.
- Modern societies emphasise achievements, but ascribed status still matters.
- Status and prestige are connected. Each status has rights and values known as prestige. Status can be ranked by prestige.
- People perform their roles based on social expectations. A child learns to behave according to how others will judge her/him.
- Role conflict occurs when someone faces conflicting expectations from different roles. For instance, a working mother may struggle to balance home and work responsibilities.
- It is often assumed that men don't face role conflict, but this is not true. In Khasi matriliny, men face conflicts between their duties to their birth family i.e. the natal family and their wife and children.
- Socialisation helps individuals learn and negotiate roles, but stereotypes often rainforce fixed roles. For example, Men as breadwinners, women as homemakers.
- Roles and status are not fixed. People strive to challenge discriminatory roles based on caste, race, or gender. However, some groups resist these changes. When individuals break social roles, they often face consequences. Thus, society operates through roles and status and mechanisms of social control.

2.5 Society and Social Control

- Social control refers to the methods a society uses to manage its members and keep them in line. It refers to the different ways a society tries to get its **recalcitrant**[5] or unruly to follow the rules.
- Functionalists see society as harmonious, while conflict theorists view it as unequal and unjust.
- From a functionalist perspective, social control has two main aspects as following
    (i) Using force to regulate behaviour and
    (ii) Enforcing shared values and norms to maintain order.

5 **Recalcitrant** It means stubbornly resistant to authority or control; uncooperative.

- Conflict theorists see social control as a way for dominant classes to impose their will on others. They argue that stability is maintained by the powerful, with laws serving the interests of the wealthy.
- Social control includes processes and strategies that regulate behaviour. It can involve both forceful methods and subtle influences.

Forms of Social Control

- Social control is categorised into formal and informal types.
- **Formal Social Control** This uses codified and systematic methods, like laws and the state. In modern societies, formal mechanisms are particularly important.
- **Informal Social Control** This is personal, uncodified and unofficial. It includes non-verbal cues, like smiles, frowns, body language as well as actions like criticism. Agencies of informal control include family, religion and kinship.

Terms Associated with Social Control

- A sanction is a reward or punishment that encourages expected behaviour.
- Social control can be positive or negative. When members of society are rewarded for following rules it is called Positive sanction.
- Negative sanction is used to discourage rule-breaking.
- Deviance refers to actions against the norms or values of a group. What is considered deviant can vary widely between cultures and change over time. For example, a woman wanting to become an astronaut might be seen as deviant at one time but celebrated at another in the same society.

Quick Test 3

1. Name one historical system of stratification.
2. What determines a person's position in a caste system?
3. What is the difference between ascribed and achieved status?
4. What concept did Weber introduce related to social classes?

Violence as a means of Social Control

- The oldest and most basic form of social control is physical violence. Even in well-functioning democracies, violence is seen as a last resort. Every state uses a police force or similar authority to maintain order. In stable societies, violence is used carefully and usually only when necessary; often, just the threat of violence is enough for daily control.
- In close-knit groups, known as Primary groups, people know each other personally and share strong loyalties. These groups have subtle but powerful ways of controlling behaviour.
- Social control can sometimes rely on deceit. For example, a young boy might gain influence over his friends by claiming he has a big brother who can intimidate others. If he doesn't have a real brother, he might pretend he does. His success depends on convincing others that his claim is true, allowing him to exert control over his peers.

NCERT Folder

1. Why do we need to use special terms and concepts in sociology?

Ans. We need to use special terms and concepts in sociology to understand the society in a better manner. Some other reasons for need of special terms and concepts in sociology are

- Special terms and concepts acts as tool of different ways to understand society. For example, Max Weber gave importance to individuals for existence of a society whereas Emile Durkheim laid emphasis on society as a whole.
- These special terms and concepts help us to overcome our narrow common sense approach towards complex social phenomena.
- These special terms and concepts help us in studying the structure, phenomena and functions of society in a scientific way.
- These terms and concepts also reflect the concern of social thinkers to understand the society in divergent ways as sociology as a discipline allows coexistence of divergent views.

2. As a member of society you must be interacting with and in different groups. How do you see these groups from a sociological perspective?

Ans. **Within Different Groups** We interact with different groups in our daily lives. The students of a classroom form a social group of that class and an individual (you) is a part of that group.

The individual has some of the classmates as his/her friends and this group of friends forms the primary group where interaction takes place with intimacy and co-operation while the rest of the class forms the secondary group.

The group of students of the class sharing common interest and ideas interact with each other in a formal manner. The friends of the individual from the class also shares common interests and ideas but with informal ways of interaction.

In Different Groups An individual also interacts with the students association which forms a secondary group based on specific goals. The individual discusses his/her school problems with the members of these groups and the members help him/her.

3. What have you observed about the stratification system existing in your society? How are individual lives affected by stratification?

Ans. The stratification system of the society mainly runs on the discrimination based on caste, creed, colour, gender, etc.

- The caste based discrimination results in having a deep impact upon the lives of the individuals and society as a whole as it creates a barrier for social liberalism and intellectualism. It hinders the occupational mobility of people and restricts the social consciousness of the masses.
- The religion based discrimination results in the communal and political tensions among the governing sections of the society. It further creates a sense of intolerance among the people which further affects the solidarity and empathy in society.
- The discrimination on the basis of region and race perpetuates the concepts of racism and regionalism within a country which further leads to disintegration of thought and land in particular.

4. What is social control? Do you think the modes of social control in different spheres of society are different? Discuss.

Ans. Social control refers to the social processes, techniques and strategies by which the behaviour of an individual or a group is regulated or controlled.

There are two types of social control as following

(i) **Formal Social Control** It is formal, official and codified. Its agents are the laws and the state.

(ii) **Informal Social Control** It is personal, unofficial and uncodified. For example, family, religion and kinship. This mode of social control is very effective in our daily life. However, it may not be adequate to enforce conformity or obedience as it culminates into social evils like honour-killing.

Yes, the modes of social control are different in different spheres of the society. As the religious sphere of the society is primarily dominated by the religious ideologies, beliefs must be subject to religious legitimacy.

The caste based society has its social control empowered by the caste system which in turns also result in the monopoly over the resources, along the lines of caste. The race based society gives primacy to the notion of 'indigenous' and 'natives' where only the former ones are considered citizens and they are the only ones to enjoy political social and economic rights.

Exam Pattern Questions

Objective Type Questions

Multiple Choice Questions (MCQs)

1. Which of the following is an example of a primary group?

(a) A team working in an office
(b) A family living together
(c) A school management committee
(d) A sports association

2. Which of the following statement is incorrect?

(a) A reference group provides a lifestyle to emulate.
(b) Peer groups exert social pressure on individuals.
(c) A caste-based movement always begins as a social group.
(d) Social stratification involves structured inequalities.

3. A ……… is an aggregation or mixture that lacks structure or organisation and whose members may be unaware of groupings' presence. It includes social classes, status groups, age and gender groups, and crowds. For example, individuals belonging to a particular social class or caste or community may not be organised as a collective body. Competency Based Que.

(a) Primary group (b) Quasi group
(c) Secondary group (d) Tertiary group

4. Reference groups are important because

(a) they represent groups with which we have personal relationships.
(b) they are goal-oriented and formal in nature.
(c) they influence aspirations and lifestyle choices, even if we are not part of them.
(d) they lack a structure or 'we' feeling.

5. Which of the following is not an example of stratification in human societies? Competency Based Que.

(a) Caste (b) Class
(c) Estate (d) Peer groups

6. There is a feeling of sacrifice and cooperation among the members of this group. Identify the group from the following options.

(a) Out-group (b) Reference group
(c) In-group (d) Peer group

7. Which among the following refers to patterns of regular and repetitive interaction between individuals or groups.

(a) Political structure (b) Social structure
(c) Primary structure (d) Secondary structure

8. How is peer pressure primarily defined in a social context? Competency Based Que.

(a) The influence of media on individual behaviour
(b) The pressure from friends to conform to specific behaviours
(c) The expectations set by authority figures
(d) The impact of cultural norms on personal choices

9. A Social Group can be defined by the characteristics of Competency Based Que.

I. Persistent interaction to provide continuity
II. A stable pattern of these interactions
III. A sense of belonging
IV. Acceptance of common norms and values

Codes

(a) I, III and IV (b) II and IV
(c) III and IV (d) All of these

10. This is a kind of primary group, usually formed between individuals who are either of similar age or who are in a common professional group. Peer pressure refers to the social pressure exerted by one's peers on what one ought to do or not. Competency Based Que.

Which of the following groups come under the peer group?

I. Friends group **II. Reference group**
III. College group **IV. Colleague group**

Codes

(a) I, III and IV (b) II and I
(c) III and IV (d) All of these

11. Social Stratification is a critical concept in Sociology because

I. It defines the unequal distribution of resources and privileges across different social groups.
II. It emphasises the significance of achieved status in determining an individual's social position.
III. It leads to the creation of rigid social hierarchies, especially in caste systems.
IV. It enables the movement of individuals between social strata, based on personal merit.

Codes

(a) I and III (b) III and IV
(c) I, III and IV (d) II, III and IV

12. **Role stereotyping is a process of reinforcing some specific role for some member of the society. For example men and women are often socialised in stereotypical roles, as breadwinner and homemaker respectively. Social roles and status are often wrongly seen as fixed and unchanging.**

What could be the reasons/ factors that can often lead to Role Stereotyping? Competency Based Que.

I. Unemployment **II. Patriarchy**

III. Illiteracy and culture **IV. Unawareness**

Codes

(a) I and III (b) II, III and IV
(c) II and IV (d) I and IV

Assertion–Reason Questions

Direction (Q. Nos. 13-16) Two statements are given in the question below as Assertion (A) and Reason (R). Read the statements and choose the appropriate option.

(a) Both A and R are true and R is the correct explanation of A.
(b) Both A and R are true, but R is not the correct explanation of A.
(c) A is true, but R is false.
(d) A is false, but R is true.

13. **Assertion** (A) Secondary groups are relatively large in size, maintain formal and impersonal relationship.

Reason (R) The primary groups are goal oriented. Schools, government office, hospitals, student's associations are its examples.

14. **Assertion** (A) Aggregates are simply collection of people who are in this same place at the same time, but share no definite connection will one another.

Reason (R) Passengers waiting at a railway station or airport or bus stop or a cinema audience are examples of aggregates.

15. **Assertion** (A) In a caste stratification system, an individual's position depends entirely on ascribed status attributes such as birth.

Reason (R) In a class society, while achievement is important, ascribed status does not play as significant a role as in a caste system.

16. **Assertion** (A) In traditional Indian society, the caste system defined an individual's social position based on purity or pollution.

Reason (R) The four-fold varna system of Brahmins, Kshatriyas, Vaishyas, and Shudras, along with numerous jatis, shaped the hierarchy in Indian society.

Case Based Questions

Read the passage given below and answer the questions that follow by choosing the correct option.

17. In a caste stratification system an individual's position totally depends on the status attributes ascribed by birth rather than on any which are achieved during the course of one's life. This is not to say that in a class society there is no systematic constraint on achievement imposed by status attributes such as race and gender.

(i) **What is a key difference between caste and class systems?**
(a) Caste systems are less rigid.
(b) Class systems are based on race.
(c) Caste systems define position more completely by birth.
(d) Class systems do not allow for any constraints.

(ii) **In a class society, which factors can constrain achievement?**
(a) Birth order
(b) Economic status only
(c) Race and gender
(d) Educational qualifications

18. Conflict theorists usually would see social control more as a mechanism to impose the social control of dominant social classes on the rest of society. Stability would be seen as the writ of one section over the other. Likewise, law would be seen as the formal writ of the powerful and their interests on society.

(i) **What aspect of social control do conflict theorists emphasise?**
(a) Its ability to foster community
(b) Its role in maintaining order through consensus
(c) Its function in enforcing the interests of the powerful
(d) Its reliance on informal social norms

(ii) **What do conflict theorists believe stability in society represents?**
(a) Mutual agreement among all classes
(b) The dominance of one section over others
(c) Complete social mobility
(d) Equality among all social groups

Answers

1. (b) A family living together
2. (c) A caste-based movement always begins as a social group.
3. (b) Quasi group
4. (c) they influence aspirations and lifestyle choices, even if we are not part of them.
5. (d) Peer groups
6. (c) In-group
7. (b) Social structure
8. (b) The pressure from friends to conform to specific behaviours
9. (d) All of these
10. (a) I, III and IV
11. (a) I and III
12. (b) II, III and IV
13. (c) A is true, but R is false.
14. (a) Both A and R are true and R is the correct explanation of A.
15. (a) Both A and R are true and R is the correct explanation of A.
16. (a) Both A and R are true and R is the correct explanation of A.
17. (i) (c) Caste systems define position more completely by birth.

    (ii) (c) Race and gender
18. (c) Its function in enforcing the interests of the powerful

    (b) The dominance of one section over others

Subjective Questions

Very Short Answer Type Questions

1. For a discipline such as, say, nuclear physics that deals with matters unknown to most people and for which no word exists in common speech, it seems obvious that a discipline must develop a terminology.

Ans. A discipline must have terminology to understand the subject matter very well. Sociology needs terminology because its subject matter is familiar and many common sense words create ambiguity.

2. We saw how certain material and intellectual developments shaped the sociological perspective as well as its concerns. Likewise sociological concepts too have a story to tell. Many of the concepts reflect the concern of social thinkers to understand and map the social changes that the shift from pre-modern to modern entailed. What was the main feature of sociology in pre-modern period?

Ans. In the pre-modern period, sociology focused on small-scale, traditional societies marked by close, often face-to-face interactions. The main feature was the emphasis on primary groups, where relationships were personal and intimate.

Sociologists studied how these societies differed from modern, large-scale societies characterized by formal, impersonal interactions.

3. What do you mean by association?

Ans. The association is also called society in sociology. It refers to a group of people organised for a particular purpose or a limited number of purposes.

4. Give the idea behind the post World War-Second period of sociology.

Ans. In post World War-Second period, sociology was greatly influenced by the structural functionalists who found society essentially harmonious. They also found sociology as a useful instrument to compare society to an organism where different parts have different functions to play for the maintenance of the whole.

5. Discuss aggregates in relation to sociology?

Ans. Aggregates are collections of people who temporarily share the same physical space. They do not see themselves as belonging together and thus, do not have continuous interaction. For example passengers travelling in the same bus or train.

6. Social classes, status groups, age and gender groups, crowds can be seen as examples of quasi groups. As these examples suggest quasi groups may well become social groups in time and in specific circumstances.

What do you meant by quasi group?

Ans. A quasi group is an aggregate or combination that lacks structure or organisation and whose members unaware or less aware of the existence of groupings.

7. Mention any two characteristics of social group?

Ans. The two characteristics of social group are as follows

(i) The social groups have persistent interaction to provide continuity.

(ii) The social groups have a stable pattern of shared interest.

8. Explain the four basic systems of stratification that have existed in human societies?

Ans. The four basic systems of stratification are slavery, caste, estate and class. Each system has unique characteristics that define social hierarchies and influence individuals' roles and opportunities within society throughout history.

9. States how is class stratification different from caste stratification?

Class stratification is different from caste stratification in following two ways.

Ans. (i) Class stratification is based on one's economic and social status whereas caste stratification is determined by birth.

(ii) Class stratification is open to all but caste stratification prevents admission of other caste members.

10. Even today acute caste discrimination exists. At the same time the working of democracy has affected the caste system. Briefly explain how? Competency Based Que.

Ans. Acute caste discrimination persists, but democracy has empowered caste groups. Discriminated castes increasingly assert their rights, gaining strength as interest groups within the democratic framework of society.

11. Weber used the term life-chances, which refers to the rewards and advantages afforded by market capacity. Inequality, Weber argued might be based on economic relations. But it could also be based on prestige or on political power.

What do you understand by prestige?

Ans. Prestige is the value given to a status or role. It ranks occupations differently across societies. For example, doctors often have higher prestige than shopkeepers, even if they earn less. Perceptions of prestige can change over time.

12. In sociology what do you mean by status?

Ans. Status refers to the position of an individual, in a group or in society. Each status has certain defined rights and duties assigned to it.

13. Role conflict is the incompatibility among roles corresponding to one or more status. When does role conflict occur? Give an example. Competency Based Que.

Ans. Role conflict occurs when expectations from multiple roles clash.

For example, a middle-class working woman must balance her responsibilities as a mother and wife with her professional duties at work.

14. It must be apparent that each individual in a modern complex society such as ours occupies many different kinds of status during the course of his/her life. Explain with the help of an example.

Ans. In modern complex societies, individuals hold multiple statuses throughout life. For example, an individual can be a student, customer, sibling, passenger and patient highlighting the diversity of social roles.

15. What role conflict do Khasi men face, and how does it affect women?

Ans. Khasi men struggle between duties to their birth families and their wives. Women feel insecure, worried their husbands might prefer their sisters' homes, adding to their emotional stress and uncertainty in the marriage.

16. Mention any two characteristics of social control.

Ans. The two characteristics of social control are as following

(i) Social control puts pressure on individual's behaviour.

(ii) Social control helps in socialisation of man.

17. Explain the meaning of deviance?

Ans. A deviance refers to mode of action, which do not conform to the norms or values held by most of the members of a group of society.

18. What are the agencies and mechanisms of formal social control in modern society?

Ans. There are agencies and mechanisms of formal social control, for example, law and the state. In a modern society formal mechanisms and agencies of social control are emphasised.

19. A sanction is a mode of reward or punishment that reinforces socially expected forms of behaviour. What are negative and positive sanctions? Competency Based Que.

Ans. Positive sanctions reward individuals for good behaviour and adherence to social norms. Negative sanctions punish rule-breaking and deviance, helping to enforce societal expectations and maintain order.

Short Answer Type Questions

1. What do you understand by social groups? State any four characteristics of social groups.

Ans. Social group is a collection of two or more persons who continuously interact, share common interest and a sense of loyality within a given society. Four characteristics of social groups are given below

(i) It has persistent interaction to provide continuity.

(ii) There is a stable pattern of these interaction.

(iii) It has a sense of belonging to identify with other members i.e. each individual is conscious of the group itself and its own set of rituals, rules and symbols.

(iv) It has shared interest and have a definable structure.

2. Explain the meaning of primary and secondary groups and bring out the difference between them.

Ans. **Primary Groups** It refers to a small group of people connected by intimate, face-to-face association and cooperation members have a sense of belonging.

Secondary Groups This group is relatively large in size and maintain formal and impersonal relationship.

The difference between Primary and Secondary group are as following

Primary Group	Secondary Group
It is small group of people.	It is relatively large in size.
It is characterised by intimate face to face and emotional relationship.	It is characterised by formal and impersonal relationships.
It is person oriented.	It is goal-oriented.
Family, village and group of friends are example of primary groups.	Schools, government offices, hospitals are examples of secondary groups.

3. Discuss the importance of primary groups in the society.

Ans. The importance of primary groups in the society is stated in the points below

- It helps in the socialisation of the individuals and maintains social control over them.
- Man comes to know about himself in the primary group and primary group also teaches the members to work in the society according to its rules.
- Psychological and emotional needs of individual are fulfilled in primary groups.
- Children and younger generations are inculcated about values, social norms, regulations and religion in the primary groups by their family members.
- Many economical needs are also fulfilled by the primary groups such as family.

4. Write the differences between In-group and Out-group in your own words.

Ans. The differences between in-group and out-group are as following

In-group	Out-group
A group with which an individual identifies himself/herself, has a sense of belongingness with.	A group to which an individual feels individual, has no sense of belongingness identification.
It is a we-group.	It is a they-group.
There is a sense of attachment towards members only.	There is a sense of indifference and at times may be even hostility towards members.
Similarity in behaviour, attitude and opinion is observed among the members of these group.	Members of out-group may show dissimilar behaviour, attitude and opinion among themselves and to the outside.
Examples of in-group are members of a private club, caste, etc.	Examples of out-group are members of different clubs, teams and caste.

5. What do you understand by reference group and peer group? Give two examples of each of them.

Ans. **Reference Group** It is a group to which one does not belong but one aspires to be like them and therefore, tries to emulate their lifestyles. They are important sources of information about culture, lifestyle, aspiration and goal attainments. Examples of reference group are celebrities and teachers.

Peer Group This group is a kind of primary group, usually formed between individuals who are either of similar age or in a common professional group. Peer groups have a very strong influence in the life of an individual.

Examples of peer group are members of school cricket team and students of sociology batch of the school.

6. Inequality of power and advantage is central for sociology, because of the crucial place of stratification in the organisation of society. Every aspect of the life of every individual and household is affected by stratification. Opportunities for health, longevity, security, educational success, fulfillment in work and political influence are all unequally distributed in systematic ways. What is social stratification? Explain its key principles. **Competency Based Que.**

Ans. Social stratification refers to the existence of structured inequalities between groups in society, in terms of their access to material or symbolic rewards.

Following are the key principles of social stratification

- Social stratification is a trait of society, not simply a reflection of individual differences.
- Social stratification carries over from generation to generation.
- Social stratification is universal but variable. For example, caste system is more prevalent in India whereas class system is more prevalent in Westernised nations.
- It not just involves inequality but beliefs as well. For instance, members of upper caste in India believe that they are better than the rest spiritually.

7. Explain how urbanisation has influenced the caste system in India. Refer to the observations made by sociologist A.R. Desai to support your answer.

Ans. Urbanisation has influenced the caste system in India by challenging traditional practices like endogamy and avoidance of contact between castes. As cities grew with modern industries and cosmopolitan spaces, people from different castes began interacting in public places such as hotels, restaurants, and public transport.

Sociologist A.R. Desai observed that although caste-based discrimination persisted, these urban settings created spaces where members of all castes, including the so-called lower castes, interacted more freely, thereby slowly reducing the rigid boundaries of caste in everyday life. However, discrimination still existed in private interactions.

8. Roles and status are not given and fixed. People make efforts to fight against discrimination roles and status for example those based on caste, race or gender. At the same time there are sections in society who oppose such changes. Likewise individual violation of roles are often punished. Society thus functions not just with roles and status but also with social control. Define social control. Enlist different perspectives about the concept and meaning of social control. Competency Based Que.

Ans. Social control refers to various means used by a society to bring its disobedient or arrogant members in conformity with the rules, standards and values prevalent in society.

Different perspectives of social control are as following

(i) **The Functionalist Sociologists** refer social control as the use of force to regulate the behaviours of the individual and the groups. They also refers to the enforcing of values and patterns for maintaining order in society.

(ii) **The Conflict Sociologists** refer social control as mechanism to impose the social control of dominant social classes on the rest of the society.

9. Status is occupied, but roles are played. We may say that a status is an institutionalised role. It is a role that has become regularised, standardised and formalised in the society at large or in any of the specific associations of society. What do you understand by role in society? Give two examples and describe the two concepts of role in society. Competency Based Que.

Ans. Role refers to specific functions that a person is expected to perform in social group.

Two examples of role in society are as following

(i) Many women in India performs dual role of mother as well as of wife.

(ii) Students performs the role of student, friend and of daughter/son.

On the basis of socialisation, role is associated with two concepts namely

(i) **Role Conflict** It is the incompatibility among role corresponding to one or more status. It occurs when contrary expectations arise from two or more roles. For example, working women very often finds that her role as professional conflicts with that of a mother and wife.

(ii) **Role Stereotyping** It refers to reinforcing of certain roles. For example, the role of breadwinner for the husband and that of homemaker for the wife is often stereotyped in advertisement and films.

Long Answer Type Questions

1. Explain different types of concepts and ideas which helps in understanding society?

Ans. Sociology is marked by different ways of understanding society and looking at dramatic social changes that the modern society brought about. The different types of concepts and ideas can be understood in the society through the following points

- In the pre-modern period, there were contrary and contesting understandings of society. Like for Karl Marx class and conflict were key concepts to understand society. Whereas social solidarity and collective conscience were key terms for Emile Durkheim.
- In the post-world war second period, sociology was greatly influenced by the structural functionalists who found society essentially harmonious. They also found sociology as a useful instrument to compare society to an organism where different parts have function to play for the maintenance of the whole.
- Some tried to understand human behaviour within sociology by starting with the individual i.e. micro interaction. Other began with macro structures such as class, caste, market, state or even communities.

- Concepts like social control or stratification begin from a larger context within which individuals are already placed.

2. Describe the important characteristics features of secondary groups.

Ans. Important characteristic features of secondary group are as follows

- Unlike the primary group which is characterised by close, intimate and face to face relations, impersonal, formal and indirect relationship exists among the members of secondary group.
- The relationship among the members of club, professional group, political party or trade unions comes under the category of secondary groups.
- The relationships of the members of the secondary groups are based on mutual interest. The basis of these relationships are located in utility or common interests.
- Individuals in secondary group do not have intimate contact with each other and normally come together for specific practical purposes only.
- A secondary group is regulated by formal rules. A formal authority is established and clear cut division of labour, responsibilities and authorities may be also made.
- The main purpose of a secondary group is to fulfill a specific function. For example, a trade union is formed to better the working conditions of the workers.

3. Discuss briefly the meaning of status. Also discuss its various forms.

Ans. Status refers to the position of an individual occupied in a group or in society. Each status has certain defined rights and duties assigned to an individual. For example, father occupies a status which has many norms of conduct as well as certain responsibilities.

In other words, status is an institutionalised role that has become regularised, standardised and formalised in the society. Status has various forms such as status set, status sequence, etc.

(i) **Status Set** In a modern society, an individual as we saw occupies multiple status which is sociologically termed as status set. It is the all of the status held by an individual at a given time. For example, a women may have status of a daughter, wife, mother, professional worker, home maker and citizen.

(ii) **Status Sequence** It refers to the status, which is attained in succession or sequence at various stages of life. For example, a son becomes a father, a grandfather and so on.

4. In traditional societies, ascribed status played a major role in determining social position. Do you think modern societies, despite being achievement-based, still place importance on ascribed status? Explain with examples.

Ans. In modern societies, while achievement-based status plays a significant role, ascribed status still holds importance. In traditional societies, ascribed status determined one's social position based on birth, such as caste, race, age or kinship and was fixed across generations. In contrast, modern societies emphasize achievements like education, profession and income to determine an individual's position. However, ascribed status continues to influence social mobility and perception, even in achievement-based systems.

For example, the caste system in India, despite urbanisation and democratic advances, still exerts its influence. Even in urban areas, individuals from lower castes face discrimination, as reflected in A.R. Desai's observation that members of the depressed classes often face prejudices, even in modern workspaces like mills.

Another example is racial and gender-based discrimination, which persists in many societies, despite legal frameworks aimed at ensuring equal opportunities. While modern societies allow for upward mobility based on achievements, ascribed status—such as caste, race, and gender—continues to impact social interactions and perceptions, thus maintaining a degree of inequality in opportunities and treatment.

5. Read the given passage and answer the questions that follow.

A role is the dynamic or the behavioural aspect of status. Status is occupied, but roles are played. We may say that a status is an institutionalised role. It is a role that has become regularised, standardised and formalised in the society at large or in any of the specific associations of society. It must be apparent that each individual in a modern complex society such as ours occupies many different kinds of status during the course of his/her life. You as a school student may be a student to your teacher, a customer to your grocer, a passenger to the bus driver, a brother or sister to your sibling and a patient to the doctor. Needless to say, we could keep adding to the list. **Competency Based Que.**

(a) Analyse the concept of 'role conflict' in modern societies.

(b) How individuals may experience conflicting expectations from different roles in their status set.

Ans. (a) Role conflict occurs when an individual faces incompatible expectations from the different roles they occupy in their status set. In modern societies, individuals often occupy multiple statuses simultaneously, such as being a student, a worker, a parent and a community member.

Each of these roles comes with its own set of expectations and when these expectations conflict, role conflict arises.

(b) A person may experience role conflict between their role as a parent and their role as a worker. As a parent, they are expected to dedicate time and attention to their children, while as a worker, they must meet professional demands, such as deadlines and office hours. This conflict can cause stress, as they struggle to balance both roles effectively.

Similarly, if an individual holds a leadership position in a community group while also having responsibilities at home, the demands from both roles can conflict, leading to stress and a sense of being overwhelmed.

6. Why social control is necessary for an orderly social life? Explain.

Ans. Social control is necessary for an orderly social life, due to following reasons

- The society regulates the individual behaviour to maintain normative social order. The social control is also important for enforcement of values and patterns for maintaining order in society.
- If the individual is effectively socialised, he confirms to the accepted ways from force of habit as well as from his desire of being accepted and approved by other persons.
- If an individual is inadequately socialised, he/she has a tendency to deviate from the accepted ways, but he is forced towards conformity by the pressures of social control.
- Many sociologists believe that, it is necessary "to bring about conformity, solidarity and continuity of a particular group or society." It is possible only through social control. Society has to make use of its mechanism to accomplish the necessary order and discipline.
- Some sociologists have put forward the view that society is a collection of group of individuals. Man lives in society because it has a utility. Through society he is able to preserve his identity and views.
- In order to preserve his identity and characteristics, he has to exercise some control for which certain rules and institutions are created. These agencies of social control are helpful for preserving the identity of the individuals and society.

7. Clarify the differences between formal and informal social control.

Ans. The differences between formal and informal social control are

Formal Social Control	Informal Social Control
Conscious efforts are made to develop means of formal social control.	Means of informal social control develop automatically and without any conscious efforts.
Means of formal social control are written and clear. Therefore, they are concrete in nature.	Means of informal social control are not written and hence are abstract in nature.
They are implemented by administration system and individuals are forced to obey these means.	They are not implemented by society but individual is criticised by every one.
If any one tries to disobey these means than he/she is punished according to rules.	No one is punished in case of non-obedience but the individual is criticised by everyone.
Law, courts, police are some of its examples.	Family, religion, folkways, customs are some of its examples.

SELF ASSESSMENT TEST

Objective Type Questions

1. Which of the following is not the characteristics of society?

(a) Its membership can be formal or informal.
(b) It has shared interests.
(c) It accepts different norms and values.
(d) It has a definable structure.

2. Which among the following is group formed for fulfillment of specific goals or purpose.

(a) Reference group
(b) Association
(c) Peer group
(d) Primary group

3. **Assertion** (A) The group whose lifestyles are emulated are known as Reference groups.

Reason (R) In the colonial period many middle class indians aspired to behave like proper Englishman.

(a) Both A and R are true and R is the correct explanation of A.
(b) Both A and R are true, but R is not the correct explanation of A.
(c) A is true, but R is false.
(d) A is false, but R is true.

Case Based Questions

1. The groups to which we belong are not all of equal importance to us. Some groups tend to influence many aspects of our lives and bring us into 'personal association' with others. The term 'primary group' is used to refer to a small group of people connected by intimate and face-to-face association and co-operation. The members of primary groups have a sense of belonging. Family, village and groups of friends are examples of primary groups. Secondary groups are relatively large in size, maintain formal and impersonal relationships. The primary groups are person-oriented, whereas the secondary groups are goal oriented. Schools, government offices, hospitals, students associations, etc., are examples of secondary groups.

(i) Which of the following term is used to refer to a small group of people connected by intimate and face-to-face association and co-operation?

(a) Quasi group
(b) Primary group
(c) Social group
(d) Political group

(ii) Which group is important sources of information about culture, lifestyle, aspiration and goal attainments?

(a) Reference groups
(b) Formal groups
(c) Informal groups
(d) Social groups

Very Short Answer Type Questions

1. Social control refers to the ways society regulates individual and group behaviour to ensure conformity to established norms. It can be either formal, like laws enforced by the state or informal, like social pressure from family and friends. Both types of control work to maintain order, but informal control is often more subtle and based on personal relationships. How does informal social control differ from formal social control?

2. In traditional caste systems, social hierarchy is rigid and transmitted across generations, whereas modern class systems are more open and achievement-based. In democratic societies, there is no legal barrier preventing a person from a lower class or caste from reaching the highest positions? What can you infer about the difference between traditional caste systems and modern class systems?

3. An ascribed status is a position a person occupies by birth, such as caste or race, while an achieved status is a social position attained through personal effort, such as educational qualifications or professional expertise.

   How does the passage suggest that ascribed and achieved statuses influence an individual's position in society?
4. Discuss the contrast between 'community' and 'society' as described by classical sociologists.
5. Differentiate between 'ascribed' and 'achieved' status.

Short Answer Type Questions

1. Social roles and status are often assumed to be fixed, but the passage argues that individuals negotiate these roles through social interaction, thereby challenging traditional views of passive socialisation.

   What inference can you make about the process of socialisation based on the passage's argument regarding the negotiation of roles and status?
2. Role conflict occurs when a person experiences incompatible expectations from different roles. For example, a working woman may face role conflict balancing her responsibilities as a mother, wife and professional.

   What can you infer about role conflict based on the example of a working woman?
3. Explain reference group with suitable example.
4. Describe the meaning of social status and write its two forms.
5. State how does social control operate in society?

Long Answer Type Questions

1. Discuss the list of the features of social stratification.
2. Status prestige are interconnected terms. Explain.
3. Sociology is the study of human social life. A defining feature of human life is that humans interact, communicate and construct social collectivities. The comparative and historical perspective of sociology brings home two apparently innocuous facts. The first that in every society whether ancient or feudal or modern, Asian or European or African human groups and collectivities exist. The second that the types of groups and collectivities are different in different societies. Any gathering of people does not necessarily constitute a social group.

   (a) What is the difference between a social group and an aggregate? Give examples of each?

   (b) How does sociology help in understanding human social life and its diversity across different societies?

03 CHAPTER

Understanding Social Institutions

An institution works according to rules established or at least acknowledged by law or by custom. They limit individuals but also create opportunities. Institutions can be seen as an end in itself i.e. valuable in themselves, like family, religion or education.

▼ **YOUR STUDY GOALS**

3.1 Introduction
3.2 Family, Marriage and Kinship
3.3 Work and Economic Life
3.4 Political Institutions
3.5 Religion as a Social Institution
3.6 Education as a Social Institution

▼ **YOUR PRACTICE GOAL**

- Objective Type Questions (23 Qs ; MCQs, A-R, Case Based Questions)
- Subjective Questions (19 VSAs , 11 SAs, 5 LAs)

3.1 Introduction

In sociology, there are different ways to understand institutions. The functionalist perspective views institutions as sets of norms and values that meet society's needs. It identifies informal institutions (like family and religion) and formal institutions (like law and education). In contrast, the conflict perspective argues that not everyone is treated equally.

Social institutions serve the interests of dominant groups-based on class, caste, tribe or gender. The dominant group not only controls political and economic institutions but also shapes the ideas accepted in society.

3.2 Family, Marriage and Kinship

- The family seems very 'natural' to us and we often think all families are like our own. It appears universal and unchanging.
- However, sociology and social anthropology have shown through research that families, marriage and kinship vary widely across cultures. They are important in every society, but their characteristics differ.

- The family (private sphere) is connected to economic, political, cultural and educational (public) aspects of society. This connection shows why it's useful to draw from different disciplines.
- Functionalists believe the family fulfills important roles that help meet society's needs and maintain social order.
- Functionalists see the nuclear family as best for industrial society. In this setup, one adult works outside while the other manages the home and children. The husband typically takes the 'instrumental' role as breadwinner and the wife takes the 'affective' role in caring for the family.
- This idea is questionable because it is unfair to women and doesn't reflect reality. Studies show that women are a large part of the workforce in industries like garment export. The assumption that men must be the heads of households is also not always true.

Variation in Family Forms

- A key debate in India is about the shift from nuclear families to joint families. Sociology challenges common beliefs. In fact, nuclear families have always existed in India, especially among poorer castes and classes.
- Sociologist A.M. Shah notes that joint families have been increasing in post-independent India. He attributes this to rising life expectancy, which has grown from about 32.5 years for men and 31.7 years for women between 1941-50 to around 55 years for both by 1981-85.
- As a result, more elderly people (aged 60 and above) are living in the population. Shah points out that most elderly individuals live in joint households.
- This is a generalisation, but it reminds us not to assume that joint families are quickly disappearing. It highlights the importance of careful studies to compare different situations.
- Research shows that family structures vary across societies. Some societies are matrilocal, where newly married couples live with the woman's family. Others are patrilocal, where they live with the man's family.
- In patriarchal families, men hold power and authority, while in matriarchal families, women have a significant role in decision-making. **Matrilineal**[1] societies exist, but matriarchal societies are less common.

Female Headed Households

Female-headed households occur when men migrate to cities, leaving women to manage farms and support their families. This can also happen when women become widows or when men remarry and stop sending money to their families. In these cases, women take on the responsibility of providing for their households. In the Kolam community, which is found in South-Eastern Maharashtra and Northern Andhra Pradesh, having a female-headed household is considered normal.

Families are Linked to other Social Spheres and Families Change

- In everyday life, we often see the family as separate from other areas like the economy or politics. However, the family and its structure are closely connected to society as a whole.
- For example, after German unification in the 1990s, marriage rates dropped significantly. This happened because the new German state removed many protections and welfare programmes that supported families. As a result, people felt economically insecure and choose not to marry. This is an example of unintended consequences.
- Family and kinship can change due to larger or macro-economic forces, but changes are not the same in all countries or regions. Also, change doesn't mean that old norms and structures disappear completely. Change and continuity often happen together.

1 **Matrilineal** Inheritance or descent traced through the mother's side of the family.

Gendered Nature of the Family

- In many families, there is a belief that a male child will support parents in old age, while a female child will leave the family when she marries. This leads families to invest more in male children.
- Despite evidence that female babies are more likely to survive than male babies, the rate of **infant mortality**[2] is higher for female children in India.

Sex ratio in India Between 1901-2011

Year	Sex Ratio	Year	Sex Ratio
1901	972	1961	941
1911	964	1971	930
1921	955	1981	934
1931	950	1991	926
1941	945	2001	933
1951	946	2011	940

- Female foeticide has caused a sharp drop in the sex ratio. The child sex ratio fell from 934 girls per 1,000 boys in 1991 to 919 in 2011. This decline is particularly severe in prosperous states like Punjab, Haryana, Maharashtra and Uttar Pradesh.
- In Punjab, the child sex ratio has dropped to 846 girls per 1,000 boys and in some districts of Haryana, it is below 800.

The Institution of Marriage

Historically, marriage has taken many forms in different societies. It serves various functions depending on the culture. The ways in which marriage partners are chosen show a remarkable variety of customs and practices.

Forms of Marriage

- Marriage comes in many forms, which can be categorised by the number of partners and the rules about who can marry whom.
- There are two main types of marriage based on the number of partners: monogamy and polygamy.
- **Monogamy** means one spouse at a time. In this system, a man can have only one wife and a woman can have only one husband. Even where polygamy is allowed, monogamy is more common.
- In many societies, people can remarry after a spouse dies or after a divorce, but they cannot have more than one spouse at the same time. This type of marriage is called **Serial monogamy**.
- Men often remarry after losing a wife, while upper caste Hindu widows historically faced restrictions on remarriage. The campaign for widow remarriage was a key issue in 19th-century reform movements. Today, nearly 10% of all women in India and 55% of women over fifty years are widows.
- **Polygamy** involves having more than one spouse at the same time. It can be divided into two forms–polygyny (one husband with multiple wives) and polyandry (one wife with multiple husbands).
- Polyandry may occur in harsh economic conditions where a single man cannot support a wife and children. In extreme poverty, limiting population can also lead to polyandry.

The Matter of Arranging Marriages: Rules and Prescriptions

In some societies, parents or relatives make the decisions about who will marry whom. In other societies, individuals have more freedom to choose their own partners.

2 **Infant Mortality** Death rate of babies under one year in a population.

Rules of Endogamy and Exogamy

- In some societies restrictions are subtle, while in some others, individuals who can or cannot be married, are clearly defined.
- Marriage rules can be classified as endogamy and exogamy.
- **Endogamy** requires people to marry within a specific cultural group, like their caste. **Exogamy**, on the other hand, means marrying outside one's own group. These concepts apply to kinship units such as clans, castes and ethnic or religious groups.
- In India, some areas practice village exogamy. This means daughters marry into families from villages far away.
- This practice helps brides adjust to their new homes without interference from their own families.

Basic Concepts, Related to Family, Kinship and Marriage

- A family is a group of people connected by kinship ties, where adult members take care of children.
- Kinship ties come from marriage or blood relationships, like those between parents, siblings and offspring.
- Marriage is a socially recognised sexual union between two adults. When two people marry, they become relatives to each other and connect with each other's families.
- The family someone is born into is called the family of orientation, while the family formed through marriage is called the family of procreation.
- Kinship can be divided into two types–consanguineous kin, who are related by blood and affines, who are related by marriage.

Quick Test 1

1. Name the type of family which consists of married couples who reside with the wife's parents.
2. What forms the basic unit of social institutions?
3. In which type of family, male holds primary power?
4. When a man marries more than one woman it refers to which form of marriage?
5. What is the rule of marriage in which one individual has to marry outside his own group known as?

3.3 Work and Economic Life

- The idea of 'work' mainly refers to paid employment.
- The informal economy includes transactions outside regular employment, often involving cash for services or direct exchanges of goods.
- Work can be defined as tasks whether paid or unpaid that require mental and physical effort. The goal of work is to produce goods and services that meet human needs.

Modern Forms of Work and Division of Labour

- In pre-modern societies, most people worked in fields or took care of livestock.
- In industrialised societies, only a small part of the population works in agriculture and farming has become industrialised, mainly using machines instead of manual labour.
- In India, a larger share of the population still works in rural agriculture or related jobs, but the service sector is also growing.
- Modern economies have a very complex **division of labour**[3]. Work is divided into many different jobs where people specialise.
- In traditional societies, non-agricultural work required mastering a craft through a long **apprenticeship**[4]. Workers would manage all parts of the production process themselves.

---

3 **Division of Labour** The specialisation of work tasks, by means of which different occupations are combined within a production system.

4 **Apprenticeship** A system where a person learns a trade from a skilled worker.

- Industrialisation changed where work happens. Before this, most work was done at home and involved all family members.
- Advances in technology, like electric and coal-powered machinery, led to the separation of work from home. Factories became central to industrial growth.
- People looking for factory jobs were trained for specific tasks and paid wages. Managers were responsible for improving worker productivity and discipline.
- A key feature of modern societies is a vast increase in economic interdependence.

Transformation of Work

- Industrial processes have been simplified into small operations that can be timed, organised and monitored easily. Mass production needs large markets. One key innovation was the moving assembly line.
- Recently, there has been a shift to 'flexible production' and 'decentralisation of work'. This change is driven by global competition, which forces companies to adapt their production to meet changing market needs.
- In the garment industry in Bangalore, for example, the production process is part of a long supply chain. Manufacturers have limited freedom, as there are over a hundred steps between the designer and the final customer, but they control only about 15 of those steps.
- If workers demand higher wages, manufacturers might move their operations elsewhere to avoid unions.
- For wage increases, it's crucial to get support from retailers. They can help create pressure on the government and local agencies for better wages and their proper enforcement. This highlights the need for an international opinion forum to support workers.
- This situation shows how the new organisation of production and global customers have changed the economics and politics of manufacturing.

3.4 Political Institutions

- Political institutions deal with how power is distributed in society. Two key concepts to understand are power and authority.
- Power is the ability of individuals or groups to carry out their will, even against opposition. It means that those who hold power do so at the expense of others.
- Power is limited in society; if some people have power, others do not. Therefore, power exists in relation to others.
- This idea of power includes many situations, from family elders assigning chores to children, to school principals enforcing rules and factory managers dividing work among employees.
- Authority is a type of power that is accepted as legitimate, meaning it is seen as right and fair. Authority is institutionalised because it is based on this **legitimacy**[5].
- People generally accept the power of those in authority because they believe it is fair and justified. Often, **ideologies**[6] support this process of legitimising authority.

Stateless Societies

- **Empirical studies**[7] of stateless societies conducted by social anthropologists over sixty years ago showed that order can be maintained without a modern government.
- Instead, these societies relied on balanced opposition among different groups. They formed alliances based on kinship, marriage and where people lived. Rites and ceremonies involved both friends and enemies.
- In contrast, the modern state has a fixed structure and formal procedures.

---

5 **Legitimacy** It is a belief that a particular political order is just and valid.
6 **Ideologies** Shared ideas or beliefs, which serve to justify the interests of dominant groups.
7 **Empirical Studies** It means factual enquiry carried out in any given area of sociological study.

The Concept of the State

- A state exists where there is a government that rules over a specific territory. This includes institutions like a parliament and civil service officials.
- The government's authority is supported by a legal system and the ability to use military force to enforce policies.
- From a functionalist view, the state represents the interests of all sections of the society. In contrast, the conflict perspective argues that the state represents the dominant groups.
- Modern states differ from traditional ones. They are defined by sovereignty, **citizenship**[8] and often nationalism. Sovereignty means the state has undisputed control over its territory.

Citizenship

- Initially, citizenship did not guarantee political participation rights.
- These rights were gained through struggles that limited or overthrew monarchs, such as the French Revolution and India's independence movement.
- Citizenship rights include civil, political and social rights.
- Civil rights involve personal freedoms like where to live, free speech, religious freedom, property ownership and equal justice.
- Political rights include the right to vote and run for office. Initially, many people, were excluded from voting based on property ownership. Women had to wait longer to gain the right to vote.
- Social rights ensure individuals have a minimum standard of economic welfare and security, such as health benefits and unemployment support.
- Socialist countries often had more extensive social provisions, while developing nations typically had few.

Nationalism

- Nationalism is a set of symbols and beliefs that create a sense of belonging to a political community. This gives individuals pride in their identity as members of a nation, such as being British or Indian.
- Although people have always identified with various social groups, nationalism emerged with modern states.
- Sociologists study power broadly, not just through formal government structures. They look at power distribution among political parties, classes, castes and communities based on race, language and religion.
- Their focus includes not only political institutions like legislatures and political parties but also non-political associations like schools, banks and religious groups.
- Sociology's scope ranges from international movements, to local village conflicts.

Quick Test 2

1. What do you understand by work?
2. The undisputed political rule of a state over territorial area is known as what?
3. Write any two civil rights.
4. The right of participate in elections and to stand for public office are included under which citizenship rights?

8 **Citizenship** A member of a political community, having both rights and duties associated with that membership.

3.5 Religion as a Social Institution

- Religion has been studied for a long time, and sociologists approach it differently than **theologians**[9]. They focus on how religions function in society and relate to other institutions.
- Sociologists conduct empirical studies without judgement and use a comparative method to avoid bias. This helps them understand religious life in connection with family, economy and politics.
- All societies have religion, but beliefs and practices differ widely. Common features of religions include
  - Symbols that inspire reverence.
  - Rituals or ceremonies.
  - A community of believers.
- Rituals, like praying or fasting, differ from everyday habits. Lighting a candle for worship is not the same as lighting a room. Ceremonies often occur in sacred places like churches and temples.
- Sociologists following Emile Durkheim, study the sacred aspect of society, which is different from the ordinary or profane.
- The sacred often involves the supernatural, though some religions, like early Buddhism, have no supernatural focus but still consider certain things sacred.

Interconnection of Religion with Society

- Religion is closely linked to power and politics. Historical movements, such as anti-caste and gender discrimination movements, show that religion is not just personal but also public.
- Classical sociologists thought modernisation would reduce religion's influence, known as secularisation.
- Max Weber explored how sociology connects religion to social and economic behaviour. He argued that Calvinism, a branch of Protestant Christianity, significantly influenced the rise of capitalism.
- Calvinists believed the world was created for God's glory, so all work should honour him, turning even ordinary tasks into acts of worship.
- They also believed in predestination, meaning one's fate in heaven or hell was decided in advance.
- Calvinists thought that money should not be spent on luxuries; they valued **frugality**[10].
- This led to viewing investment as a sacred duty. Investment is central to capitalism, involving the use of money to produce goods and make profits, which generate more capital.
- Thus, Weber argued that Calvinism had a real impact on economic development.
- Religion cannot be isolated from social forces. Political, economic, and gender factors shape religious behavior, while religious norms influence social understandings.
- Religion is an essential part of society and interconnected with many other aspects. Sociologists aim to explore these connections.

Preists of Nasik

Many outside factors have changed the traditional lives of religious specialists in Nasik. After Independence, priests' families have started sending their children to school and training them for non-traditional jobs. Like other pilgrimage sites, Nasik also developed additional centers for religious activities. Pilgrims would regularly take home sacred water from the Godavari in copper pots made by coppersmiths. They also bought items to give as gifts. Nasik was known for skilled craftsmen in brass, copper, and silver. However, since the demand for these goods is irregular, not all adult males can rely on this work. Many craftsmen have turned to industry and business, both small and large scale.

9 **Theologians** It means scholars who study and interpret religious doctrines and beliefs.

10 **Frugality** It means careful use of resources, avoiding waste and unnecessary spending.

3.6 Education as a Social Institution

- Education is a lifelong process that includes both formal and informal learning.
- Sociology views education as a way to pass down cultural heritage. Simple societies do not require formal schooling; children learn through activities with adults.
- In complex societies, there is a need for specialised skills, making formal education necessary.
- Modern societies are based on universal values, unlike simple societies that focus on family or tribal values.
- Schools promote uniformity and standardisation, such as through school uniforms, to promote equality.
- Emile Durkheim stated that societies require a common base of ideas and practices that education should impart to all children. Education prepares children for specific jobs and instills core societal values.
- Functionalist sociologists argue that education maintains social structure and develops culture, placing individuals in roles based on their abilities.

Education and Social Inequality

- Sociologists who recognise societal inequality see education as a major factor in social stratification.
- This can widen the gap between the elite and the masses, as children from privileged school may gain confidence while those in underprivileged schools may not.
- Many children cannot attend school or drop out. For example, during planting season, SC and ST children's attendance may drop down to zero due to household responsibilities. Girls in these communities often miss school for domestic work, like collecting cow dung for sale.
- This highlights how gender and caste discrimination impact educational opportunities, shaping children's chances for good jobs.

Quick Test 3

1. Write any two characteristics of all religions.
2. Identify the concept which describes the process where religion become less influential?
3. What is secularisation?
4. Who argued that calvinism influenced the growth of capitalism?

NCERT Folder

1. Note what are the marriage rules that are followed in your society? Compare your observations with these made by other students in the class. Discuss.

Ans. In my society, marriage rules often emphasise endogamy, where individuals are enocouraged to marry within their caste or religious group. However, exogamy is also practiced, particularly in inter-caste or inter-religious marriages, though these are less common.

Comparison

- Unlike the village exogamy mentioned in the content, where daughters marry far from their natal homes, marriages in my society do not always involve such significant geographical separation.
- The emotional aspect of leaving the natal home is similar, and this is also expressed through customs and songs in my culture.

Discussion

Observations from classmates may reveal variations, such as societies practicing more freedom in partner choice or stricter adherence to endogamy. It highlights the diversity of marriage rules across cultures.

2. Find out how membership, residence pattern and even the mode of interaction changes in the family with broader economic, political and cultural changes, for instance migration?

Ans. Social relations are the base of group structure. Modern society is changing rapidly and so is its structure and composition. Change is a universal and continuous process. Due to industrialisation, urbanisation, globalisation, information and technology, easy availability of electric and electronic gadgets and means of commutation has tremendous influence on our communication and social interaction.

Modern society is not significantly relationship oriented instead it is time focused society. Therefore, with broader economic, political and cultural changes migration within the country as well as outside the country is a common phenomena and due to low cost calls, skype, whatsapp and other sources the mode of social interaction has changed.

3. Write an essay on 'work'. Focus on both the range of occupations, which exist and how they change?

Ans. 'Work' is mainly assessed in terms of its monetary value and the addition to the economic structure of the country. The 'Formal economy' and its development is also considered as 'work' but the aspects of 'Informal economy' are not taken into the assessment which results in oppression of particular sections of the society.

The range of occupations start from the household, agriculture, industry, etc. These range of occupations have changed tremendously due to the impact of capitalism and changing social narratives of the country. The occupations changed to being more industrialised or money oriented due to economic transformation of the society.

The agricultural sector has shown a tremendous decline in regards with the human capital as the increasing inclination is towards the industrial sectors. The changing occupational patterns are subject to environment, stipends and other governing factors of the society.

The recent change in employment sectors like equal pay, minimum wage, etc. has created a change in the occupational structure of the respective countries and gave rise to a new type of discourse on the lines of occupational equality.

4. Discuss the kind of rights that exist in your society. How do they affect your life?

Ans. There are three kinds of rights that exist in our society

(i) **Political rights** such as participation in the formation of the government by casting vote. Political rights include the right to participate in elections and to stand for public office. Participation in the formation of government by casting votes.

In most countries governments were reluctant to admit the principle of universal franchise. In the early years, not only women but a large section of male population was excluded as holding a certain amount of property was an eligibility criterion. Woman as such had to wait longer for the right to vote.

(ii) **Civil rights** such as freedom of speech, choice of religion, the right to equal justice before the law. The citizen has the freedom to live anywhere in the state territory and has the right to own property irrespective of his/her gender.

(iii) **Social rights** such as health benefits, unemployment allowance, and setting of minimum level of wages. The citizen can enjoy a minimum standard of economic welfare and security.

These rights help in the smooth functioning of life of individuals, as they help in the growth of personality. For instance, the individual can go for higher studies of his/her subject of interest, he/she can learn any form of music and dance and can also practice in any religion. Therefore, the individual has the right to make his/her own choice and can also demand justice by appealing to the court.

5. How does sociology study religion?

Ans. Sociology studies religion as an institution and conducts it in three ways as following

(i) It conducts an empirical study of how religions actually function in society and its relationship to other institutions.

(ii) It uses a comparative method.

(iii) It investigates the religious beliefs and practices in relation to other aspects of the society.

According to socialist study, religion has certain beliefs, norms, rules and regulations that are expected to be followed by its members, which govern and regulate their behaviour.

Classical sociologists believed that as societies have modernised, the influence of religion on the lives of individuals has decreased, which has led to secularism.

Many thinkers of sociology have presented their theories upon religion and their origin. For example, Max Weber in his study, the Protestant Ethic and the Rise of Capitalism viewed that capitalism was a result of Calvinism and their thinking of increasing the economic activity, in order to please the God.

Similarly, other sociologists of religion presented the view of differentiating the sacred from the profane that existed in religious societies.

Further religion is considered to have a public character, as it holds strong ties with other institutions like politics, economics, education and marriage and kinship.

6. Write an essay on school as a social institution. Draw from both your reading as well as your personal observations.

Ans. The need for education gave rise to schools, and sociology terms this a process of transmission or communication of group heritage, which is common to all the societies. The schools function in order to discipline and regulate human behaviour.

Hence, it becomes a permanent and binding character. Furthermore, Ginsberg defines the established institutions as "the recognised and established usage governing the relations between individuals and groups" and schools are established institutions that provide formal education to students.

The institution of school is imperative for the establishment of the educational premise which results in the maximum and integrated development of an individual. The school is responsible for the inculcation of social, cultural and moral norms within the identities of the students.

Exam Pattern Questions

Objective Type Questions

Multiple Choice Questions (MCQs)

1. In which form or type of family women play a major role in the decision making?

(a) Nuclear family (b) Patrilineal family
(c) Matriarchal family (d) Extended family

2. According to functionalists, what role does the husband typically play in a nuclear family?

(a) Affective role (b) Instrumental role
(c) Emotional caregiver (d) Primary educator

3. The decline in the child sex ratio in prosperous Indian states like Punjab and Haryana is primarily due to

(a) Migration to urban areas
(b) Preference for matriarchal family structures
(c) High infant mortality rates among boys
(d) Female foeticide

4. According to sociologist ...., the number of joint families has gradually increased in post-independence India. According to him, the rising life expectancy in India is a contributing factor. Over the period 1941–50 to 1981–85, it increased for men from 32.5 to 55.4 years and for women from 31.7 to 55.7 years. As a result, the proportion of people aged 60 and up in the total population has risen.

(a) A.M. Shah (b) Emile Durkheim
(c) Herbert Spencer (d) Georg Simmel

5. Identify the incorrect statement from the following.

(a) Female-headed households are only found in tribal societies.
(b) The nuclear family is best suited for industrial societies according to functionalists.
(c) Joint families in India have increased due to rising life expectancy.
(d) The family is linked to economic, political and cultural spheres.

6. Which of the following best describes the informal economy?

(a) Work that is recorded in official employment statistics.
(b) Paid employment in registered companies.
(c) Transactions outside regular employment, often involving cash or barter.
(d) Government-sponsored jobs in the public sector.

7. One of the main features of modern societies is an enormous expansion of .... We are all dependent on an immense number of other workers-stretching right across the world–for the products and services that sustain our lives. With few exceptions, the vast majority of people in modern societies do not produce the food they eat, the houses they live in or the material goods they consume. Competency Based Que.

(a) Political interdependence
(b) Economic interdependence
(c) Social interdependence
(d) None of the above

8. Right to equal justice before law is known as which right?

(a) Civil (b) Political (c) Judicial (d) Social

9. Which of the following rights includes the right to own property?

(a) Social Rights
(b) Civil Rights
(c) Political Rights
(d) None of these

10. **"The dominant social section not only dominates political and economic institutions but also ensures that the ruling class ideas become the ruling ideas of a society."** **Competency Based Que.**

Which of the following factors make the Dominant caste dominant?

I. Social status in society   II. Land rights
III. Decisive role in politics
IV. Large population in a region

Codes

(a) I, III and IV   (b) I, II and III
(c) II and IV   (d) All of these

11. **"Marriage has a large variety of forms. These forms can be identified on the basis of the number of partners and rules governing who can marry whom."** **Competency Based Que.**

Identify the type of marriage with the help of the options given below.

I. It restricts the individual to one spouse at a time.
II. Under this system, at any given time a man can have only one wife and a woman can have only one husband.
III. The individuals are permitted to marry again, often on the death/divorce of/with the first spouse.

Codes

(a) Monogamy (b) Polygamy (c) Endogamy (d) Exogamy

12. **Which of the following best describes a key feature of modern industrial production?**

(a) Mastery of all parts of the production process by workers.
(b) Use of electric and coal-powered machinery for home-based work.
(c) Simplification of processes into small operations monitored for efficiency.
(d) Decentralisation of work into individual households.

13. **What does the concept of sovereighty mean in the context of modern states?**

(a) The state ensures equal social rights for all citizens.
(b) The state has undisputed control over its territory.
(c) The state provides economic welfare to its citizens.
(d) The state promotes alliances based on kinship and marriage.

14. **Which of the following is an example of a matrilineal society?**

(a) A society where inheritance is traced through the father.
(b) A society where newly married couples live with the wife's family.
(c) A society where men hold all decision-making power.
(d) A society with patriarchal norms and joint families.

15. **According to Max Weber, which belief of Calvinism contributed to the rise of capitalism?**

(a) The idea that money should be spent on luxuries
(b) The belief in predestination and viewing success in work as a sign of God's approval
(c) Rejecting the need for frugality in economic activities
(d) Encouraging people to focus on family values rather than economic growth

Assertion-Reason Questions

Direction (Q. Nos. 16-20) Two statements are given in the question below as Assertion (A) and Reason (R). Read the statements and choose the appropriate option.

(a) Both A and R are true and R is the correct explanation of A.
(b) Both A and R are true, but R is not the correct explanation of A.
(c) A is true, but R is false.
(d) A is false, but R is true.

16. **Assertion** (A) Work in the informal economy is not always recorded in official employment statistics.

Reason (R) Much of the work done in the informal economy involves direct exchanges of goods and services, rather than paid employment.

17. **Assertion** (A) In traditional societies, work was often done collectively at home.

Reason (R) Before industrialisation, work was primarily agricultural and the family played a central role in production.

18. **Assertion** (A) Sovereignty refers to the undisputed political rule of a state over a given territorial area.

Reason (R) These states were achieved largely through struggles, which limited the power of monarchs or actively overthrow them.

19. **Assertion** (A) Religious rituals are distinct from the habits and procedures of ordinary life, as they are oriented toward religious symbols.

Reason (R) The act of lighting a candle or diya for religious purposes carries a completely different significance than simply lighting a room.

20. **Assertion** (A) Education is a life-long process, involving both formal and informal institutions of learning.

Reason (R) Children learnt customs and the broader way life by participating in activities with their adults.

Case Based Questions

Read the passage given below and answer the questions that follow by choosing the correct option.

21. According to the functionalists the family performs important tasks, which contribute to society's basic needs and helps perpetuate social order. The functionalist perspective argues that modern industrial societies function best if women look after the family and men earn the family livelihood. In India studies however suggest that families need not become nuclear in an industrial pattern of economy (Singh 1993: 83). This is but one example to show how trends based on experiences of one society cannot necessarily be generalised.

(i) According to the functionalist perspective, what is the role of women in the family?
(a) To work outside the home and earn money
(b) To take care of the family and children
(c) To assume the role of the breadwinner
(d) To manage economic and political affairs

(ii) Which family structure does the functionalist perspective believe is best suited for industrial societies?
(a) Extended family (b) Nuclear family
(c) Joint family (d) Polygamous family

22. One of the main features of modern societies is an enormous expansion of economic interdependence. We are all dependent on an immense number of other workers-stretching right across the world–for the products and services that sustain our lives. With few exceptions, the vast majority of people in modern societies do not produce the food they eat, the houses they live in or the material goods they consume.

(i) Which of the following best describes the economic system in modern societies?
(a) Economic isolationism
(b) Economic self-sufficiency
(c) Economic interdependence across global workers
(d) Decline in trade and outsourcing

(ii) How does the global labour force contribute to modern societies?
(a) By producing and delivering goods and services that sustain daily life
(b) By restricting the flow of goods and services to local markets
(c) By creating a self-sufficient economy
(d) By encouraging local farming and crafts

23. Marriage has a large variety of forms. These forms can be identified on the basis of the number of partners and rules governing who can marry whom. In terms of the number of partners that can legitimately enter into matrimony, we have two forms of marriage, namely, monogamy and polygamy. Monogamy restricts the individual to one spouse at a time. Under this system, at any given time a man can have only one wife and a woman can have only one husband.

(i) Which form of marriage is more widely practiced, even where polygamy is permitted?
(a) Polygamy (b) Serial Monogamy
(c) Monogamy (d) Bigamy

(ii) In which form of marriage is remarriage permitted after the death of a spouse or divorce, but only one spouse is allowed at a time?
(a) Polygamy
(b) Serial Monogamy
(c) Monogamy
(d) Bigamy

Answers

1. (c) Matriarchal family 2. (b) Instrumental role
3. (d) Female foeticide 4. (a) A.M. Shah
5. (a) Female-headed households are only found in tribal societies.
6. (c) Transactions outside regular employment, often involving cash or barter.
7. (b) Economic interdependence
8. (a) Civil 9. (b) Civil Rights
10. (b) I, II and III 11. (a) Monogamy
12. (c) Simplification of processes into small operations monitored for efficiency.
13. (b) The state has undisputed control over its territory.
14. (b) A society where newly married couple live with the wife's family.
15. (b) The belief in predestination and viewing success in work as a sign of God's approval.
16. (a) Both A and R are true and R is the correct explanation of A.
17. (a) Both A and R are true and R is the correct explanation of A.
18. (a) Both A and R are true and R is the correct explanation of A.
19. (a) Both A and R are correct and R is the correct explanation of A.

20. (b) Both A and R are true, but R is not the correct explanation of A.

21. (i) (b) To take care of the family and children
(ii) (b) Nuclear family

22. (i) (c) Economic interdependence across global workers
(ii) (a) By producing and delivering goods and services that sustain daily life

23. (i) (c) Monogamy
(ii) (b) Serial Monogamy

Subjective Questions

Very Short Answer Type Questions

1. Each one of us has a status and a role or roles, but these are not simply what we as individuals choose. They are not like roles a film actor may or may not opt to do. There are social institutions that constrain and control, punish and reward. What is social institution?

Ans. An established and structured pattern of behaviour or of relationship that is accepted as a fundamental part of a culture can be referred to as social institutions. For example, family, marriage, kinship, etc.

2. Mention one function of economic institution.

Ans. Economic institutions coordinate activities of individuals with regard to production, distribution and consumption of goods and services in the society.

3. The functionalist perspective argues that modern industrial societies function best if women look after the family and men earn the family livelihood. What inference can you draw about the implications of this view on gender roles and societal expectations?

Ans. This view reinforces traditional gender roles, portraying women as caregivers and men as breadwinners. It suggests societal expectations are rooted in predefined roles, limiting individual choices. Such a perspective may perpetuate inequality, hindering progress towards gender equity and ignoring the evolving dynamics of modern societies where roles are more fluid.

4. What do you mean by patriarchal family? Explain with example.

Ans. In this kind of family, male member holds the primary power. For example, Fathers or father figures hold authority over women and children.

5. Write any one social function of the family.

Ans. Socialisation of a child takes place in the family. Child learns, in family, the ways of behaving with others and becomes a good citizen. Family also protects our culture and transmits it to next generation.

6. The family is described as being linked to economic, political, cultural and educational spheres. What does this suggest about the interconnectedness of private and public domains in society?

Ans. The family's connection to economic, political, cultural and educational spheres shows that private family life affects and is influenced by public matters. For example, a family's financial situation can impact education choices and cultural values can shape political views, highlighting how personal and societal life are closely linked.

7. The sociologist A.M. Shah remarked that the joint family has steadily increased in post-independent India due to rising life expectancy. How does this observation challenge the common belief about the erosion of joint families?

Ans. A.M. Shah's observation challenges the belief that joint families are disappearing in modern India. He suggests that rising life expectancy, meaning people live longer, actually supports the growth of joint families. Older generations need care, leading to more families living together instead of breaking apart as often assumed.

8. Forms of marriage based on rules governing eligibility/ inegilibility of mates is classified as endogamy and exogamy. Discuss the rules of endogamy and exogamy of marriage.

Ans. The rules of endogamy and exogamy of marriage are discussed below

(i) **Endogamy** It requires an individual to marry within a culturally defined group of which he or she is already a member. For example, caste

(ii) **Exogamy** It is a reverse of endogamy as it requires the individual to marry outside his/her own group.

9. It is stated that village exogamy ensured geographical distance and reduced interference of the bride's kin in her new home. What social or cultural purposes might this practice serve?

Ans. Village exogamy, where people marry outside their village, helps maintain distance between the bride's family and her new home. This practice reduces interference from the bride's relatives, allowing the couple to establish their own family life. It promotes independence, strengthens social ties and reduces conflict between families.

10. In how many parts kinship can be divided?

Ans. Kinship can be divided in two parts as following
(i) Affinal kinship (ii) Consanguinal kinship

11. What do you understand by consanguineous kinship?

Ans. Relation by the bond of blood is called Consanguineous kinship. For example, the bond between parents and their children and that of between siblings is consanguineous kinship.

12. Sociology and social anthropology have over many decades, conducted field research across cultures to show how the institutions of family, marriage and kinship are important in all societies and yet their character is different in different societies.

How do a relationship establish between the family, kinship and marriage?

Ans. A family is a group of persons directly linked by kin connections. When two young people marry, they become kin to one another. Parents, brothers, sisters and other blood relations become relatives of the newly married couple through marriage ceremony.

13. What do you understand by work?

Ans. The most widely understood sense of work in modern day, is paid employment.

14. Many types of work do not conform to the idea of paid employment much of the work is done in the informal economy. What is informal economy? **Competency Based Que.**

Ans. The term informal economy refers to transactions outside the sphere of regular employment, sometimes involving the exchange of cash for services provided, but also often involving the direct exchange of goods and services.

15. Modern states are defined by sovereignty, citizenship and most often, ideas of nationalism. In the light of the above statement, define sovereignty? **Competency Based Que.**

Ans. The undisputed political rule of a state over a given territorial area is known as Sovereignty.

16. Discuss what do you understand by nationalism?

Ans. Nationalism refers to a set of symbols and beliefs providing the sense of being part a single political community. Thus, individuals feel a sense of pride and belongingness.

17. Religion exists in all known societies, although religious beliefs and practices vary from culture to culture. In the light of the statement state some common characteristics of the states. **Competency Based Que.**

Ans. Some characteristics that all states share are
- Set of symbols, invoking feelings of reverence or awe.
- Specific rituals or ceremonies.
- A community of believers.

18. Sociologists of religion, following Emile Durkheim, are interested in understanding this sacred realm which every society distinguishes from the profane. In what manner has Emile Durkheim explained the term 'sacred realm'? **Competency Based Que.**

Ans. Emile Durkheim explained the 'sacred realm' as things or places set apart from everyday life, often linked to supernatural powers. Societies believe that certain objects, like trees or temples, are sacred because they are connected to these higher forces.

19. Discuss functionalist view of education.

Ans. The functionalist view states that socialisation function of education also serves to promote social control and to curb deviant behaviour.

Short Answer Type Questions

1. State the functionalist and conflict view of understanding social institutions.

Ans. A functionalist view understands social institution as a complex set of social norms beliefs, values and role relationships that arises in response to the needs of society. Social institutions exist to satisfy social needs. Accordingly, we find informal and formal institutions in societies. Institutions such as family and religion are examples of informal social institutions while law and education are formal institutions.

A conflict view holds that all individuals are not placed equally in a society. All social institutions whether familial, religious, political, economic, legal or educational will operate in the interest of the dominant sections of society-be it caste, tribe or gender.

2. Marriage has a large variety of forms. These forms can be identified on the basis of the number of partners and rules governing who can marry whom. Discuss various types of marriage form that exist in society.

Types of marriage form that exist in society are as follows **Competency Based Que.**

Ans.
- Monogamy restricts the individual to one spouse at a time. Under this system, at any given time a man can have only one wife and woman can have only one husband. In many societies, individuals are permitted to marry again often on the death of first spouse or after divorce. But they cannot have more than one spouse at one and same time. Such monogamous marriages are termed as serial monogamy.
- Polygamy denotes marriage to more than one partner at one time and takes the form of either.

- Polyandry, one wife with two or more husbands. Usually, where economic conditions are harsh, polyandry may be one response of society, since in such situations, a single male cannot adequately support a wife and children.
- Polygyny one husband with 2 or more wives.

3. What is kinship? How is the system of kinship determined?

Ans. The kinship represents one of the basic social institution and plays a significant role in the socialisation of individuals and the maintenance of group solidarity. It is a relation between two or more persons that is based on common ancestry (descent) or marriage (affinity) is known as kinship.

Kinship is one of the main organising principles of society. It is one of the basic social institutions found in every society. This institution establishes relationship between individuals and groups. People in all societies are bound together by various kinds of bonds. The most basic bonds are based on marriage and reproduction. Kinship refers to these bonds and all other relationships resulting from them.

The kinship system is determined by following factors are as following

- Rules of social behaviour
- Providing of social help and security
- Maintenance of socio-cultural relationship
- Regulates social behaviour

4. "In modern societies, most people are not involved in producing the food they eat or the clothes they wear. What does this suggest about the complex interdependence of work in the modern economy?"

Ans. In modern societies, most people don't directly produce food or clothes. Instead, they depend on others for these things. This shows how interdependent work is in today's world. Different people and industries are responsible for various tasks, such as farming, manufacturing and retail. Each person or group specialises in one part of the process and all these tasks come together to provide goods and services. This complex web of interdependent work ensures that people can access the products they need, even if they aren't directly involved in making them.

5. Discuss political institution and its concepts.

Ans. Political institutions are concerned with the distribution of power in society. Political institutions are institutions of formal social control. They are mechanism or agencies related to the exercise of legitimate power for maintaining order within a society.

(i) **Power** It is the ability to influence or control the behaviour of people. In other words, an individual or group does not hold power in isolation, they hold it in relation to others.

(ii) **Authority** Power is exercised through authority. Authority is accepted as legitimate means as right and just. It is institutionalised due to legitimacy.

6. Discuss the concept of a modern state.

Ans. The modern state has a fixed structure and formal procedures.

The modern states are very different from traditional state. They are defined also by sovereignty, citizenship and ideas of nationalism that it acquires.

State exists where there is a political apparatus of government ruling over a given territory. Government authority is backed by a legal system and by the capacity to use military force to implement its policies.

The functionalist perspective sees the state as representing the interests of all sections of the society. On the other hand, the conflict perspective sees the state as representing the dominant sections of the society.

7. What are the citizenship rights in the modern state or welfare state?

Ans. Citizenship rights include civil, political and social rights.

Civil rights involve the freedom of individuals to live where they choose, freedom to speech and religion, the right to own property and the right to equal justice before law.

Political rights include the right to participate in elections and to stand for public office. In most countries, government were reluctant to admit the principle of universal franchise. For instance, women had to wait longer for the vote.

As regards social rights, these include the right of every individual to enjoy a certain minimum standard of economic welfare and security. They include such rights as health benefits, unemployment allowance, setting of minimum level of wages. The broadening of social or welfare rights led to the welfare state, which was established in Western societies.

8. Define the concept of power. Give examples to show how power works.

Ans. Power is the ability of individuals or groups to carry out their will even when opposed by others. There is fixed amount of power in a society and if some wield power others do not. In other words, an individual or group that does not hold power in isolation, they hold it in relation to others. This notion of power is fairly inclusive and extends from family.

For example, elders in the family have the power to assign domestic duties to their children, principals have power to enforce discipline in school, a manager of factory has the power to distribute work among executives and political leaders have power to regulate programmes of their parties. In each case, an individual or group has the power to the extent to which others abide by their will. In this sense, political activities or policies is concerned with power.

9. Religion has been a subject of study and reflection for a very long time. Discuss the perspectives to understand the religion. **Competency Based Que.**

Ans. Sociologists study religion as both a belief system and a social institution. In sociology, religions can be studied under three point of views

(i) The empirical method says that the sociologist does not have a judgement approach to religious phenomena.

(ii) The comparative method brings all societies on level with each other. It helps to study without bias and prejudice.

(iii) The sociological perspective means that religious life can be made intelligible only by relating it to domestic life, economic life and political life.

10. Studying religion sociologically lets us ask questions about the relationship of religion with other social institutions. Religion has had a very close relationship with power and politics.
Explain the relation of religion with power and politics. **Competency Based Que.**

Ans. Power and politics have always had a tight association with religion. For example, there have been religious movements for social change throughout history, such as anti-caste or anti-gender discrimination movements. Religion is not only a matter of an individual's private beliefs; it also has a public aspect. And it is this public nature of religion that has a significant impact on other social institutions.

11. Education is characterised by aspiration for progress and betterment of human being. How? **Competency Based Que.**

Ans. Education is often seen as a fundamentally optimistic human endeavour characterised by aspirations for progress and betterment. This happens due to following reasons

- It socialises the man to play important roles in the society. An individual through education learns the basic rules, regulations, norms and values of society.
- Education becomes hindrance to stereotype thinking of society. It also raises the issue of inequality, women empowerment and achieve these through education.
- Education everywhere has led the formation of social personalities. Education helps in transmitting culture through proper molding of social personalities.
- The curriculum of the school, its extracurricular activities and the informal relationships amongst students and teacher communicate social skill and values. All these can be achieved through education only.

Long Answer Type Questions

1. 'Types of families and their forms are based on various parameters.' How can you find the list of types of family and family forms? **Competency Based Que.**

Ans. Different types and structures of families in society have been listed below

(i) Types of family on the basis of marriage. Family has been classified into three major types
- Polygamous or polygynous family
- Polyandrous family
- Monogamous family

(ii) Types of family on the basis of the nature of residence. Therefore, family can be classified into three main forms
- Family of matrilocal residence
- Family of patrilocal residence
- Family of changing residence

(iii) Types of family on the basis of ancestry or descent. Therefore, family can be classified into two main types
- Matrilineal family
- Patrilineal family

(iv) Types of family on the basis of size or structure and the depth of generations. Therefore, family can be classified into two main types
- Nuclear or the single unit family
- Joint family

(v) Types of family on the basis of the nature of relations among the family members. Hence, family can be classified into two main types
- The conjugal family which consists of adult members among them exists sexual relationship.
- Consanguine family which consists of members among whom there exists blood relationship like brother and sister, father and son, etc.

2. What do you understand by kinship system? Discuss its importance in social life.

Ans. It is a method of organising marriage relations between groups. A woman be as wife, as daughter-in-law and so on through her marriage goes into another group and a male through his marriage be as a husband, son-in-law and so on. The kinship system is not only an organisation of transacted marriage, but it is also a system of relation between the individuals in the family and families are organised.

The Importance of Kinship System in Social Life

The kinship system occupies an important place in the society and makes relationship with other groups or sometime with other societies. The importance of kinship system in social life can be understood through following points

- Kinship is an important aspect of a family life. People in the family have definite rights and obligations according to their status. A kin is more quickly available for help than any other person or agency. It is because the kin has emotional relationship with another kin.
- Kins provide assistance in economic affairs or other activities which need co-operation from others. When social functions like marriage ceremonies and religious functions take place in the family, kins are necessarily invited and their presence is expected. It is also obligatory on their part to provide services as and when needed.
- In the events of crises also, people depend greatly on their relatives for aid. Blood relatives have greater significance as a person feels much closer to them than those who are related by marriage.
- Different kins have different obligations to carry out on different occasions in the family. For example, in Hindu family, the role of the eldest brother is very important. When a person dies, the eldest son of the deceased is supposed to perform the funeral pyre.
  It is customary that the eldest son would be heir after the death of the father and would get the larger share in case the property is divided among the offsprings.
- The kinship system assists in maintaining solidarity in the family. However, tensions and conflicts among the kins due to discriminatory rights also did exist and even now exist in the traditional Indian joint families especially of the propertied class.

3. Discuss the modern form of work and division of labour.

Ans. The modern form of work and division of labour can be understood properly through following points

- In modern time, the highly complex division of labour exists and work has been divided into enormous number of different occupations in which people are specialised.
- Modern society also witnesses a shift in the location of works, but this was not the case before industrialisation where people worked collectively at their home.
- Advancement in industrial technology, such as machinery operating on electricity and coal contributed to the separation of work and home. Factories owned by capitalist entrepreneurs became the focal point of industrial development.
- The workers were trained to perform specialised tasks and they received wages accordingly. Managers supervised the work, and their task was to enhance worker productivity and discipline.
- In every society, a vast number of population do not produce the food they eat, the houses they live in, and the material goods they consume. It means the population is dependent on many other workers for the products and services that sustain our lives.

4. Cite the differences between simple and complex modern societies in respect to education or learning.

Ans. The simple society is called as Informal society on the other side complex modern society is called as Formal society.

Simple Society	Complex Modern Society
The simple society provides more informal education.	The modern society provides more formal education.
In this society, child can learn mainly from family or elder, etc.	In this society, child can learn mainly from teachers, specialised trained people.
Division of labour is based on the age and sex in the simple society.	Division of labour is based on qualifications and skills in the complex modern society.
There is only oral communication established in the simple society.	Both oral and written communication are established in this society.
In this society, usually the whole family is involved in the same work, for example agriculture.	The working place and family are separate units in this society.
The values in the society are laid down by rules and norms.	The universal values are followed in modern society.

5. The empirical method means that the sociologist does not have a judgemental approach to religious phenomena. The comparative method is important because in a sense it brings all societies on level with each other. It helps to study without bias and prejudice. The sociological perspective means that religious life can be made intelligible only by relating it to domestic life, economic life and political life. Religion exists in all known societies, although religious beliefs and practices vary from culture to culture.

(a) What are the key characteristics that all religions seem to share? Discuss each characteristic briefly.

(b) In what ways do sociologists study religion using the empirical and comparative methods?

Ans. (a) All religions seem to share three key characteristics

(i) **Symbols** Religions use symbols that invoke feelings of reverence or awe, such as the cross in Christianity or the crescent in Islam. These symbols hold deep spiritual significance.

(ii) **Rituals** Religious rituals, like praying, fasting or lighting candles, are acts that honour the divine and are distinct from everyday habits.

(iii) **Community of Believers** Religions foster a sense of belonging, where individuals come together to practice and uphold shared beliefs, often in sacred spaces like churches or temples. These elements bind believers to their faith and each other.

(b) Sociologists study religion using the empirical method by conducting objective, data-driven research to observe how religions function in society. They avoid making judgemental conclusions, focusing instead on the actual practices, beliefs and behaviours associated with different religions.

The comparative method involves comparing religious beliefs, rituals, and institutions across various societies to identify similarities and differences. This approach helps sociologists avoid bias and gain a broader understanding of religious life, placing each society's religious practices in context with others, thus offering a more inclusive, neutral perspective on religion's role in different cultures.

SELF ASSESSMENT TEST

Objective Type Questions

1. What is polyandry?

(a) One husband and one wife
(b) One wife with two or more husband
(c) One husband with two or more wives
(d) Husband married after his wife's death

2. Which concepts are critical to the understanding of political institution?

(a) Power
(b) Authority
(c) Both (a) and (b)
(d) None of these

3. **Assertion** (A) Religious rituals are often carried out both individually and collectively, with some ceremonies practiced in special places like churches, mosques or temples.

Reason (R) Rituals in religious contexts are always individual and do not involve group participation or special places.

(a) Both A and R are true and R is the correct explanation of A.
(b) Both A and R are true, but R is not the correct explanation of A.
(c) A is true, but R is false.
(d) A is false, but R is true.

Case Based Questions

1. The family, marriage, and kinship are fundamental institutions in all societies, though their forms vary. Families can be nuclear, consisting of parents and their unmarried children, or joint, where multiple generations live together. Patrilocal families require couples to reside with the groom's parents, while matrilocal families involve living with the bride's parents. Authority within families can be patriarchal, where men dominate decision-making, or matriarchal, where women hold similar power. Inheritance, too, can follow patrilineal or matrilineal lines. Female-headed households, like those among the Kolams, emerge when women manage homes due to male migration, widowhood, or lack of financial support from men.

(i) In which type of family does a newly married couple live with the groom's parents?

(a) Matrilocal family (b) Patrilocal family
(c) Extended family (d) Matriarchal family

(ii) What is a distinguishing feature of a female-headed household?

(a) It is always formed due to widowhood.
(b) Women manage the family in the absence of male support.
(c) It is only found among urban communities.
(d) Men retain authority while women provide support.

Very Short Answer Type Questions

1. It is mentioned that polygyny is more prevalent in conditions of wealth and polyandry in economic hardship. What inference can you draw about the relationship between economic conditions and marital customs?

2. The declining child sex ratio in states like Punjab and Haryana is attributed to female foeticide. What does this trend indicate about gender bias and societal attitudes toward female children?

3. "Many forms of work are not included in official employment statistics, such as work in the informal economy. Why is it important to recognise the different types of work that exist outside paid employment?"

4. Give the meaning of the term 'decentralisation of work'.

Short Answer Type Questions

1. Family and Kinship have undergone a change due to economic processes. Discuss with examples.

2. Power is exercised through authority. Discuss.

3. "Power in society is often tied to authority. How do concepts like power and authority influence the way people comply with commands in different settings, such as a family or a school?"

4. "The rise of the service sector in India has shifted the type of work people do. What are some examples of these shifts and how have they affected the economy?"

Long Answer Type Questions

1. Discuss the concept behind family, marriage and kinship.

2. How does political institution play a significant role for developing an economic structure for the society?

3. Education is a life-long process, involving both formal and informal institutions of learning. Here we are however confining ourselves only to school education. We are all aware how important getting admission into a school is. We also know, for many of us, school is a step towards higher education and finally employment. For some of us, it may mean acquiring some necessary social skills. What is common in all cases is that there is a felt need for education. Sociology understands this need as a process of transmission/communication of group heritage that is common to all societies.

(a) How does sociology understand the need for education as a process of communication of group heritage?

(b) What are the key distinctions between education in simple societies and modern complex societies?

04

CHAPTER

Culture and Socialisation

In everyday language, culture usually refers to the arts or the lifestyles of specific groups or countries. Sociologists and anthropologists study how culture exists in social contexts.

YOUR STUDY GOALS

4.1 Introduction

4.2 Diverse Setting, Different Cultures

4.3 Culture and Identity

4.4 Socialisation

YOUR PRACTICE GOAL

- Objective Type Questions (22 Qs ; MCQs, A-R, Case Based Questions)
- Subjective Questions (15 VSAs, 9 SAs, 3 LAs)

4.1 Introduction

Culture represents a shared understanding learned through social interaction. This shared understanding helps define a group and gives it an identity.

Cultures are not fixed; they are always changing and evolving. Elements of culture can be added, removed, or altered. This makes cultures **dynamic**[1] and adaptable. The ability to create a common understanding and draw meanings from signs and symbols differentiates humans from other animals.

4.2 Diverse Settings, Different Cultures

- Humans live in many natural settings, and different social setups. In these various environments, people develop different strategies to deal with natural and social conditions. This leads to the creation of diverse cultures.
- The differences in coping strategies were clear during the tsunami on 26th December, 2004. This disaster affected parts of the Tamil Nadu and Kerala coasts and the Andaman and Nicobar Islands in India.
- People living on the mainland and the islands had a more modern lifestyle. The fisherfolk and service workers in the islands were caught off guard and faced great destruction and loss of life.

1 **Dynamic** Constantly changing or evolving; characterised by continuous activity.

- In contrast, the tribal communities on the islands, like the Onges, Jarawas, Great Andamanese and Shompens, had no access to modern technology. However, they were able to sense the disaster through their experience and moved to higher ground to save themselves.
- This shows that access to modern science and technology does not make modern cultures better than tribal cultures. Therefore, cultures cannot be ranked as superior or inferior. They can only be evaluated based on their ability to cope with challenges from nature.

Defining Culture

- The term 'culture' is often used to describe refined tastes in classical music, dance or painting. This refined taste was seen as a way to separate cultured people from the 'uncultured' masses.
- Sociologists view culture differently. They see it as a way of life that everyone in society participates in. Each social group develops its own culture.
- British scholar **Edward Tylor** defined culture as a complex whole, which includes knowledge, beliefs, art, morals, law, customs and other habits acquired by people in society.
- **Clifford Geertz** suggested we treat human actions like words in a book, seeing them as messages. He said, "Man is an animal suspended in webs of significance he himself has spun." For Geertz, culture consists of these webs, focusing on meaning rather than just causes.
- **Leslie White** emphasised that culture adds meaning to objective reality. For example, some people consider water from a specific source to be holy.
- **Tylor's** definition mostly includes non-material aspects. This doesn't mean he ignored material culture. Tylor was a museum curator and studied artifacts from many societies he hadn't visited. His definition aimed to include intangible aspects of culture for a complete understanding.
- **Malinowski** learned the value of long-term study when he was stranded on an island during World War I. This experience helped establish the tradition of 'field work.'
- **Alfred Kroeber** and **Clyde Kluckhohn** published a survey called Culture: A Critical Review of Concepts and Definitions in 1952, highlighting various definitions of culture.
- When comparing these definitions, you may notice recurring words like 'way', 'learn' and 'behaviour'. Each word is used differently, showing shifts in emphasis. Some definitions focus on mental aspects, while others refer to the total way of life.

A sample of the various definitions as given is presented below

Culture is ...

(i) a way of thinking, feeling, believing.
(ii) the total way of life of a people.
(iii) an abstraction from behaviour.
(iv) learned behaviour.
(v) a storehouse of pooled learning.
(vi) the social legacy the individual acquires from his group.
(vii) a set of standardised orientations of recurrent problems.
(viii) a mechanism for the normative regulation of behaviour.

Differences between Malinowski and Taylor's Definition on Culture

- Edward Tylor defines culture as 'a complex whole' that includes knowledge, beliefs, art, morals, laws, customs and other habits learned by people in society. He focuses on non-material aspects like beliefs and values and studied culture through artifacts in museums, without much interaction with people.
- Bronislaw Malinowski defines culture as a mix of material and non-material things, like tools, goods, ideas, and values. He emphasises how culture helps meet people's needs and studied it by living with communities to understand their way of life directly.

Dimensions of Culture

Culture can be understood through three distinct dimensions

(i) **Cognitive** This involves how we process information to give it meaning. For example, recognising our cell phone's ringtone or identifying a political cartoon.

(ii) **Normative** This refers to rules of conduct. For example, not opening others' letters or performing death rituals.

(iii) **Material** This encompasses activities that rely on materials,including tools and machines. Examples are chatting online or using rice-flour paste to create kolam designs.

Understanding material culture, especially art, requires knowledge from cognitive and normative dimensions. Our understanding of social processes draws on all these areas. In communities with low literacy, it may be normal for a third party to read private letters aloud.

Cognitive Aspects of Culture

- The cognitive aspects of culture are harder to recognise than its material and normative aspects. Cognition involves how we understand information from our environment.
- In literate societies, ideas are recorded in books and preserved in libraries or archives. In non-literate societies, **legends**[2] and **lore**[3] are memorised and passed down orally.
- Writing influences how art is produced and consumed. Walter Ong, in his book *Orality* and *Literacy*, notes that only 78 of about 3,000 languages have written literature. He argues that unwritten material has specific characteristics. There is a lot of repetition of words, to make it simpler to remember.
- Audiences in oral performances tend to be more engaged than readers of unfamiliar texts. Written texts are usually more elaborate.
- Historically, literacy has been accessible mainly to the privileged. Sociological studies explore how to make literacy relevant for those whose families have not attended school.
- Today, we rely more on written, audio and visual records. However, students of Indian classical music are still encouraged to memorise what they learn instead of writing it down.
- The impact of electronic media and instant access to information on attention span and cognitive culture is not fully understood.

Normative Aspects of Culture

- The normative dimension includes folkways, mores, customs, conventions and laws. These are values or rules that guide social behavior in different contexts.
- Norms are implicit rules, while laws are explicit rules. For example, a family rule may prohibit children from being outside after sundown. It is specific to families and may not be applicable to all families.
- Sociologist Pierre Bourdieu noted that understanding another culture's norms requires recognising implicit meanings. For example, to show gratitude, one should not offer a return gift too quickly, as it may seem like paying off a debt.
- A law is a formal rule defined by the government that all citizens must follow. Laws apply to society as a whole, and violating them leads to penalties.
- Laws are the most formal definitions of acceptable behaviour. Different schools may have their own norms for students, but laws apply to everyone under state authority.
- Unlike laws, norms can vary by social status. Dominant groups often enforce norms that can discriminate, such as those preventing Dalits from drinking from the same water sources or restricting women's freedom in public.

---

2 **Legend** Traditional stories often rooted in historical events or figures.

3 **Lore** It means traditional knowledge or stories passed down through generations orally.

Material Aspects of Culture

- The material aspect of culture includes tools, technologies, machines, buildings, transportation and means of production and communication.
- In urban areas, the use of mobile phones, music systems, cars, buses, ATMs, refrigerators and computers shows our reliance on technology.
- In rural areas, devices like transistor radios and electric motor pumps for irrigation also highlight the adoption of technology to boost production.
- Culture has two main dimensions: material and non-material. The cognitive and normative aspects are non-material.
- The material dimension is important for increasing production and improving quality of life.
- For culture to function effectively, both dimensions must work together. However, when material or technological changes occur rapidly, non-material aspects such as values and norms may lag behind. This creates a situation called **culture lag**, where non-material dimensions fail to keep up with technological advances.

Quick Test 1

1. It is a common understanding learnt and develop through social interaction with others in society. Identify what is being talked about?
2. In which societies ideas are in the form of legends and myths?
3. Who wrote the book, 'Orality and Literacy'?
4. Name the non-material dimensions.

4.3 Culture and Identity

- Identities are not inherited; they are shaped by individuals and groups through their interactions with others. In modern society, people play multiple roles.
- It is not enough to simply perform these roles; they must also be recognised and acknowledged. Recognition often occurs through the specific language used among role players.
- In any culture, there are different subcultures, like those of elite and working-class youth. Subcultures have their own styles, tastes and ways of interacting. They can often be identified by their speech, dress, music preferences and group behaviour.
- Subcultures can act as cohesive[4] units, giving members a sense of identity. Within these groups, there can be leaders and followers, but all members share common goals.
- These positive activities help create a good image for the members in their community, boosting their self-esteem and encouraging better performance. As a result, the group's identity becomes distinct, gaining acceptance and recognition from the neighbourhood.

Ethnocentrism

- Ethnocentrism arises when different cultures come into contact with one another. It means judging the behaviours and beliefs of other cultures based on your own cultural values. This often leads to the belief that your culture is superior to others.
- Ethnocentrism shows a sense of cultural superiority. This is clear in colonial situations. Thomas Babbington Macaulay's 1835 statement to the East India Company illustrates this. He said we should create a class of Indians who think and act like the English.
- Ethnocentrism is the opposite of cosmopolitanism. Cosmopolitanism values different cultures. It celebrates and accepts cultural differences.

4 Cohesive It characterised by elements that work together to create unity and solidarity within a group.

- The English language is a good example. It includes many foreign words. Hindi film music is also popular because it mixes Western pop with Indian traditions like bhangra and ghazal.
- Modern societies appreciate cultural differences. They welcome influences from other cultures. These influences blend uniquely with local traditions.
- In our global world, modern communication connects cultures and a cosmopolitan view allows various influences to enrich one's own culture.

Cultural Change

- Cultural change is how societies change their cultural patterns. It can happen for internal or external reasons.
- **Internal Changes** New farming methods can improve food production and quality of life in farming communities.
- **External Changes** Conquest or colonisation can deeply impact a society's cultural practices.
- Cultural change can also occur due to changes in the environment, contact with other cultures or adaptation. For example, if forest communities lose access to forests, it can severely affect their way of life. Tribal communities in North-East and middle India have been particularly hurt by losing forest resources.
- Cultural change can be evolutionary (gradual) or revolutionary (rapid). Revolutionary change happens when a culture undergoes a quick and significant transformation. This can result from political actions, new technologies or ecological changes.
- For example, the French Revolution in 1789 changed society by ending the monarchy and promoting values like liberty and equality. Recent advancements in media have also influenced culture.

Quick Test 2

1. How does ethnocentrism influence cultural interactions?
2. How do natural environmental changes impact cultural practices?
3. What is meant by 'Hinglish' and why is it significant in modern communication?
4. What role does media play in cultural change?

4.4 Socialisation

- When a baby is born, they know nothing about society. As they grow, they learn what behaviours are good or bad. Socialisation is the process through which a baby becomes a self-aware person, learning the cultural norms of their community.
- The birth of a child also changes the lives of parents and grandparents, introducing new relationships and learning experiences. Similarly, the life of a young child changes with the birth of a sibling.
- Socialisation is a life-long process even though the most critical process happens in the early years, the stage of primary socialisation. Secondary socialisation extends over the entire life of a person.
- Socialisation greatly influences individuals, but it's not just passive learning. Even newborns show their needs by crying, asserting their will. Family routines often change when a new child is born.
- A child belongs to a family and larger kin groups, like clans, religious and linguistic communities[5]. They can be part of either a nuclear or extended family. Each group imposes certain behaviours and values. Children perform different and multiple roles, like being a son or daughter.
- Learning about norms and values starts early and continues throughout life. Different families may have unique norms based on caste, region or social class. The language a person speaks also reflects their background, influenced by their family's socio-economic status and culture.

5 Linguistic Communities It is a group of people who share a common language or habit.

Agencies of Socialisation

- Children are socialised by various agencies, including family, school, peers, neighbourhood, work groups, and factors like social class, caste, region and religion.

Family

- Family structures vary greatly. Some children live in nuclear families with just their parents and siblings, while others are part of extended families with grandparents, aunts, uncles and cousins. In nuclear families, parents are often the main influence, while in extended families, other relatives can play significant roles.
- In traditional societies, a person's social position is usually determined by the family they are born into. Even in modern contexts, a family's region and social class significantly impact how children are socialised.
- Children often adopt behaviours from their parents and community. However, they don't always follow their parents' views blindly, especially in today's rapidly changing world.
- This variety of socialising influences leads to differences in perspectives between children, teenagers and their parents.

Peer Groups

- An important socialising agency is the peer group, which consists of friends of similar ages. In some small, traditional cultures, these groups are formalised into age-grades.
- Even without formal groups, children aged four or five often spend a lot of time with their peers.
- The term 'peer' means 'equal,' and friendships among young children are generally equal. While stronger children might try to dominate, interactions are more balanced compared to family relationships.
- In families, parents enforce rules and expectations, while in peer groups, children can explore and test different behaviors.
- Peer relationships are important throughout life. Informal groups of similar-aged people, like those at work, continue to shape attitudes and behaviours as individuals grow.

Schools

- Schools are formal organisations where specific subjects are taught. However, they also serve as socialising agencies in more subtle ways. Alongside the official curriculum, there is something called a 'hidden curriculum' that shapes children's learning and behaviour.
- For example, in some schools in India, girls are expected to sweep the classroom, while boys are rarely asked to do this. Some schools try to change this by having both boys and girls perform tasks that are not typically assigned to them.

Mass Media

- Mass media has become a vital part of our daily lives. In today's world electronic media, such as television, continues to grow and evolve, print media still plays a significant role. In the 19th century, conduct books in various languages guided women on being better homemakers.
- Media helps make information more accessible, even reaching remote villages without roads or literacy centers.
- A study in Britain showed that the time spent by children watching television is the equivalent of almost a hundred school days a year and that adults are not far behind them.
- However, the impact of media is not always clear, especially regarding links between on-screen violence and aggressive behaviour in children.
- While predicting the media's influence is difficult, its reach is undeniable. Indian television shows and films have large audiences in countries like Nigeria and Afghanistan. The Mahabharat series was even watched by English speaking children in London.
- Recently, non-print digital media, especially the internet, has gained significant attention, particularly in urban areas.

Other Socialising Agencies

- In addition to families, schools and media, work is another important setting for socialisation. In all cultures, work plays a significant role, but it's especially noticeable in industrial societies where many people go to jobs outside their homes.
- In traditional communities, people often worked close to home, either by farming the land nearby or having workshops in their houses.

Socialisation and Individual Freedom

- Socialisation doesn't completely make people conform. Conflicts can arise between different socialising agencies, like home and school or home and peer groups.
- While our cultural backgrounds greatly influence our behaviour, it doesn't mean we lose our individuality or free will.
- In fact, socialisation helps shape our personalities and values and allows us to develop a sense of self-identity. Through socialisation, we gain the ability to think and act independently, which contributes to our uniqueness.
- A few years ago, the **Shaktimaan** serial led to incidents where children tried jumping off buildings, resulting in tragic accidents. Clinical psychologists explain that children often learn by imitation, a behaviour commonly seen in people.

Socialisation and Gender

- Boys often used the streets for various activities, like playing and riding bikes. For girls, the street served a different purpose.
- Girls mainly used it just to get home from school. Girls typically travelled in groups, possibly due to fears of being attacked. This highlights how socialisation can differ based on gender.

Quick Test 3

1. What is the opposite of ethnocentrism?
2. Which type of socialisation refers to early years of childhood?
3. Name any one socialising agency which socialise a child.

NCERT Folder

1. How does the understanding of culture in social science differ from the everyday use of the word 'culture'?

Ans. The use of the word 'culture' in everyday life is limited. It refers to the artistic performances such as dance, music, painting, drama, etc. But sociology understands culture in a scientifically prescribed way that is not only limited to drawing and painting. Culture has shaped the society.

In sociological terms, culture implies the common understanding which is learnt and developed through social interaction and then passed onto the next generation. Therefore, in everyday use, the term culture is used for individuals, whereas in sociology, it is used to denote the entire group or the society.

Edward Taylor was the first sociologist to define culture that includes abstract and intangible dimensions. Later, Bronislaw Malinowski defined culture, which included the use of materials as well.

2. How can we demonstrate that the different dimensions of culture comprise a whole?

Ans. There are three dimensions of cultures that are cognitive, normative and material that comprise as a whole. They are discussed as below

(i) **Cognitive** It refers to how we learn to process what we see and hear so as to give it a meaning. For example, looking at a flag and associating it with the country to which it belongs or symbolising the waving of hand as a may of saying goodbye. Thus, every culture has given a different meaning to different actions.

(ii) **Normative** It refers to the rules of conduct. Every society has some rules according to which its members have to behave. As a result, this behaviour and action of the individuals become the culture of that society.

(iii) **Material** It includes any activity which is made possible by the means of materials. It also includes tools and machines, which is said to be a part of the culture. In the present industrial societies, advanced technology and machines are used. Some societies use them in abundance such as, USA while some do not make much use of it, such as Afghanistan. Thus, use of various materials in different ways for various purposes shows the culture of that society.

Therefore, culture can be identified as material and non-material. For the proper and integrated functioning of the culture, both material and non-material dimensions work together as a whole. The use of materials having different notions and ways of understanding different signs and symbols with certain rules of conduct as a whole describes the culture of that society.

3. Compare two cultures with which you are familiar. Is it difficult not to be ethnocentric?

Ans. The two cultures with which we are familiar are as following

(i) Urban culture (ii) Rural culture

The urban culture represents the life in a city, while the rural culture represents the life in a village. In a city, there are industries for people to work with machines. On the other hand, in a village people work in farms to produce crops. The life in villages is simpler and traditional as compared to that of the life in a city. In a city, there is an emphasis on individualism, while in villages more importance is given to groups.

Hence, the way of life, culture, occupation and thinking is different in urban and rural areas.

Difficulty in Being Ethnocentric

Ethnocentrism means giving value to one's own culture and consider the other culture as inferior.

Yes, it is difficult not to be ethnocentric because people mostly give value and superiority to one's own culture.

If we compare the villages and cities, it would be obvious that the villagers carry the belief that their culture is better because it is embedded with societal norms, values and traditions.

On the other hand, the city dwellers would consider their culture superior because it is modern and liberal. Historically, the colonialists considered their culture superior and better to that of the colonised countries. The belief of ethnocentrism generates differences and wars between many ethnic and racial groups.

Therefore, it is correct to say that it is difficult for people not to be ethnocentric even in contemporary societies.

4. Discuss two different approaches to studying cultural change.

Ans. The two different approaches of cultural change are as following

(i) **Evolutionary** Its change is slow. For example, in the case of education. In ancient times, the individuals were often taught orally. Gradually, with the discovery of paper, writing and publication of books started.

Eventually, new subjects were introduced according to the need of the society. Further, with the introduction of industrialisation, focus on professional courses also increased. With the introduction of information technology and globalisation, the new ways of teaching emerged. Finally, several instruments or gadgets like computer and use of internet were invented which lead to cultural change in the society.

(ii) **Revolutionary** Contrary to evolutionary, revolutionary change is fast. For example, revolutionary change takes place through political intervention, as in the case of France. After the French Revolution, the estate system of ranking was destroyed. The values of liberty and equality in the society were established. This was a radical change in the society and its culture.

5. Is cosmopolitanism something you associate with modernity? Observe and give examples of ethnocentrism.

Ans. Cosmopolitanism means valuing other cultures for their difference. A cosmopolitan perception is always ready to adapt other cultures and share its own culture with others.

In this process of sharing, neither foreign culture becomes the legitimate part of one's own culture, nor does the indigenous culture lose its base. Hence, it respects every culture. Cosmopolitanism is associated with modernity, in contemporary period, as it is emerging in most parts of the world. Since modernity has to deal with time, cosmopolitanism is phenomenon of the modern world.

Ethnocentrism, on the other hand, refers to the standard cultural values that are considered more superior to that of cultural values of others. For example, the British people were ethnocentric as they regarded the Indian culture as primitive and orthodox. Similarly, the people belonging to cities consider the people of villages inferior to them.

The above examples show that unlike cosmopolitanism, ethnocentrism ranks the culture as superior or inferior.

6. What in your mind is the most effective agent of socialisation for your generation? How do you think it was different before?

Ans. Mass Media as an Effective Agent of Socialisation

In contemporary time, the mass media has emerged as a strong agent of socialisation. Earlier, family and the peer groups were the socialising agent in an individual's life. Now, due to penetration of information technology, people spend more time with computers and television sets, than their families and friends.

Children have started adopting new ways from televisions. For example, they choose their own career and lead a self-chosen lifestyle. They stay connected with their friends through internet and they even depend on the internet for their studies.

Hence, their dependence on visual media is much more than that of print media. Even women, men and old age people are getting affected by mass media. Magazines, newspapers, radio, advertisements, etc. provide information on various aspects such as health, decoration, eating habits, etc.

Mass media has affected the society and also promoted globalisation. It has decreased the distance between different parts of the world.

Life Before Mass Media

Life before introduction of mass media was very different as people had very little information of the rest of the world. There was no television, radio, newspaper or internet. People in earlier days had to make a lot of efforts together to get information and also to spread it.

Exam Pattern Questions

Objective Type Questions

Multiple Choice Questions (MCQs)

1. Who is the founder of the functional school of anthropology?

(a) Lesli White
(b) Edward Taylor
(c) Clifford Geertz
(d) Bronislaw Malinowski

2. Which of the following groups was able to foresee the tsunami and take action to protect themselves?

(a) The fisherfolk of Kerala
(b) The service personnel in Tamil Nadu
(c) The 'primitive' tribal communities of the islands
(d) The modern cities on the mainland

3. Who had placed a comparable emphasis on culture as a means of adding meaning to objective reality?

(a) Edward Taylor
(b) Bronislaw Malinowski
(c) Leslie White
(d) Clifford Geertz

4. The term 'Culture' is defined as Competency Based Que.

I. Learned behaviour
II. A way of thinking, feeling, believing
III. The total way of life of a people
IV. School learning

Codes

(a) I, II and III
(b) I and IV
(c) II and IV
(d) All of these

5. Which of these constitute three dimensions of culture?

(a) Cognitive, emotional and material
(b) Practical, normative and material
(c) Cognitive, normative and material
(d) Material, practical and emotional

6. .... refers to how we learn to interpret what we hear or see in order to give it significance (for example, recognising the ring of a mobile phone as ours or recognising a politician's cartoon). True, our growing knowledge of social processes will draw from both of these sources. However, in a society where few people have acquired the cognitive ability of literacy, having private letters read out by a third party can become the standard.

(a) Normative
(b) Material
(c) Cognitive
(d) None of these

7. Which of the following is a normative aspect of culture?

(a) Tools and machines used in daily life
(b) Written records of historical events
(c) Folkways, customs and conventions
(d) Rituals and formal documents of law

8. Which of the following statements about subcultures is true?

(a) Subcultures are identified by distinct styles, tastes and associations.

(b) Subcultures are primarily defined by their preference for different types of food.
(c) Subcultures are homogeneous and share the same practices across society.
(d) Subcultures cannot exist within larger cultural groups.

9. Which of the following is not true regarding cultural change?
(a) Cultural change can be caused by internal factors such as new methods of farming.
(b) External intervention, such as conquest or colonisation, does not affect cultural practices.
(c) Cultural change can occur through adaptation and contact with other cultures.
(d) Ecological changes can drastically alter the way of life for a community.

10. "Cultural change is the way in which societies change their patterns of culture. The impetus for change can be internal or external. In regard to internal causes, for instance, new methods of farming or agriculture can boost agricultural production, which can transform the nature of food consumption and quality of life of an agrarian community."
Cultural change can be an important factor in **Competency Based Que.**
(a) adapting new ideas and technologies
(b) increasing farm productivity
(c) Both (a) and (b)
(d) None of the above

11. The English language has emerged as a leading vehicle of international communication through its constant inclusion of foreign words into its vocabulary. Again the popularity of Hindi film music can be attributed to its borrowings from Western pop music as well as from different traditions of Indian folk and semi-classical forms like the bhangra and ghazal.
Which of the following can be a reason for such cultural influence? **Competency Based Que.**
(a) Educational reach (b) Cultural assimilation
(c) Increasing population (d) Tour and travel

12. The process of socialisation which takes place in school and other institutions is known as ....
(a) Personality development (b) Primary socialisation
(c) Both (a) and (b) (d) Secondary socialisation

13. It is only when cultures come into contact with one another that the question of ethnocentrism arises. Ethnocentrism is the application of one's own cultural values in evaluating the behaviour and beliefs of people from other cultures.
Which of the following statements are correct about ethnocentrism?
I. Ethnocentrism is the opposite of cosmopolitanism.
II. Standard or norm are considered superior to that of the beliefs and values of other cultures.
III. It is a sense of cultural superiority.
Codes
(a) Only I (b) II and III (c) I and III (d) Only III

14. Cultural assimilation can be challenging for multicultural societies because
I. it requires individuals to abandon their cultural practices to fully integrate.
II. it may lead to the erosion of traditional cultural values.
III. different cultural groups may find it hard to accept one dominant culture.
IV. assimilation efforts can create tensions between the state and minority communities.
Codes
(a) I and III (b) II and IV
(c) I, II and III (d) I, II, III and IV

15. Which of the following scholars emphasised the importance of meaning in culture by describing human actions as 'webs of significance'?
(a) Edward Tylor (b) Clifford Geertz
(c) Bronislaw Malinowski (d) Leslie White

Assertion-Reason Questions

Direction (Q. Nos. 16-20) Two statements are given in the question below as Assertion (A) and Reason (R). Read the statements and choose the appropriate option.
(a) Both A and R are true and R is the correct explanation of A.
(b) Both A and R are true, but R is not the correct explanation of A.
(c) A is true, but R is false.
(d) A is false, but R is true.

16. Assertion (R) Ethnocentrism arises when people from different cultures evaluate each other's behaviour based on their own cultural values.
Reason (R) Ethnocentrism leads to the appreciation of cultural differences and promotes harmonious relationships between cultures.

17. Assertion (A) Cutural change is the way in which societies change their patterns of culture.
Reason (R) Cultural change can occur through changes in the natural environment, contact with other cultures or processes of adaptation.

18. Assertion (A) Cultural influences shape an individual's behaviour and values.
Reason (R) Socialisation begins with the family, where a child learns cultural norms and values that define their role in society.

19. Assertion (A) Peer groups are friendship groups of children of a similar age.

Reason (R) In peer groups, by contrast, child discovers a different kind of interaction within which rules of behaviour can be tested out and explored.

20. **Assertion** (A) Malinowski's definition of culture includes both material and non-material aspects, such as tools, goods, ideas, and values.

Reason (R) Malinowski emphasised the need to understand culture by living with communities and observing their way of life directly.

Case Based Questions

Read the passage given below and answer the questions that follow by choosing the correct option.

21. The capacity of individuals to develop a common understanding with others and to draw the same meanings from signs and symbols is what distinguishes humans from other animals. Creating meaning is a social virtue as we learn it in the company of others in families, groups and communities. We learn the use of tools and techniques as well as the non-material signs and symbols through interaction with family members, friends and colleagues in different social settings.

(i) Which of the following according to the sociologist, is not something that separates people, but rather a way of life in which everyone in society participates.
(a) Ecosystem
(b) Culture
(c) Community
(d) Religion

(ii) What is the role of family members, friends and colleagues in the learning process?
(a) They help in coping with natural conditions.
(b) They teach the use of tools and techniques.
(c) They play a role in teaching non-material signs and symbols.
(d) They are responsible for social conflicts.

22. The cognitive aspects of one's own culture are harder to recognise than its material aspects (which are tangible or visible or audible) and its normative aspects (which are explicitly stated). Cognition refers to understanding, how we make sense of all the information coming to us from our environment. In literate societies ideas are transcribed in books and documents and preserved in libraries, instititutions or archives. But in non-literate societies legend or lore is committed to memory and transmitted orally.

(i) In literate societies, how are ideas typically preserved and transmitted?
(a) Through oral traditions and storytelling.
(b) Through books, documents and libraries.
(c) Through ritual and festive occasions.
(d) Through visual and auditory means.

(ii) What does Walter Ong suggest about material that is not written down?
(a) It becomes more elaborate over time.
(b) It contains fewer words and simpler ideas.
(c) It is more easily forgotten.
(d) It has specific characteristics, including repetition for memory.

Answers

1. (d) Bronislaw Malinowski
2. (c) The 'primitive' tribal communities of the islands
3. (c) Leslie White
4. (a) I, II and III
5. (c) Cognitive, normative and material
6. (c) Cognitive
7. (c) Folkways, customs and conventions.
8. (a) Subcultures are identified by distinct styles, tastes and associations.
9. (b) External intervention, such as conquest or colonisation, does not affect cultural practices.
10. (c) Both (a) and (b)
11. (b) Cultural assimilation
12. (d) Secondary socialisation
13. (b) II and III
14. (d) I, II, III and IV
15. (b) Clifford Geertz
16. (a) Both A and R are true and R is the correct explanation of A.
17. (a) Both A and R are true and R is the correct explanation of A.
18. (a) Both A and R are true and R is the correct explanation of A.
19. (b) Both A and R are true, but R is not the correct explanation of A.
20. (a) Both A and R are true, and R is the correct explanation of A.
21. (i) (b) Culture
    (ii) (c) They play a role in teaching non-material signs and symbols.
22. (i) (b) Through books, documents and libraries
    (ii) (d) It has specific characteristics, including repetition for memory.

Subjective Questions

Very Short Answer Type Questions

1. What is culture?

Ans. Culture is the common understanding which is learnt and developed through social interaction with others in society. Culture is always changing and evolving.

2. Why is culture said to be dynamic as a functioning units?

Ans. Culture is the common understanding which is learnt and developed through social interaction with others in society. A common understanding within a group separates it from others and gives it an identity. But cultures are always changing and evolving. Elements are constantly being added, deleted, expanded and rearranged.

This makes cultures dynamic as functioning units.

3. Give any one sociological definition of culture.

Ans. According to Bronislaw Malinowski, "the culture comprises inherited artefacts, goods, technical process, ideas, habits and values."

4. A modern society is appreciative of cultural difference and does not close its doors to cultural influences from abroad. But such influences are always incorporated in a distinctive way, which can combine with elements of indigenous culture.

What are the main elements of culture?

Ans. Customs, beliefs, traditions, knowledge, rituals, ideals, etc. are main elements of culture.

5. Who is the founder of functional school of anthropology?

Ans. Bronislaw Malinowski is the founder of functional school of anthropology.

6. Give the characteristics of culture.

Ans. Following are the main characteristics of the culture

- Culture is learned and it is an acquired behaviour.
- Culture is shared (cannot be possessed by an individual in isolation) and transmitted amongst the members of a society. It binds the members of society.
- Culture is dynamic. It constantly changes and makes each society and group unique or distinct.

7. Ethnocentrism is the application of one's own cultural values in evaluating the behaviour and beliefs of people from other cultures. This means that the cultural values projected as the standard or norm are considered superior to that of the beliefs and values of other cultures. What do you mean by norm in sociology?

Ans. Norms are unwritten rules. They are present to regulate the behaviour of members in a society. They are prescriptions which have to be followed by society. If they aren't followed it can lead to chaos and disorder in society. They are as important as written rules.

8. In a culture there can be many sub-cultures, like that of the elite and working class youth. What is sub-culture? Competency Based Que.

Ans. Sub-culture is defined as a group of people within a larger culture. They are marked by style, taste and association. They borrow and often distort, exaggerate or invert the symbols, values and beliefs of the larger culture to distinguish themselves.

9. What is material dimension of culture?

Ans. The material dimension of culture includes any activity which is made possible by the means of materials which is said to be a part of the culture. For example, using internet as chatting, etc.

10. What is non-material dimension of culture?

Ans. The non-material dimension of culture refers to the abstract or intangible elements of culture, such as the ways of thinking and patterns of behaviour. It includes normative and cognitive dimensions of culture.

11. Thomas Babbington Macaulay's famous Minute on Education (1835) to the East India Company in India exemplifies ethnocentrism when he says, "We must at present do our best to form a class who may be interpreters between us and the millions whom we govern, a class of persons Indian in blood and colour but English in tastes, in opinions, morals and intellect" What is meant by ethnocentrism? Competency Based Que.

Ans. It is defined as the application of one's cultural values in evaluating behaviour and beliefs of people from other culture. It is a sense of feeling of cultural superiority against the beliefs and values of other cultures.

12. Describe the cosmopolitan outlook to culture.

Ans. A cosmopolitan outlook does not seek to evaluate the values and beliefs of people according to one's own. It celebrates and accommodates different cultural propensities within its fold and promote cultural exchange and borrowings enrich one's own culture.

13. Socialisation is a lifelong process even though the most critical process happens in the early years. What do you understand by socialisation? Competency Based Que.

Ans. Socialisation refers to the way by which the values and norms of the society or group become a part of the individual's own way of thinking and feeling.

14. Does socialisation give birth to individual freedom?

Ans. Yes, socialisation gives birth to individual freedom. In modern societies, one's biological gender no longer determines the functions that an individual can perform. It allows greater freedoms and opportunities to all people to express their individual talents and interests.

15. Mass media has increasingly become an essential part of our everyday life. While today the electronic media like the television is expanding, the print media continues to be of great importance.
What is the importance of the mass media in Indian context? Competency Based Que.

Ans. The media can make the access to information more democratic. Electronic communication is something that can reach even to a village not connected by road and where no literacy centres have been set up.

Short Answer Type Questions

1. Sociologists look at culture not as something that distinguishes individuals, but as a way of life in which all members of society participate. Give different interpretations of culture as provided by various thinkers and scholars. Competency Based Que.

Ans. According to Edward Taylor, "The culture or civilisation taken in its wide ethnographic sense, is that complex whole which includes knowledge, belief, art, morals, law, custom and any other capabilities and habits acquired by man as a member of society."

According to Bronislaw Malinowski, (founder of functional school), the culture comprises inherited artefacts, goods, technical process, ideas, habits and values.

Leslie White had placed a comparable emphasis on culture as a means of adding meaning to objective reality, using the example of people regarding water from the particular source as holy.

2. Our understanding of material culture, especially art, is incomplete without knowledge acquired from the cognitive and normative areas. Discuss the cognitive and normative dimensions of culture. Competency Based Que.

Ans. Cognitive dimension refers to how we learn to process what we see and hear so as to give it a meaning. For example, looking at a flag and associating it with the country to which it belongs.

The cognitive dimension of culture refers to ideas which include beliefs, knowledge, myths, superstitions, etc. of society.

The normative dimension includes social rules and social expectations, i.e., the norms and values of a society. The normative dimension consists of folkways, customs, conventions and laws. These are values or rules that guide social behaviours in different contexts.

Normative dimension usually vary across societies and even within the same society across different social groups. A social norm is not necessarily an actual behaviour. Most of human actions are governed by norms.

3. What do you understand by law in normative dimension of culture?

Ans. Laws are a formal sanction defined by government as a rule or principle that its citizens must follow. Laws are applicable to the whole society and violation of these, attracts penalties and punishments.

Laws are the formal standardised expressions of norms. Laws are derived from the authority of the state, which are the most formal definitions of acceptable behaviour. While different schools may establish different norms.

In few cases, where laws are contrary to norms, the enforcement of law becomes difficult. For example, norms that did not allow dalits from drinking water from the same vessel or even source.

4. Differentiate between Law and Norm.

Ans.

Law	Norm
A law is a formal sanction defined by the government as a rule or principle that its citizens must follow.	Norms are specific to a particular family and may not be applicable to other families.
Laws are based on explicit rules. The violation of law attracts penalties and punishments.	Norms are based on implicit rules. The violation of norms doesn't lead to penalties and punishments.
Laws which are derived from the authority of the state are the most formal definitions of acceptable behaviour. Laws would apply to all those accepting the authority of the state.	Norms can vary according to the status. They are not permanent in nature. For example, Dominant sections of the society apply dominant norms and often these norms are discriminating.

5. The cultural identity can often be done through the recognition of the particular language. How?

Ans. Identities are not inherited but fashioned both by the individual and the group through their relationship with others. The language becomes an identity for an individual. Therefore, language becomes another important aspects to understand culture. The social identity is to appreciate how language and culture are intricately interwined, mutually dependent and socially constructed. Recognition and acknowledgment can often be done through the recognition of the particular language that is used among role players, like

- Students in schools have their own way of referring to their teacher, other students, class performances.
- Women are known to create their own language and thought in their own private space beyond the control of men.

6. How is culture related to identity?

Ans. One's identity is shaped by their culture. Culture influences the way we behave, it influences the personality of individuals. Personality can be shaped by nature and nurture. Each person has status in the society and has corresponding roles which are played as per the culture of that society.

Carrying out the roles is not important as the society accepting and acknowledging that particular role. Each group has its own culture which differs from place to place, society to society. They create their own codes rules etc. which have a certain meaning to that particular group.

7. Cite the difference between ethnocentrism and cosmopolitanism.

Ans. The differences between ethnocentrism and cosmopolitanism are

Ethnocentrism	Cosmopolitanism
It is the application of one's own cultural value in evaluating the behaviour and beliefs of people from other cultures.	It celebrates and accommodates different cultures within its fold and promote cultural exchange and borrowing to enrich one's own culture.
It is sense of cultural superiority as they are prejudicial towards other culture.	It is respecting other culture and trying to learn from other culture.
Ethnocentrism avoids mingling with other cultures.	Cosmopolitanism has much more forward thinking as compared to ethnocentrism.

8. Explain the role of socialisation in personality formation.

Ans. Role of socialisation in personality formation is discussed below

- Socialisation is a lifelong process but the most important aspect of this process starts during infancy period. By the time individuals become adult, the major part of socialisation is completed.
- Socialisation makes a human individual a social being. Without socialisation, individuals would not behave like human beings.
- Even the human style of speaking and modes of communication are the function of socialisation.
- The process of socialisation and personality development begins right from the time when the newly born baby first come into contact with his family members.
- From the childhood itself, an individual learns and internalises the role structure and develops his/her own 'self'. Internalisation takes place through the process of socialisation. Much of the personality of an individual is shaped in this way.
- There is another part of culture which an individual learns consciously. This learning process starts at a later stage when the formal teaching in school starts. There he learns about a more complicated part of culture such as cultural heritage, etc.

9. Peer groups are extremely important agents of socialisation. Discuss.

Ans. Peer groups are friendship groups of children of a similar age. In some cultures particularly small traditional societies peer groups are formalised as age grades. Even without formal age grades, children over four or five usually spend a great deal of time in the company of friends of the same age. A forceful or physically strong child may to some extent try to dominate others.

Yet there is a greater amount of give and take compared to the dependence inherent in the family situation. Because of their power parents are able to enforce codes of conduct upon their children. In peer groups, by contrast a child discovers a different kind of interaction within which rules of behaviour can be tested out and explored. Peer relationships often remain important throughout a person's life.

Long Answer Type Questions

1. Cultures cannot be ranked but can be judged adequate or inadequate in terms of their ability to cope with the strains imposed by nature. What does the response of tribal communities to natural disasters reveal about the value of different cultural knowledge systems?

Competency Based Que.

Ans. The response of tribal communities, such as the Onges and Jarawas, to natural disasters illustrates the value of experiential knowledge over modern technological advancements. During the tsunami, these communities, lacking modern science, effectively foresaw or predicted the calamity and moved to higher ground, demonstrating their deep understanding of their environment. This highlights that access to modern technology does not inherently confer superiority; rather, cultures can be assessed based on their adaptability and effectiveness in crisis situations. The ability of tribal cultures to survive and respond to natural threats shows that all cultures possess unique strengths. It emphasises the importance of diverse knowledge systems and the need to evaluate cultures based on their contextual resilience rather than a hierarchy of development.

2. While socialisation has an important impact on individuals it is not a kind of 'cultural programming', in which the child absorbs passively the influences with which he or she comes into contact. Even the most recent newborn can assert her/his will. She/he will cry when hungry. And keep crying until those responsible for the infant's care respond. You may have seen how normal, everyday schedules of the family get completely reorganised with the birth of a child. You have already been introduced to the concepts of status/role, social control, groups and social stratification.

(a) **What is socialisation and why is it important in a child's development?**

(b) **How does socialisation continue throughout a person's life?**

Ans. (a) Socialisation is the process through which a child learns the norms, values, behaviours and social skills appropriate to their culture and society. It begins at birth and continues throughout life. This process is crucial for a child's development as it helps them understand their roles in various social contexts, such as family, school and community. Through socialisation, children learn how to interact with others, develop their identity and acquire the necessary tools to function as responsible members of society. Without socialisation, children would not understand how to behave or communicate effectively in a social environment.

(b) Socialisation continues throughout a person's life as they learn and adapt to different roles in various situations. While early socialisation happens in childhood, it doesn't stop there. As people grow, they experience new roles, such as becoming a student, employee, spouse or parent. Each stage of life brings new lessons about behaviour, values and social expectations. For example, a person may learn how to interact with colleagues at work, raise children or take care of elderly parents. This ongoing process helps individuals adjust to changes in their environment and maintain relationships with others in society.

3. While socialisation has an important impact on individuals, it is not a kind of 'cultural programming', in which the child absorbs passively the influences with which he or she comes into contact. Discuss the characteristics of socialisation.

Ans. Characteristics of socialisation are discussed below

- **Process of Learning** Socialisation is a matter of learning and not of biological inheritance. In the socialisation process, the individual learns the folkways, mores, sanction and other patterns of culture as well as skills ranging from the language to manual dexterity.
- **Life-long Process** The process of socialisation starts right from the time of birth and continuous till the death of the individual.
- **Process of Cultural Assimilation** An individual not only learn the folkways mores etc. but he inhibits and assimilate the aspects.
- **Process of Cultural Transmission** Socialisation is a process through which society transmits the cultural heritage from any generation to another.
- **Process of becoming a Functional Member of Society** The process of becoming a functional member of society is called socialisation. It involves learning the norms, values, behaviours and roles necessary to participate effectively in social life.

SELF ASSESSMENT TEST

Objective Type Questions

1. Which of the following statements is incorrect about socialisation?

(a) Socialisation is a life-long process that starts from the moment of birth.
(b) Socialisation only occurs in the early years of life and has no impact on adulthood.
(c) Socialisation is influenced by family, school, peer group and other social institutions.
(d) Socialisation helps individuals understand and perform various roles within society.

2. Which of the following is not the agent of socialisation?

(a) School (b) Family
(c) Computer (d) Media

3. Assertion (A) Normative dimension of culture refers to rules of conduct.

Reason (R) It includes not opening other people letters, performing rituals at death.

(a) Both A and R are true and R is the correct explanation of A.
(b) Both A and R are true, but R is not the correct explanation of A.
(c) A is true, but R is false.
(d) A is false, but R is true.

Case Based Questions

1. Culture, in sociology, is not just about refined tastes in arts but encompasses the way of life shared by all members of a society. Edward Taylor defined culture as a 'complex whole' including knowledge, belief, law, and customs. Bronislaw Malinowski emphasised material and non-material culture, suggesting it includes artifacts, values, and habits. Clifford Geertz highlighted the interpretative nature of culture, calling it 'webs of significance' spun by humans. Definitions of culture vary, encompassing learned behaviours, legacies, mechanisms for behaviour regulation, and ways of thinking. These diverse perspectives led Kroebor and Kluckhohn to publish *Culture : A Critical Review of Concepts and Definitions* in 1952.

(i) Which scholar defined culture as 'the complex whole which includes knowledge, belief, art, morals, law, custom, and other capabilities acquired by man'?

(a) Bronislaw Malinowski (b) Edward Taylor (c) Clifford Geertz (d) Alfred Kroebor

(ii) What concept is central to Clifford Geertz's understanding of culture?

(a) Culture as a means of adding meaning to objective reality
(b) Culture as a collection of artifacts and goods
(c) Culture as webs of significance spun by humans
(d) Culture as the normative regulation of behaviour

Very Short Answer Type Questions

1. The birth of a child leads to various changes in the lives of the parents, including the reorganisation of their daily schedules. How does this statement reflect the impact of socialisation on parents?

2. The process of socialisation is not a passive absorption of culture, as even a newborn can assert their will by crying when hungry. What can we infer about the nature of socialisation from this example?

Short Answer Type Questions

1. Explain main features of culture.

2. What are the major components of culture? Explain.

3. Describe the concept of revolutionary change with suitable examples.

4. Cultural change can occur due to environmental shifts, contact with other cultures or adaptation. How does this statement highlight the dynamic nature of culture in response to both internal and external factors?

Long Answer Type Questions

1. In sum there are two principal dimensions of culture–material and non-material. While the cognitive and normative aspects are non-material, the material dimension is crucial to increase production and enhance the quality of life. For integrated functioning of a culture the material and non-material dimensions must work together. But when the material or technological dimensions change rapidly, the non-material aspects can lag behind in terms of values and norms.

(a) Why is it important for the material and non-material dimensions of culture to work together for integrated functioning?

(b) What is the material aspect of culture and how does it impact daily life in both urban and rural areas?

2. Explain the role of socialise agencies in personality formation.

3. Identities are not inherited but fashioned with by the individual and the group. Discuss.

PART B
UNDERSTANDING SOCIETY

01

CHAPTER

Changes in technology and available jobs have transformed social relations, with social institutions such as caste, kinship networks, gender and religion playing significant roles in organising work and marketing products.

Social Change and Social Order in Rural and Urban Society

▼ **YOUR STUDY GOALS**

1.1 Introduction
1.2 Social Change
1.3 Technology and Economy
1.4 Politics
1.5 Culture
1.6 Social Order
1.7 Social Order and Social Change in Rural Areas

▼ **YOUR PRACTICE GOAL**

- Objective Type Questions (21 Qs ; MCQs, A-R, Case Based Questions)
- Subjective Questions (10 VSAs, 6 SAs, 3 LAs)

1.1 Introduction

- In modern life, change is one of the most obvious features. Sociology itself began to understand the rapid changes in Western European society from the 17th to 19th centuries.
- Humans have existed for around 500,000 years, but civilised societies[1] have only been around for about 6,000 years. Change has happened faster in the last 50 years. And in the last 20 years, the world may have changed even more than in the previous 30.

1.2 Social Change

- **Social Change** is a broad term used to define the significant changes in society that alter the basic structure of society over time.
- It needs to be both **intensive** (big impact) and **extensive** (affecting a large part of society).

1 **Civilised Societies** It means a country or group of people with a well-developed system of government, culture and a way of life.

- Social change is often classified by its causes, nature or speed. For example, **evolutionary change** happens slowly over a long time.
- Charles Darwin's theory of evolution showed how life forms adapt over centuries to survive. It focused on the survival of the fittest i.e. that only the strongest or best adapted will survive, while those who can't adapt will eventually die off.
- Darwin suggested that humans evolved from sea creatures (like fish) to land mammals, going through stages that included monkeys and chimpanzees, until finally developing into Homo sapiens (Humans). His ideas about natural evolution were applied to society, called **Social Darwinism**, which emphasises the need for societies to adapt to survive.
- In contrast, **revolutionary change** is much faster and occurs suddenly. It is often used in political context when one group overthrows another, like in the French Revolution (1789-93) or the Russian Revolution (1917).
- The term can also refer to sudden changes in other areas, like the 'industrial revolution' or the 'telecommunications revolution'.

Types of Social Change Based on Nature or Impact

On the basis of their nature or impact, types of changes are as follows

Structural Change

- Structural change affects the structure of society or its institutions or the rules by which these institutions are run. For example, the introduction of paper money changed how financial markets worked.
- Before paper money, coins were made of precious metals like gold and silver. The value of the coin was based on the value of the metal. However, the value of paper money was not intrinsic i.e. not based on the paper itself, but on trust.
- This shift led to the creation of the credit market and changed banking and finance. This led to changes in the organisation of economic life.

Changes in Values and Beliefs

- Changes in values and beliefs can also cause social change.
- In the past, children were seen as small adults and expected to work from a young age. Factories used child labour and children started working as early as five or six. In the 19th and early 20th centuries, views on childhood changed. Laws were made to ban child labour and make education compulsory.
- Child labour still exists in some industries (such as carpet weaving, small tea shops or restaurants, matchstick making and so on), but it is illegal and employers can be punished.
- Social change can have internal (endogenous) or external (exogenous) causes.

Types of Social Change Based on Causes or Sources

There are five broad types of sources or causes of social change; environmental, technological, economic, political and cultural.

Environment

- Nature, ecology and the physical environment have always influenced society, especially in the past. People in deserts couldn't practice settled agriculture like those in fertile areas.
- Their food, clothing, patterns of social interaction and livelihoods were shaped by the physical and climatic conditions of their environment. This was true for people in cold climates, port towns, trade routes and river valleys.

- However, technology has reduced the impact of nature on society, allowing people to adapt to different environments. Technology also changes nature and our relationship to it.
- Natural disasters, like earthquakes, floods, or tsunamis, can drastically alter societies. These changes are often permanent and irreversible. For example, the 2004 tsunami destroyed livelihoods and changed the social structure of coastal villages.
- Environmental factors can also be constructive. The discovery of oil in the Middle East transformed countries like Saudi Arabia and Kuwait, just like the gold rush in California. Without oil wealth, these countries would be very different.

Quick Test 1

1. What are the two principal dimensions of culture?
2. What does the term 'revolutionary change' mean?
3. Why is child labour illegal in many countries today?
4. How does technology reduce the influence of the environment on society?

1.3 Technology and Economy

- Technological and economic changes have caused significant social changes, especially in modern times.
- Technology helps us adapt to or control nature and when combined with the power of markets, it can have a major social impact, like natural events such as tsunamis or the discovery of oil. A key example of this is the Industrial Revolution.
- The steam engine had a huge impact, allowing industries to use a powerful energy source that worked continuously, unlike animals or humans.
- Steamships made ocean travel faster and more reliable, changing international trade and migration.
- Railways helped expand trade and industry across the American continent and Asia. In India, the railways have played a key role after their introduction in 1853.
- A technological invention or discovery may produce limited immediate effects and the full social impact of a technological change becomes clear only later.
- For example, gunpowder and paper had little immediate effect when they were first discovered in China, but later they became crucial in Europe for warfare and printing, reshaping society.
- Similarly, new textile machines in Britain, along with market forces and **imperialism**[2], led to the collapse of India's advanced handloom industry.
- Economic changes that aren't directly technological can also cause social change. For example, Plantation agriculture, which focused on growing single crops like sugarcane, tea or cotton, created a high demand for labour.
- This led to the rise of slavery and the slave trade between Africa, Europe and the Americas between the 17th and 19th centuries. In India, tea plantations in Assam involved the forced migration of labour from areas like Jharkhand and Chhattisgarh.
- Today, changes in tariffs and international trade agreements made by international organisations like the World Trade Organisation (WTO) can either destroy industries or boost others.

2 **Imperialism** It is a political system in which a rich and powerful country controls other countries (colonies) which are not as rich and powerful as itself.

1.4 Politics

- In the past, kings and queens were seen as the main forces of social change. However, they were actually part of larger political, social and economic trends.
- Political forces have been crucial in driving social change, with warfare being one of the clearest examples. Conquerors could bring change, but sometimes the conquered society changed the conquerors as well.
- A modern example is the relationship between the United States and Japan. After the US defeated Japan in World War II, it occupied Japan and introduced changes, including land reforms.
- By the 1970s, Japans industrial techniques, especially in car manufacturing, surpassed those of the US.
- By the 1970s and 1990s, Japanese industry dominated globally and forced changes in US and European industries.
- Big industries like steel, cars, and heavy machinery faced big problems and had to change their ways, following Japanese technology and management methods. At the same time, Japan also led in new areas like electronics.
- Japan revolutionised the global industrial landscape, not through warfare, but through economic and technological means.
- Political changes can also impact society at home. The Indian independence movement not only ended British rule but also transformed Indian society.
- In 2006, the Nepali people's rejection of the monarchy also led to major changes. More generally, political changes redistribute power across different social groups, impacting society deeply.
- Universal adult franchise or the right of all adults to vote, is one of the biggest political changes in history. Voting was once restricted to wealthy men or those from high-status social groups. Women were excluded from voting.
- Over time, through struggles, **universal suffrage**[3] was achieved. It forces governments to seek the approval of the people to maintain legitimacy, leading to massive social changes.

1.5 Culture

- Culture refers to the values, beliefs and ideas that shape people's lives. Changes in these cultural elements often lead to changes in society.
- One major cultural force that has led to social change is religion. Religious beliefs and practices have organised societies and changes in religion have transformed them.
- Some scholars define civilisations in terms of religion and view history as the interaction between different religions.
- For example, Max Weber's study showed how Protestant beliefs helped establish capitalism. In India, Buddhism and the Bhakti Movement influenced social and political life, including the caste system.
- In the modern era, women's struggles for equality have led to significant social changes.
- During World War II, women in Western countries took on factory jobs traditionally held by men, which helped support their claims for equality.
- As cities grew, women became key decision-makers in household spending, which caught the attention of advertisers. As a result, ads began to target women more specifically.
- Now, it's economically important for advertisers and manufacturers to consider what women think and feel, something that wasn't as important in the past.

3 **Universal Suffrage** It means the right of all adult citizens to vote in an election.

- Sports have also played a role in social change. Cricket, originally an aristocratic British pastime, spread globally, particularly in former British colonies. It became a symbol of national or racial pride.
- For example, the England-Australia rivalry reflected Australia's resentment as a colonised nation. Similarly, the West Indies cricket team's dominance in the 1970s and 1980s expressed **racial pride**.
- Social change is influenced by many factors–internal or external, deliberate or accidental. Economic and technological changes can have cultural effects and politics may be influenced by the environment.
- While social change is often better understood after it happens, we also need to recognise and adapt to it as it occurs.

Quick Test 2

1. What does Darwian theory of evolution focus on?
2. Mention the most famous instance of social change brought about by technology.
3. Which type of change involves rapid and dramatic shifts in power?
4. Identify the resource which drastically transformed societies in the middle East?

1.6 Social Order

- Social change is better understood with social order. Social order is the resistance to change within society.
- Social order helps maintain stability, as societies need to reproduce themselves over time and keep things predictable. People follow the same rules, and actions have similar results, which ensures stability.
- However, societies resist change for more concrete reasons. Societies are often stratified[4], with different groups holding varying levels of power, wealth and status.
- The powerful groups usually resist changes that could reduce their advantages, while the disadvantaged groups want change to improve their situation. 'Normal' conditions usually favour the rich and powerful and they are able to resist change. This is the reason why societies are generally stable.
- Social order is not just about resisting change; it's also about maintaining a certain structure of relationships, values and norms.
- Social order can be maintained in two ways: when people agree to follow norms willingly or when they are forced to obey them. Every society employs a combination of these methods to sustain social order.
- Socialisation or learning societal norms, helps people accept social order. However, socialisation is not completely efficient; people may change their minds about what is right or wrong over time, questioning or even rediscovering old beliefs.
- Power is the ability to make others do what you want, regardless of their own desires. When power is stable and accepted, it leads to domination, where certain groups or individuals are consistently in control.
- In normal times, dominant groups, institutions or individuals have a strong influence on society. While they are not completely unchallenged, opposition usually happens only in unusual or extraordinary situations.
- Even though domination means people may be forced to do things they don't want to, it often appears smooth and without conflict in everyday life.

4 **Stratified** It means to organise something or different parts of something in layers.

Domination, Authority and Law

Role of Domination, Authority and Law in Social Order

- Domination essentially refers to the power of an individual to exercise a certain degree of influence on another individual.
- This power of the dominant works through legitimacy which is the degree of acceptance involved in power relations.
- A legitimate power ensures conformity to the existing norms of right, propriety and justice.
- The legitimate power for Max Weber is authority, a power that is justified or proper. For example, a police officer, a judge, a teacher, etc. hold authority because of their official job description.
- Authority is also held/exercised by religious leaders, scholars, artists, writers and other intellectuals in a form that is not strictly defined or formalised.
- The difference between formal, codified authority and informal authority is important when understanding the concept of law.
- **Law** is explicitly codified written norms and rules that every citizen living in a society must follow irrespective of the fact that he/she agrees with it or not.
- Thus, domination works through power which is legitimate and supported by law. However, all power is not legitimate.

Contestation, Crime and Violence

- Domination, power, legitimate authority, and law do not always guarantee obedience or conformity.
- Society is marked by contestation. Contestation refers to broad forms of disagreement, not just specific conflicts or competition. It's about general protest or refusal to accept certain norms or rules in society.
- One example of contestation is youth counter cultures, where young people protest against social norms by changing things like their hairstyles, clothing, language or lifestyle.
- Contestation also includes more traditional forms like elections, where political parties compete. It also includes protests or disagreements with laws and authorities.
- Open societies allow people to disagree or protest, but there are limits (both implicit and explicit) to this dissent. If an individual crosses these boundaries, law enforcement may intervene.
- Even though Indians share a common identity, people can still disagree. Different political parties may have different views and even with shared traffic rules, people argue on the roads.
- It means that society can tolerate different opinions, but how much disagreement is allowed depends on the social and historical context.
- A crime is an act that breaks the law. The moral value of an act is not decided just by whether it breaks the law. For example, breaking an unjust law can be seen as morally right.
- Mahatma Gandhi broke the British salt law as part of the Civil Disobedience movement. While he was committing a crime by breaking the law, he did it for a higher moral cause and was supported by many people.
- Violence is considered illegal unless it's authorised by the state (like by police). The state has a monopoly on the legitimate use of violence and all other violence is illegal. Violence is clearly a threat to social order. It goes against both the law and important social norms.
- Violence in society often reflects serious problems and is a challenge to the state's authority. It shows the breakdown of social order and legitimation.

Social Order and Change in Village, Town and City

- Most societies can be divided into rural and urban areas. The way people live and organise their societies is very different in these two sectors.
- Sociologically, villages came from changes in society as people shifted from nomadic lifestyles to settled agricultural ones.
- As people began farming in one place, they started to accumulate wealth and produce more than they needed to survive. This created social differences.
- The more advanced division of labour also created the need for occupational specialisation.
- The main way to distinguish between rural and urban areas is based on two things–population density and the amount of agricultural work. Cities have higher population density, while villages have more people working in farming-related jobs.
- Villages are usually smaller in terms of the number of people, but they are spread out over a larger area. In contrast, cities and towns are more compact, with a higher concentration of people in a smaller space.
- Villages are more focused on agriculture. Most people in villages work in farming, and most of the products and income come from agriculture. Cities and towns, on the other hand, are more focused on non-agricultural activities.
- The difference between a town and a city is mainly about size. Cities are larger settlements with more infrastructure than towns.
- An **'urban agglomeration'** refers to a city and its surrounding areas, including suburbs and satellite settlements. A 'metropolitan area' can include several cities or a larger, continuous urban region.
- Urbanisation is the process where more people live in cities and towns instead of rural areas. This process is happening worldwide, especially in developed countries and is also taking place in developing nations, though at different speeds.
- According to a **United Nations Report** (2014), 54 per cent of the world's population lives in urban areas, a proportion that is expected to increase to 66 per cent by 2050.
- In India, the urban population has been increasing over time. In 1901, only about 11% of the population lived in cities and by 1951 it was around 17%. By 2001, about 28% lived in urban areas and by 2011, the percentage had risen to 37.7%.

Quick Test 3

1. What is the relationship between social change and social order?
2. Why does society resist change?
3. How does socialisation contribute to maintaining social order?
4. Define the term 'legitimacy' in the context of social power.
5. How does the concept of crime relate to the law?

1.7 Social Order and Social Change in Rural Areas

- Villages are smaller and people often know each other personally. Social structures are more traditional, with strong influences from caste, religion and customs.
- Change happens more slowly in villages because of these traditional structures. Villages are more resistant to change compared to towns. Changes in the sense of shifts in power are slow and late to arrive in rural areas because the social order is stronger and more resilient[5].

5 **Resilient** A strong enough to deal with illness, a shock, change etc.

- People in villages have less freedom to express dissent because there is no anonymity. If someone disagrees with the dominant group, they can easily be identified and punished.
- In villages, dominant groups control most jobs and resources. The poor depend on them for employment and support, making it difficult to challenge the established power structure.
- Villages have small populations and organising large protests is difficult. Any attempt to protest is quickly noticed and suppressed by the powerful.

Impact of Social and Agriculture Changes on Rural Society

- Villages are more isolated than towns and cities, making change slower. However, improvements in communication (like telephones and television) and transportation have connected villages to the outside world, reducing the cultural lag and speeding up social change.
- Changes in agriculture, like land reforms or new technologies, have a significant effect on rural society. For example, land reforms after independence shifted land from absentee landlords to local farmers.

Dominant Castes and Shift in Rural Power Structures

- Land reforms increased the political and social power of intermediate castes (called 'dominant castes'). These groups gained control over land and became politically influential because their votes mattered for winning elections, especially in rural areas.
- M.N. Srinivas has named these groups as the 'dominant castes'.
- The dominant castes are now facing challenges from lower and more backward castes, who are asserting their rights. This has led to social unrest in states like Andhra Pradesh, Bihar, Uttar Pradesh and Tamil Nadu.

Social Order and Social Change in Urban Areas

- Technological advances in agriculture, like new machinery or different cropping patterns, can change labour demands and thus change the relative bargaining strength of different social groups like landlords and labourers.
- Economic changes, such as price fluctuations or natural disasters, can have major effects on rural society. For example, an increase in the farmer suicides in India.
- Large-scale government programmes, such as the Mahatma Gandhi National Rural Employment Guarantee Act (MGNREGA), have a significant impact on rural areas by providing employment and improving living conditions.

Economic, Technological and Governmental Influences on Rural Areas of 2005

- Cities have existed for a long time, but large-scale urban living is modern. Historically, trade, religion, and military needs decided city locations, often on trade routes, near harbours or in strategic military spots.
- Religious centers attracted people and supported urban economies. Examples in India include trading towns like Tezpur and Kozhikode and religious cities like Varanasi and Madurai.
- Cities and modern life go together, offering opportunities for individualism and personal growth. Unlike villages, cities offer more freedom, though only the wealthy experience full freedom.
- Most city dwellers face economic and social constraints. Cities also examplify group identities based on race, religion, caste, ethnicity and class.

Challenges of Urban Living and Housing Patterns

- High population density in cities lead to challenges in housing, transport, public services and safety. Class, ethnicity and religion tensions further complicate matters.
- A lack of affordable housing for the poor leads to homelessness and the rise of **'street people'**[6] living in public spaces.
- Slums are overcrowded areas without basic services, where homes are often made from materials like plastic sheets, cardboard or even concrete, but are still inadequate for proper living conditions.
- In slums, lack of property rights allows strongmen ('dadas') to control territory and engage in illegal activities.
- Wealthy neighbourhoods or gated communities, are separated by walls and have controlled entry and exit. They have their own services such as electricity and water supply.
- Housing patterns affect the economy. Traffic congestion and pollution are major problems, worsened by reliance on private cars.
- Commuters can form political groups and sub-cultures, like Mumbai's suburban train commuters, who engage in activities like singing, playing games or celebrating festivals.

Social Changes and Urban Space Utilisation

- Social change in cities is linked to how space is used. City centers, once the heart of urban life, declined in the late 20th century as affluent or wealthy people moved to suburbs.
- Now, many Western cities are reviving city centers through gentrification, where poorer areas are converted into middle-class neighbourhoods.

Real Estate, Transport and Population Growth in Urban Areas

- As real estate prices go up, developers try to improve areas to make more profit. If successful, rents rise and the area becomes more prosperous. But sometimes, the effort fails and the neighbourhood falls back to its old status.
- Transport changes also influence social life. Cities with good public transport, like London or New York, have a different social dynamic compared to car-dependent cities like Los Angeles. In India, the new Metro Rail in Delhi may change the city's social life.
- The biggest challenge for cities, especially in rapidly urbanising countries, is managing population growth due to migration and natural increase.

Quick Test 4

1. Who controlled most resources in rural villages post-independence in India?
2. What makes dissent difficult in rural areas?
3. Identify the urban phenomena which involves wealthy neighbourhoods being separated by gates?
4. What is the process of revitalising lower class neighbourhoods called?
5. How are housing patterns linked to the economy of city?

6 **Street People** It means the people who live and survive on the street and footpaths, under bridges and flyovers, abandoned buildings and other empty places.

NCERT Folder

1. Would you agree with the statement that rapid social change is a comparatively new phenomenon in human history? Give reasons for your answer.

Ans. Yes, the statement that rapid social change is a comparatively new phenomenon in human history is correct. Human beings have existed on planet earth for approximately five lakh years, but they have had a civilised existence for only about 6000 years out of which we have seen constant and rapid changes in the last 100 years.

2. How is social change to be distinguished from other kinds of change?

Ans. Social change is a general term that refers to almost any kind of change that is not qualified by some other terms, such as economic or political change. However, it does not mean that it includes any and all changes. Social changes are changes which transform things fundamentally or which significantly alters the underlying structure of an object or situation over a period of time.

Social change is a very broad and complex term. It is connected to different levels or layers of the society. It includes not just formal but also informal structures including class, caste, race, etc. which affects the fundamental structure or order of a social set-up. Thus, it can be called a mix of the various types of changes that affect the society. This is mainly the reason why social change is distinguished from other types of changes.

3. What do you understand by structural change? Explain with examples other than those in the text.

Ans. **Structural Change** It refers to transformations in the structure of society. It is generally with reference to rules on the basis of which certain types of institutions operate and function. The changes that actually happen in the prevailing institutions of society is referred to as structural change.

For example

- The introduction of the Triple Talaq Bill has significantly transformed the Muslim structures of marriage and thus changes the status quo.
- Article 17 of the Indian Constitution prohibits untouchability. Now, all practices of untouchability are illegal and their social status has been uplifted.
- In the economic sense, the Goods and Services Tax and demonetisation are example of structural change which impacts monetary production and usage as well as corruption.

4. Describe some kinds of environment related social changes.

Ans. Nature, ecology and physical environment have always had a significant influence on the structure and shape of society. This was particularly true in the past when human beings were unable to control or overcome the effects of nature. For example, people living in a desert environment were unable to practice settled agriculture.

So their food, their clothes, their livelihood and their patterns of social interaction were all determined by the physical and climatic conditions of their environment.

Sudden and catastrophic events such as earthquakes, volcanic eruptions, floods or tidal waves like the tsunami that hit Indonesia, Sri Lanka, the Andaman Islands and parts of Tamil Nadu in December 2004 can change societies quite drastically. These changes are permanent and don't allow a return to the way things were.

Environmental or ecological factors need not only be destructive, they can be constructive as well. For example, the discovery of oil in the region of West Asia or the Middle East, the discovery of gold in California, etc. had completely changed the societies of the region.

5. What are some kinds of changes brought about by technology and the economy?

Ans. The changes brought by technology and the economy are given below

- Technology and economy have revolutionised the way society has progressed over the years. Since the year 1750, many technological machines were invented that led to the advent of Industrial Revolution.
- Production in industries started growing rapidly on a large scale that not only empowered man to control certain aspects of nature but also his economic condition.
- Dams were constructed to control the fury of floods. The introduction of steam engines allowed easy migration and transportation which in turn allowed industrialisation. Thus, social structure started transforming.
- Globalisation slowly transformed the world into one single economic village.
- Division of labour and specialisation of labour became the new norm of modern societies. However, such changes in the pattern of technology also brought certain negative things along. Labour was replaced by machines and unemployment rose in the society. In this manner that social changes were brought about by technology and economy.

6. What is meant by social order and how is it maintained?

Ans. Social Order It refers to the way that the various components of society-social structures and institutions, social relations such as social interaction and behaviour, and cultural aspects like norms, beliefs and values-work together to maintain the existing state of affairs.

Social order is not just resistance to change it is also the active maintenance and reproduction of particular pattern of social relations and of values and norms.

Ways of Maintaing Social Order

There are two ways of maintaining social order as follows

(i) First is when people spontaneously want to abide by a set of rules and norms. The shared values and norms are accepted and internalised by people through socialisation.

(ii) Second is when people are compelled through some form of power or coercion to ensure that institutions and individuals obey the norms. If any individual or organisation challenges the dominant order, they are suppressed or punished.

7. What is authority and how is it related to domination the law?

Ans. Authority Max Weber has defined authority as legitimate power considered to be justified or proper. Authority in society is based upon economic factors.

In other words, an individual assumes authority because of his/her official job description which gives a certain legitimate power. All other then must follow their authority in proper domain. For example, a judge authority works in court, while outside the court, he is under the authority of a police man.

Relation of Authority with Domination and Law

Domination works through legitimate power or authority/a major portion of which constitutes the law. Similarly/law is a system of rules through which human behaviours are controlled and regulated. Without authority, law cannot be formed and implemented and without law authority is not normalised.

8. How are a village, town and a city distinguished from each other?

Ans. Villages Villages are a unit of the rural community, where rural life upholds itself and perform its functions. It is simple community spread out or scattered over a relatively larger area. It has a lower density of population most of whom are engaged in agriculture linked occupations.

A village is often characterised by personalised relationships where every member knows every other member of a society. However, such a set up is not well connected to the world because of which social changes are slow and gradual.

Town/Cities Cities and towns have a higher density of people living per unit area. Majority of people living in town or cities are engaged in non-agricultural pursuits. Cities and towns are generally characterised by industrialisation and urbanisation where they have become commercial hubs.

As a result, the life of an individual is complex and multi-dimensional such that social changes are quick and drastic.

Town and cities differ only on administrative basis. A town and a city are same sorts of settlements that differ only in terms of size.

9. What are some features of social order in rural areas?

Ans. Rural areas which are quite distinct from the urban areas have some very peculiar features of social order that are summarised as under the followings

- **Agriculture the Sole Occupation** Land is the prime asset of a rural society upon which the entire economic system and development of people as well as villages rests.
- **Simplicity in Living** People residing in rural areas do not aspire much in terms of living conditions and lead a simple life.
- **Less Population and Homogeneity** Population size of rural areas is very small compared to urban areas. People have common traditional customs and rituals resulting in increased homogeneity in their cultures. Also there is no significant difference in the income level of the people in the rural areas.
- **Strong Resilience** The relative power of the dominant sections is more pronounced in a rural set up. They govern the economic sources, thus making the social order resilient to change.
- **Impact of Innovation** As the rural society is dependent on the agrarian mode of livelihood, all agricultural technological innovations have a great impact on the social order of rural areas.

10. What are some of the challenges to social order in urban areas?

Ans. The social order in the urban regions face some major complex problems most of which is related to a lack of space.

- **Spatial Problems** High population density in a city makes the urban social order focus on ensuring the spatial viability of the city. This includes ensuring housing, transportation, coexistence of residential, public and industrial areas as well as public health, sanitation, policing, public safety and monitoring the needs of urban governance. Thus, it poses many challenges of planning, implementation and maintenance which are intensified because of the stratification of the society on the basis of groups and labour.

- **Communal Rivalry** The urban landscape is also a home to communal rivalry that results from segregation prevalent in the residential areas of the society. For example, the communal tensions between Hindus and Muslims or the Godhra riots in Gujarat in 2002.
- **Housing Patterns and Transportation** The housing patterns are linked intricately to the economy of the city. The location of residential areas relative to industrial and commercial workplaces severely affects the urban transport. If the residential areas are located at a larger distance from the industrial areas, the transport system must be created and maintained. Transportation impacts the quality of life of working people and commuting becomes a way of life. Further, reliance on private road transport also creates problems of traffic congestion and vehicular pollution.

Exam Pattern Questions

Objective Type Questions

Multiple Choice Questions (MCQs)

1. Which of the following is not true about social change?

(a) Social change refers to significant transformations affecting a large section of society.
(b) Evolutionary change occurs slowly over an extended period of time.
(c) Revolutionary change is always destructive and does not bring any positive outcomes.
(d) Changes in values and beliefs can lead to structural transformations in society.

2. Evolutionary change was first proposed by

(a) Max Weber (b) Charles Darwin
(c) M.N. Srinivas (d) Emile Durkheim

3. Which of the following is not true about evolutionary change?

(a) It refers to slow changes over long periods of time.
(b) It often involves adapting to natural circumstances.
(c) Evolutionary change always results in revolutionary transformations.
(d) Darwin's theory of evolution inspired the concept of social Darwinism.

4. What is the main effect of revolutionary change in society?

(a) Gradual adaptation to new environments
(b) Sharp and total transformations
(c) Decrease in technological innovations
(d) Increased influence of natural disasters

5. "Social change is such a general term that it can be and often is, used to refer to almost any kind of change not qualified by some other term, such as economic or political change." In your opinion which of the following can be considered as a social change?

Competency Based Que.

I. Changes in values and belief
II. Women empowerment
III. Adapting scientific temper

Codes

(a) I and II (b) Only III (c) Only I (d) I, II and III

6. Which of the following is an example of structural change mentioned in the passage?

(a) Introduction of paper money
(b) Spread of child labour in industries
(c) Tsunami disaster in Tamil Nadu
(d) Invention of new technology

7. Political changes come through which of the following?

(a) Mass dissent of people
(b) Technological innovations
(c) Redistribution of power
(d) Coercion

8. "Women's struggles have also been helped or hindered by other historical circumstances. For example, during the Second World War, women in Western countries started to work in factories doing jobs that they had never done before."

Why women were forced to go out for work?

Competency Based Que.

(a) To fight the inflation and support the family with extra income
(b) They were skilled and well educated
(c) They wanted to explore new things in life
(d) There was no male breadwinner due to participation in war.

9. Which of the following is an important means of cultural change?

(a) Religion (b) Gender
(c) Sports (d) Caste

10. The term 'dominant castes' was coined by whom among in follwing?

(a) M.N. Srinivas (b) Andre Beitille
(c) Ramaswamy (d) A.R. Desai

11. Social change is an important concept in sociology because

I. It refers to changes that alter the underlying structure of society over time.
II. Social change includes all minor and superficial changes in society.
III. Structural and value-based changes impact the organisation of society.
IV. It explains both slow evolutionary changes and rapid revolutionary transformations.

Codes

(a) I and III (b) II, III and IV
(c) I, III and IV (d) I, II and III

12. The combination of authority, law and domination results in which among the following?

(a) Consent and cooperation (b) Dissent
(c) Violence and crimes (d) Conformity

13. Culture is used as a short label for a very wide field of

I. Ideas II. Values
III. Beliefs IV. Ethics

Codes

(a) I and II (b) I, III and IV
(c) II and IV (d) All of these

14. .... includes a continuous urban settlement that is many times the size of a single city.

(a) Urban agglomeration (b) Town
(c) Metropolitan city (d) Commercial city

15. Lack of proper housing facilities results in

(a) Homelessness (b) Slums
(c) Communal rivalry (d) Both (a) and (b)

Assertion-Reason Questions

Direction (Q. Nos. 16-18) Two statements are given in the question below as Assertion (A) and Reason (R). Read the statements and choose the appropriate option.

(a) Both A and R are true and R is the correct explanation of A.
(b) Both A and R are correct, but R is not the correct explanation of A.
(c) A is true, but R is false.
(d) A is false, but R is true.

16. Assertion (A) Land reforms in India, particularly the redistribution of land ownership, had an immediate social impact by empowering intermediate castes.

Reason (R) The land reforms transferred land rights from absentee landlords to those who were actively managing and cultivating the land, often leading to an increase in the political and social power of these intermediate castes.

17. Assertion (A) Mass transit systems in cities are essential for transporting large numbers of workers to and from their workplaces.

Reason (R) High population density in urban areas makes it difficult for people to commute without an organised public transportation system.

18. Assertion (A) Legitimacy implies conformity to existing norms of right, propriety and justice.

Reason (R) Legitimacy refers to the degree of acceptance that is involved in power relations.

Case Based Questions

Read the passage given below and answer the questions that follow by choosing the correct option.

19. Sudden and catastrophic events such as earthquakes, volcanic eruptions, floods or tidal waves (like the tsunami that hit Indonesia, Sri Lanka, the Andaman Islands and parts of Tamil Nadu in December 2004) can change societies quite drastically. These changes are often irreversible, that is, they are permanent and don't allow a return to the way things were.

(i) Which of the following is an example of a catastrophic event that can drastically change societies?

(a) The discovery of new technologies
(b) A volcanic eruption
(c) The development of new trade routes
(d) The spread of a new language

(ii) How might environmental factors like natural disasters influence the future development of a region?

(a) They might encourage new technologies that prevent further disasters
(b) They may lead to permanent changes that reshape the region's economy and society
(c) They typically lead to a restoration of the pre-disaster conditions
(d) They have little to no long-term effect on the development of a region

20. Culture is used here as a short label for a very wide field of ideas, values, beliefs, that are important to people and help shape their lives. Changes in such ideas and beliefs lead naturally to changes in social life. The commonest example of a socio-cultural institution that has had enormous social impact is religion. Religious beliefs and norms have helped organise society and it is hardly surprising that changes in these beliefs have helped transform society. So important has religion been, that some scholars have tended to define civilisations in religious terms and to see history as the process of interaction between religions.

(i) **According to Max Weber, how did the Protestant ethic contribute to social change?**
(a) By promoting religious tolerance
(b) By encouraging a shift from socialism to capitalism
(c) By helping to establish the capitalist social system
(d) By abolishing the caste system

(ii) **What social change did Buddhism influence in ancient India?**
(a) Economic policies
(b) Political and social life
(c) Caste system
(d) Women's rights

21. Changes in modes of mass transport may also bring about significant social change in cities. Affordable, efficient and safe public transport makes a huge difference to city life and can shape the social character of a city apart from influencing its economic fortunes. Many scholars have written on the difference between cities based on public transport like London or New York and cities that depend mainly on individualised car based transport like Los Angeles. It remains to be seen, for example, whether the new Metro Rail in Delhi will significantly change social life in that city.

(i) **What role does affordable, efficient and safe public transport play in a city?**
(a) It only affects economic development.
(b) It has no impact on social life.
(c) It can shape the social character of a city and influence its economic fortunes.
(d) It decreases the population growth in cities.

(ii) **Which cities are commonly compared based on their modes of public transport?**
(a) Los Angeles and Tokyo
(b) London and New York
(c) Paris and Berlin
(d) Delhi and Mumbai

Answers

1. (c) Revolutionary change is always destructive and does not bring any positive outcomes.
2. (b) Charles Darwin
3. (c) Evolutionary change always results in revolutionary transformations.
4. (b) Sharp and total transformations
5. (d) I, II and III
6. (a) Introduction of paper money
7. (c) Redistribution of power
8. (d) There was no male breadwinner due to participation in war.
9. (a) Religion
10. (a) M.N. Srinivas
11. (c) I, III and IV
12. (a) Consent and cooperation
13. (d) All of these
14. (c) Metropolitan city
15. (d) Both (a) and (b)
16. (a) Both A and R are correct and R is the correct explanation of A.
17. (a) Both A and R are correct and R is the correct explanation of A.
18. (a) Both A and R are true and R is the correct explanation of A.
19. (i) (b) A volcanic eruption
(ii) (b) They may lead to permanent changes that reshape the region's economy and society
20. (i) (c) By helping to establish the capitalist social system
(ii) (b) Political and social life
21. (i) (c) It can shape the social character of a city and influence its economic fortunes.
(ii) (b) London and New York

Subjective Questions

Very Short Answer Type Questions

1. What do you understand by social change?

Ans. Social change is a type of change in which the social relationships remain organised, controlled and stable. Changes then takes place in the underlying structure of an object or situation over a period of time.

2. Sometimes changes in economic organisation that are not directly technological can also change society. In a well-known historical example, plantation agriculture–that is, the growing of single cash crops like sugarcane, tea or cotton on a large scale–created a heavy demand for labour. How did this economic change contribute to the social structures and political dynamics of the 17th to 19th centuries? Competency Based Que.

Ans. The expansion of plantation agriculture in the 17th to 19th centuries fuelled the demand for cheap labour, leading to the establishment of slavery. This economic change reinforced social hierarchies, with enslaved people at the bottom and influenced political dynamics, as colonial powers structured economies around forced labour and trade.

3. The creation of the World Trade Organisation (WTO) and its role in shaping global trade policies has had significant effects on various industries worldwide. How have international agreements like these led to sudden booms or downturns in different sectors?

Ans. International agreements like the WTO have opened markets, leading to booms in sectors such as technology and agriculture by promoting free trade. However, they also caused downturns in industries like textiles or manufacturing, where competition increased and local businesses struggled to adapt.

4. Explain the meaning of authority?

Ans. Authority is defined by Max Weber as legitimate power or power that is considered to be justified and proper. Authority implies that people have legitimate power because of their official description of their position which they could use only in their domain.

5. What do you understand by crime?

Ans. The notion of crime is derived from law. A crime is an act that violates an existing law or goes beyond the boundary of legitimate dissent.

6. What is violence?

Ans. Violence is the extreme form of contestation that not only goes against law but also against social norms. It is a product of social tensions that acts as a challenge to the authority of the state.

7. In economic and administrative terms, the distinction between rural and urban settlements is usually made on the basis of two major factors. List down these factors Competency Based Que.

Ans. The distinction between rural and urban settlements is typically based on two key factors: population density and the proportion of economic activities related to agriculture. Urban areas tend to have higher population densities and more diversified economies, whereas rural areas are more dependent on agriculture.

8. City centres are experiencing a revival now in many major Western cities as attempts to regenerate community life and the arts bear fruit. A related phenomenon is gentrification. What is gentrification? Competency Based Que.

Ans. The phenomenon of gentrification refers to the revival of the city centre under which they are going through a phase of revival of community life. It is a process that takes place with the conversion of previously lower class into middle and upper class.

9. City life and modernity go very well together; in fact, each may be considered an intimate expression of the other. Comment. Competency Based Que.

Ans. City life and modernity are closely linked, with cities offering anonymity and opportunities for personal growth. Unlike rural areas, which often limit individuality, cities provide the amenities and institutions that support diverse lifestyles. This makes the city a perfect environment for modern individuals to explore and express themselves freely.

10. Briefly explain the concept of 'gated communities'.

Ans. Gated communities are upscale neighbourhoods surrounded by walls or gates, controlling who can enter or leave. These communities often provide their own services like water, electricity and security, creating a self-contained living environment, commonly found in Indian cities.

Short Answer Type Questions

1. Although social change sums such a common and obvious fact about modern life, it is - comparatively speaking - a very new and recent fact. Define social change and mention its types. Competency Based Que.

Ans. Social change refers to the change in the system in which human social relationship remains organised, controlled and stable. It is a universal phenomenon wherein only the rate of change varies.

Social change is significantly a very complex and broad term. Therefore, it has been often defined in terms of its types. Social changes has been characterised into various types depending on different basis. They are

(i) On the basis of pace
- Evolutionary change
- Revolutionary change

(ii) On the basis of impact
- Structural change
- Change in values and beliefs

(iii) On the basis of cause/source
- Environmental change
- Technology and economy change
- Political change
- Cultural change

2. Write a short note on Social Darwinism.

Ans. The term 'Social Darwinism' emerged with the concept of evolutionary changes that was proposed by Charles Darwin. Darwin stated that evolution refers to changes that take place slowly over a long period of time. He used evolution to propose how living organism evolve over time by adapting to their environment. He proposed the idea of 'survival of the fittest'.

According to the Darwinian theory, only those survive who are best adapted to their situations and those who do not or are slow die in the long run. Although this theory referred to natural process, it was understood in sociological process giving way to the concept of Social Darwinism.

3. Contestation, crime and violence are always present in a social order. Elaborate. Competency Based Que.

Ans. The existence of dominant authority does not necessarily mean obedience and conformity. People can have different opinions even if they follow the same law. Hence, there is always a scope of dissent. There are contestations or continuous disagreements as well as dissents in a society. Societies generally allow dissent but only to a certain extent.

If the limit is crossed, it becomes a crime which allows for a reaction usually from the law enforcement agencies.

The notion of crime then is derived from law. A crime is an act that violates an existing law or goes beyond the boundary of legitimate dissent. There also exists an extreme form of contestation that not only goes against law but also against social norms. It is a product of social tensions that acts as a challenge to the authority of the state.

Apart from self defence, all acts of violence are against the state, becoming a crime. The state thus can punish an individual for violating its monopoly over its legitimate and legal use of violence.

4. A technological invention or discovery may produce limited immediate effects, as though it were lying dormant. Justify. Competency Based Que.

Ans. Although technological inventions produce a quick impact in society, in many cases it may produce limited impact. It is only with some later economic changes that the invention may become significant.

For example, the discovery of writing paper and gunpowder in China was not of much global significance for many centuries until it came under the context of modernising Western Europe. Gunpowder changed the technology of warfare while the paper-print revolution changed the society for the better.

5. State, how do social stratification and vested interests contribute to resistance to social change in society?

Ans. Social stratification creates unequal access to resources, power and status, leading to resistance to social change from dominant groups. Those in power, such as the rich and powerful, benefit from stability and wish to maintain their privileged positions. Conversely, subordinated groups, who face disadvantages, seek change to improve their circumstances. The dominant groups resist change because it threatens their status, while oppressed groups are more likely to support change. This unequal positioning creates a natural resistance to social change, preserving the existing social order.

6. The introduction of new labour saving machinery or new cropping patterns may alter the demand for labour and thus change the relative bargaining strength of different social groups like landlords and labourers. Even if they don't directly affect labour demand, technological or economic changes can change the economic power of different groups and thus set in motion a chain of changes. How can the introduction of new labour-saving machinery or changes in cropping patterns affect the demand for labour?

Ans. The introduction of labour-saving machinery or changes in cropping patterns can reduce the demand for manual labour, potentially displacing agricultural workers. This shift impacts the bargaining power between social groups, such as landlords and labourers. Additionally, economic shocks like fluctuating agricultural prices, droughts or floods can destabilise rural economies, contributing to challenges such as farmer suicides in India.

Conversely, large-scale development programmes like the Mahatma Gandhi National Rural Employment Guarantee Act (MGNREGA) of 2005 can offer employment opportunities, improve livelihoods and help restore economic stability in rural areas, providing crucial support to the rural poor.

Long Answer Type Questions

1. The meaning of social events or processes often becomes clear through contrasts, just as the letters on the page that you are reading become legible because they contrast against the background. In the same way, social change as a process acquires meaning against the backdrop of continuity or lack of change. It may sound odd, but change makes sense as a concept only if there are also some things that are not changing, so that they offer the possibility of comparison or contrast. In other words, social change has to be understood together with social order, which is the tendency within established social systems that resists and regulates change.

(i) In this context, briefly explain how does social change relate to social order and why is stability is important in maintaining societal functions?

(ii) Why stability is important in maintaining societal functions? Competency Based Que.

Ans. (i) Social change is often understood through contrast, much like how letters become legible against a background. Change acquires meaning when placed alongside continuity or stability, as without some things remaining constant, the concept of change itself wouldn't make sense. Social change is linked with social order, the force that resists or regulates change within a society.

(ii) Stability is important for maintaining societal functions because it ensures predictability and order within a society. When stability exists, individuals can rely on established rules and norms, which fosters cooperation and coordination. It helps maintain economic growth, social relationships and institutions, ensuring that people can function effectively within their communities. Stability also allows societies to reproduce themselves over time, ensuring continuity in social structures, values and behaviours, which are essential for the smooth functioning of daily life and for the preservation of cultural identity.

2. By far the most common way of classifying social change is by its causes or sources sometimes the causes are pre-classified into endogenous and exogenous causes. Briefly discuss any three sources or causes of social change. Competency Based Que.

Ans. Factors behind social change in the society are as follow

(i) **Factor Related to Technology** Technology related factors are an important part of material culture and they carry their own importance. Traditionally, in the absence of technology, society functioned differently but the modern means of communication have completely changed life and society. Production increased due to the developments in technology and more efficiency in production was brought about with the use of machines.

It affected the social order and brought about significant social changes.

(ii) **Political Factors** Any redistribution of power in a social set-up brings about changes in the society. The shift from monarchy to democracy to the acceptance of the universal adult franchise is the biggest example of how warfare or revolutions impact the social order.

(iii) **Cultural Factors** An individual's beliefs and ideas are very significant to any social order. Hence, changes in the religious beliefs, cultural roles and many cultural motifs like games and sports bring about slow but major changes in the society.

3. The combination of technological and economic change has been responsible for immense social changes, especially in the modern period. Technology affects society in a wide variety of ways. Explain Competency Based Que.

Ans. The combination of technological and economic changes has driven huge social transformations, particularly in the modern era. Technological advancements, like the steam engine during the Industrial Revolution, altered industries and social structures. Steam power enabled large-scale production and continuous energy use, shifting economies from agrarian to industrial. It also revolutionised transportation, with steamships and railways speeding up global trade and migration, reshaping social geography. These changes were not only economic but also cultural and demographic, as urbanisation increased and new social classes emerged.

However, the full impact of technological innovations is not always immediate. Some inventions, such as gunpowder and paper, had limited initial effects until later economic contexts enabled their wider social significance. Similarly, the industrialisation of textiles in Britain, combined with imperialism and market forces, led to the destruction of India's handloom industry, showcasing how technological and economic changes can reshape societies globally.

SELF ASSESSMENT TEST

Objective Type Questions

1. The new spinning and weaving machines destroyed which industry of the Indian subcontinent with technological innovations in the textile industry in Britain?

(a) Transport
(b) Handloom
(c) Silk
(d) Cotton

2. **Assertion** (A) Religious places like temples and pilgrimage sites were essential to the development of urban economies in ancient India.

Reason (R) Large numbers of pilgrims visiting religious cities provided a steady flow of resources, boosting local economies and supporting urban growth.

(a) Both A and R are correct and R is the correct explanation of A.
(b) Both A and R are correct, but R is not the correct explanation of A.
(c) A is correct, but R is incorrect.
(d) A is incorrect, but R is correct.

3. What is 'Social Darwinism'?

(a) A theory about the evolution of life forms
(b) A theory emphasising the importance of adaptive change in society
(c) A social structure change due to technological advancements
(d) A political change brought about by economic disparity

Case Based Questions

1. Social order refers to the set of rules and norms that resist and regulate change in society. It is actively maintained through shared values internalised during socialisation and through power or coercion to ensure compliance. Max Weber defined authority as legitimate power justified within a specific domain, such as a judge's authority in court or a teacher's authority in school. Laws codify these norms, ensuring conformity across society irrespective of personal agreement.

(i) Max Weber described legitimate power as

(a) coercion
(b) domination
(c) authority
(d) socialisation

(ii) Social order is primarily maintained through

(a) questioning norms
(b) internalised norms and coercion
(c) informal agreements
(d) political revolutions

Very Short Answer Type Questions

1. The combination of technological and economic changes has led to significant social changes, especially during the modern period. Consider the role of the steam engine in the Industrial Revolution.

How did the steam engine contribute to social and economic transformations during this time?

2. The introduction of universal adult franchise was a significant political change. How did this political change impact social structures and power distribution in different societies, especially with the right to vote being extended to all adults?

3. Religion has historically played a crucial role in shaping social structures. Discuss how the influence of the Bhakti Movement in medieval India brought about social changes, particularly in relation to the caste system.
4. Define authority as given by Max Weber.
5. What do you understand by the term 'legitimation'?

Short Answer Type Questions

1. "Universal Adult Franchise brought about a major political change." Justify
2. Distinguish between evolutionary and revolutionary forms of social change.
3. Technological changes, like the advent of the photocopying machine, have had a significant social impact. Reflect on how the widespread use of photocopying technology has affected society and communication. Can you identify other technological changes that have had similar consequences?
4. "Authority is defined by legitimate power." Explain.

Long Answer Type Questions

1. Nature, ecology and the physical environment have always had a significant influence on the structure and shape of society. This was particularly true in the past when human beings were unable to control or overcome the effects of nature. For example, people living in a desert environment were unable to practise settled agriculture of the sort that was possible in the plains, near rivers and so on. So the kind of food they ate or the clothes they wore, the way they earned their livelihood and their patterns of social interaction were all determined to a large extent by the physical and climatic conditions of their environment.
   (a) How did the physical environment influence the lifestyle of people in the past?
   (b) Give an example of how geographical location influenced societies in the past.
2. The concept of social order is interlinked with the concepts of domination authority, law, contestation, crime and violence. Elaborate.

02

CHAPTER

Sociology is called the child of the ´age of revolution´. It was born in 19th-century Western Europe after revolutionary changes in the revious three centuries that changed how people lived.

▼ **YOUR STUDY GOALS**

2.1 The Context of Sociology
2.2 Karl Marx
2.3 Emile Durkheim
2.4 Max Weber

▼ **YOUR PRACTICE GOAL**

- Objective Type Questions (21 Qs ; MCQs, A-R, Case Based Questions)
- Subjective Questions (12 VSAs, 10 SAs, 3 LAs)

Introducing Western Sociologists

2.1 The Context of Sociology

- Three revolutions helped create sociology: First, the Enlightenment, or the 'age of reason'. Second, the French Revolution, which sought political sovereignty. Third, the Industrial Revolution, which introduced mass manufacturing.
- These events changed European society and affected the rest of the world as it interacted with Europe.

The Enlightenment

- In the late 17th and 18th centuries, Western Europe saw new ways of thinking called the **Enlightenment**[1].
- These ideas placed humans at the center of the universe and made rational thought a key part of being human. The ability to think critically turned people into 'knowing subjects' who produced and used knowledge.
- Only those who could think and reason were seen as fully human. Those who could not, like natives of primitive societies, were considered less evolved.

1 **Enlightenment** A period in 18th century Europe when philosophers rejected the supremacy of religious doctrines and established reason as the means to truth.

- Society, made by humans, could be understood through reason. To establish the importance of reason, the ideas of nature, religion and gods had to be replaced. The Enlightenment helped create the secular, scientific and humanistic attitudes we have today.

The French Revolution

- The French Revolution (1789) brought political sovereignty to individuals and nation-states.
- The Declaration of Human Rights declared all citizens equal and challenged inherited privileges.
- It freed individuals from the control of religious and feudal institutions. Peasants, many of whom were serfs or bounded labourers tied to **aristocratic estates**[2], were freed from their bonds.
- Taxes paid to feudal lords and the church were abolished. As citizens of the republic, people were given rights and equality before the law.
- The state had to respect individual privacy and could not interfere in people's domestic lives. A division was created between the public sphere of the state and the private sphere of the household.
- Religion and family became more private, while education became more public.
- The ideals of liberty, equality and fraternity became the guiding principles of the modern state.

The Industrial Revolution

- The Industrial Revolution began in Britain in the late 18th and early 19th centuries and laid the foundations for modern industry.
- It had two main aspects. First, it applied science and technology to production, especially with new machines and power sources. Second, it introduced new ways to organise labour and markets on a much larger scale than before.
- Machines like the Spinning Jenny and steam engines improved production and led to factories and mass manufacturing. Goods were now made on a huge scale for global markets and raw materials came from all over the world. Modern industry became a worldwide phenomenon.
- These changes also transformed social life. Factories in cities needed workers, so many people moved from rural areas to urban centers in search of jobs. Low wages meant that men, women and even children worked long hours in dangerous conditions.
- Industry made cities more important than rural areas. Cities grew, but so did poverty, with the rich living in better areas and the poor in slums.
- The rise of modern industry led to new forms of governance. State started controlling health, sanitation, crime and development.
- This created a need for new knowledge, leading to the rise of social sciences, including sociology.
- Sociology emerged partly to analyse the changes in industrial society. It was seen as the 'science of the new industrial society'. With modern industrial society came the ability to study social behaviour scientifically. The data collected by the state to manage society became the basis for sociological theory.

Quick Test 1

1. Name the revolutions responsible for the development of sociology?
2. What does the declaration of Human Rights Assert?
3. To whom did the peasants pay the taxes in Europe?
4. Declaration of which rights asserted the equality of all citizens?

2 **Aristocratic Estates** It is a form of government that places power in the hands of a small, privileged rulling class, the aristocrats.

2.2 Karl Marx

- Karl Marx was from Germany but spent most of his productive years in exile in Britain. His radical ideas led to his exile from Germany, France and Austria. Although he studied philosophy, Marx was not a philosopher. He was a social thinker who wanted to end oppression and exploitation.
- Marx believed scientific socialism could achieve this goal. He analysed capitalist society to show its weaknesses and to help bring about its downfall.
- Marx argued that human society progressed through different stages–primitive communism, slavery, feudalism, and capitalism. Capitalism was the latest stage, but Marx believed it would eventually give way to socialism.
- Capitalist society was marked by **alienation**[3] at several levels.
  - People were more alienated from nature.
  - Capitalism alienated people from each other, as it made society more individualistic and market-driven.
  - Workers were alienated from the products they created because they didn't own them.
  - Workers also had no control over the work process, unlike skilled craftsmen of the past. Finally, all these forms of alienation made people feel disconnected from themselves and struggle to find meaning in life.
- Even though capitalism was oppressive, Marx saw it as a necessary stage in history. It created the conditions for a future free from exploitation and poverty.
- Marx believed that the working class would unite to overthrow capitalism and create a free and equal socialist society. To understand capitalism, Marx studied its political, social and economic aspects.

Class Struggle

- Marx's idea of the economy was based on the mode of production, which is a system of production linked to a historical period. It also shows the way of life of a particular era. Primitive communism, slavery, feudalism and capitalism were all modes of production.
- The mode of production consists of a base (economic factors) and a superstructure (social, cultural and political institutions). The base includes productive forces (land, labour, technology, energy sources) and production relations (ownership and control of production).
- Production relations refer to all the economic relationships and forms of labour organisation which are involved in production. Production relations are also property relations or relationships based on the ownership or control of the means of production.
- For example, in primitive communism, productive forces were nature and simple tools, while production relations were based on community property.
- The superstructure is built on top of the economic base and includes institutions like religion, art and law. Marx argued that people's beliefs came from the economic system they lived in. How people earned their living shaped their ideas, not the other way around. This idea went against the dominant thinking of Marx's time, which believed that ideas shaped the world.
- Marx focused on economic structures and processes because he believed they formed the foundation of every social system throughout human history. He argued that understanding how the economy works could help us change society in the future. Marx believed this change would come through class struggle.

---

3 **Alienation** A process in capitalist society by which human beings are separated and distanced from (or made strangers to) nature, other human beings, their work and its product and their own nature or self.

Views of Marx on Class Conflict

- For Marx, the most important way to classify people was based on their role in the production process.
- He believed that people in the same position in the production process would form a class. People in these classes shared common interests, even if they didn't recognise it.
- Classes were formed through historical processes and were shaped by changes in production conditions and conflicts between existing classes.
- As the mode of production (technology and social relations) changed, conflicts arose, leading to class struggles.
- For example, the rise of capitalism created a new working class. The destruction of the **feudal agricultural system**[4] left peasants and serfs without land, forcing them to move to cities for work. They became a large group of property-less people who had to work for a living. This shared position in the production process made them a class.
- Marx believed class struggle was the driving force of change in society. In 'The Communist Manifesto', Marx and Engels wrote that "the history of all hitherto existing societies is the history of class struggle".
- They described how, in different historical periods, oppressor and oppressed classes fought. In capitalism, the bourgeoisie (capitalists) owned the means of production, while the working class had nothing but their labour to sell.
- However, conflict doesn't automatically happen just because classes are opposed. People must become aware of their class interests and the interests of the other class. This awareness or 'class consciousness', is needed for class conflict to happen.
- Class conflict can lead to a revolution, where the working class overthrows the ruling class and creates a new society.
- Economic processes often lead to class conflict, but social and political factors are also necessary for revolution.
- Ideology is one reason why the relationship between economic and political processes is complicated. Ruling classes promote ideologies that justify their dominance. For example, poor people might be told they are poor because of fate or past sins, not because they are exploited.
- However, ideologies can be challenged by alternate ideologies.
- According to Marx, consciousness spreads unevenly among classes i.e. not all classes become aware of their situation in the same way. How a class acts in a certain time can't be predicted.
- Economic processes usually cause class conflicts. But these conflicts also depend on politics and society. If the conditions are right, class conflicts can lead to revolutions.

Quick Test 2

1. In the capitalist society who decides the means of production?
2. Marx's conception of the economy was based on which concept?
3. What did Marx argue was the driving force for societal change?
4. Why are dominant ideologies not always successful?

4 **Feudal Agricultural System** It was a land-based economic and political system in dedival europe where the rulling class, or aristocracy, controlled arabic land and exploited the peasant who framed it.

2.3 Emile Durkheim

- Emile Durkheim is considered as the founder of sociology as a formal discipline. In 1913, he became the first Professor of Sociology in Paris.
- Durkheim believed that moral codes were key to understanding society. These codes shaped individual behaviour and kept society together.
- Durkheim wanted to understand religion in a more secular (non-religious) way. He was able to do this in his final book, The Elementary Forms of Religious Life.
- He saw society as a 'social fact'–a force greater than the individual, formed by social ties. These ties created social solidarity, pressuring individuals to follow group norms and expectations. This limited individual behaviour, making it predictable and patterned.
- Durkheim argued that by studying these behaviour patterns, we could understand the unseen social forces like ideas, values and norms.
- He believed these moral facts could be studied scientifically, just like physical facts. For him, moral codes reflected the social conditions of a society. Therefore, the moral rules of one society could be different from those of another.
- Durkheim aimed to make sociology a scientific discipline by showing that society could be studied through its moral facts, similar to how natural sciences study physical facts.

Durkheim's Vision of Sociology

- Durkheim's vision of sociology as a scientific discipline had two key features.
- First, sociology studied social facts, which were different from what other sciences studied. Social facts are phenomena that arise from collective life. These include things like social institutions (e.g., religion, family) or values (e.g., friendship, patriotism).
- They can only exist in a group and are more than just the sum of individuals. For example, a football team is not just a collection of players; it's something more. Sociology studies this 'emergent' level of social life.
- Second feature of Durkheim's sociology was that it was empirical. This meant sociology relied on observable, measurable evidence, like natural sciences.
- Social facts are abstract, so we cannot directly see things like a community or nation. Durkheim showed that even though we cannot directly observe social facts, we can study them through behaviour patterns.
- One famous example of this is Durkheim's study of suicide. While each suicide is unique, the overall suicide rate in a community is a social fact.
- Social facts are things that are external to the individual but still shape their behavior. They include laws, education, religion, beliefs and collective practices. These social facts are not tied to any one person but are shared by the group.

Division of Labour in Society

- In his first book, 'Division of Labour in Society', Durkheim explained how society evolves from primitive to modern. He classified societies on the basis of the social solidarity they had.
- Primitive societies are based on mechanical solidarity. This means people are similar to each other and share similar roles. These societies are small and everyone knows each other. They are not tolerant of differences and breaking community rules is punished harshly.
- Laws are repressive, meant to prevent deviation and protect the community.

- Modern societies have organic solidarity. This means people are different from each other and are interdependent. These societies are large and relationships are more impersonal. People depend on each other for survival and their roles are more specialised.
- Laws in modern societies are restitutive–they aim to repair harm, not punish. In primitive societies, the law focused on revenge and harsh punishment.
- In modern societies, people form voluntary groups with specific goals. These groups don't control every part of a person's life, so individuals can have multiple roles and identities. People depend on each other for basic needs and this increases interaction. In large societies, impersonal rules are needed to manage social relations because personalised relations can no longer be maintained in a large population.
- Durkheim's work in the Division of Labour shows his aim to create sociology as a new scientific discipline. His study of social solidarity laid the foundation for sociology as the science of society.

Quick Test 3

1. Who founded sociology as a formal discipline?
2. Who wrote the book 'The Elementary Forms of Religious Life'?
3. Who argued that society was a social fact which existed as a moral community over and above the individual?
4. What type of social lies exist in societies based on organic solidarity?

2.4 Max Weber

Max Weber was a leading German social thinker. Despite poor health, he left a rich legacy of sociological work.

He wrote on many topics but focused mainly on understanding social action, power and domination. One of his key concerns was the process of **rationalisation**[5] in modern society. He also studied how different religions influenced this process.

Max Weber and Interpretive Sociology

- Weber believed the goal of social science was to understand social action. Social action is human behaviour that has meaning.
- Unlike natural sciences, which study objective facts, social sciences focus on subjective meanings. Sociologists need to understand what actions mean to the people performing them. To do this, they must put themselves in the actor's shoes and imagine their perspective.
- This approach is called 'empathetic understanding'. It's not about sympathy, but understanding people's feelings and motivations. Sociologists must understand without letting their own opinions affect the process. Weber called this 'value neutrality'. Sociologists should describe others' beliefs and actions without judgment.
- Weber also introduced the idea of the 'ideal type'. An ideal type is a model that highlights the key features of a social phenomenon. It helps with analysis, but it's not meant to be an exact copy of reality. Ideal types may exaggerate some characteristics to help explain them better.
- Weber used the ideal type to study how certain religious ethics influenced social changes.
- For example, he suggested that Protestant ethics helped develop capitalism in Europe. He also used ideal types to define three types of authority–traditional, charismatic and rational-legal.

---

5 **Rationalisation** The process of making things more efficient and predictable through rules.

- Traditional authority is based on customs, charismatic authority comes from personal qualities and rational-legal authority is based on laws. Modern society is dominated by rational-legal authority, seen in bureaucracy.

Bureaucracy

Bureaucracy is a system where the public and private worlds are separated. Public behaviour is regulated by rules. Bureaucracy limits the power of officials and gives them clear responsibilities, but they don't have absolute power.

Bureaucratic authority has these main features

(i) **Functioning of Officials** Officials have clear duties defined by laws and rules. They follow commands from higher authorities and carry out tasks regularly. Only qualified people are hired for these tasks. Positions are independent of the person in the role and continue even when the person changes.

(ii) **Hierarchical Ordering of Positions** There is a clear hierarchy in bureaucracy. Higher officials oversee lower ones. If someone disagrees with a decision, they can appeal to a higher authority.

(iii) **Reliance on Written Documents** Bureaucracy relies on written records. These documents help manage the organisation and store decisions made. The public domain is separate from an official's private life.

(iv) **Office Management** Bureaucracy requires skilled and trained personnel to manage operations properly.

(v) **Conduct in Office** Officials must follow strict rules and regulations in their work. Their behavior is governed by these rules and separate from their personal life. These rules are legally recognised and officials can be held accountable.

Weber saw bureaucracy as a modern form of political authority. It recognised the skills and training of officials while limiting their power. The legal structure made officials accountable and kept their actions in the public domain.

Quick Test 4

1. Mention three types of authorities described by Max Weber.
2. Who are included in the property-less new social group?
3. Name the solidarity based on modern society.
4. Who decides rules and regulations of official conduct?

NCERT Folder

1. Why is Enlightenment important for the development of sociology?

Ans. The late 17th and 18th century Europe was marked by emergence of radical ways of thinking about the world. This phase was referred to as Enlightenment where new philosophies established the human being at the centre of the universe. Rational thought eventually became centre of human being and human thinking.

It was the ability to think rationally and critically that transformed humans into both producer and user of knowledge. The power of reasoning in humans changed everything. Reasoning eventually became defining feature of the human world.

Thus, it became necessary to displace the nature, religion and divine acts of God from the central position which were prevalent in the previous world. Thus, Enlightenment helped to develop attitudes of mind in a secular, scientific and humanistic manner.

This development influenced society as it was a product of human interaction. Thus, Enlightenment helped sociology to grow as a rational and scientific subject with critical analysis and provided better understanding of the world.

2. How was Industrial Revolution responsible for giving rise to sociology?

Ans. The Industrial Revolution brought many changes in the society. The invention of new machines led to evolution in the organisation of labour and markets. The factory system and manufacturing on mass scale led to changes in modes of production around the world.

The growth of industries, urban space, slums and modern form of government was a social consequence of these developments. As a result, the Industrial Revolution caused significant changes in society, which ultimately gave rise to the concept of sociology. The scientific analysis of development and study of social behaviour in industrialised societies were the main subjects of sociology. This was made possible by empirical observation and study of the information about social indicators generated by the state.

3. What are the various components of a mode of production?

Ans. Karl Marx's philosophy of capitalism was based on the notion of modes of production which was associated with the historical period.

The various modes of production at a general level are

- Primitive communism
- Slavery
- Feudalism
- Capitalism

At a specific level, the base of production is economic and includes productive forces and production relations. The productive relations refer to economic relationships and forms of labour organisation that are involved in production. Property relations are based on the ownership of means of production.

4. Why do classes come into conflict, according to Marx?

Ans. According to Karl Marx, the groups with similar interests and common objectives form same classes. This formation of classes is based on a historical process. It means that in every society, class identity among the people was present.

With the change in modes of production, technology and social relations, these classes became antagonist to each other, thus resulting in class conflict. For example, in a capitalist society, there is a conflict between the capitalists and the working class. In such a society, both of them are in a direct opposition to each other and hence the class conflict arises between classes.

5. What are social facts? How do we recognise them?

Ans. **Meaning of Social Facts** According to Emile Durkheim, sociology is the study of social facts. Social facts are things that are external to an individual and constrain their behaviour. They are general in nature.

They are combined representations of social behaviour of a group of people. Social institutions like law, education and religion also constitute social facts alongwith beliefs, feelings and collective practices.

Recognition of Social Facts In order to prove that sociology is based on social facts, Durkheim carried out the study on 'suicide'. According to it, suicide is a personal choice that an individual commits, but the average rate of suicide in society reflects social behaviour thus, making it a social fact. Hence, social facts can be recognised through social behaviour and the aggregate patterns of social behaviour.

6. What is the difference between 'mechanical' and 'organic' solidarity?

Ans. The differences between mechanical and organic solidarity are

Mechanical Solidarity	Organic Solidarity
It is majorly found in primitive societies.	It is found in modern societies.
Its basis is similarity of its individual members.	Its basis is heterogeneity of its members.
It is found in those societies that have less population.	It is found in societies that have a large population and greater impersonal relationships.
It is basically a group of people who are self-sufficient in their own ways and are engaged in similar type of activities.	The people in this group are not self-sufficient but are dependent on other groups for their survival.
This type of society is not very tolerant of differences and violent.	This type of society is tolerant and is independent of each other.
It has repressive laws that prevent deviation or opposition from the norms of the community.	It has components of restitutive law, which means that it tries to correct the wrong done by the criminals in the society.
The individual in this kind of society is totally submerged in the collectivity.	In this society, the individual is given a certain degree of autonomy.

7. Show with examples, how moral codes are indicators of social solidarity?

Ans. The following examples show how moral codes are indicators of social solidarity

- **Moral Codes are Imposed by Collective Agreement** According to Durkheim, the social solidarity was to be found in the codes of conduct imposed on individuals by collective agreement. In the everyday life, we can see such practices. For example, in Western societies, people generally wear black dress for funeral.
- **Moral Conduct Codes are Manifestations of Particular Social Conditions** It means that morally appropriate condition for one society can be inappropriate for another. For example, pecking (kissing on cheek) is morally appropriate in Western societies, but not in India. According to Durkheim, the prevailing social conditions could be derived from moral codes.
- **Moral Codes can Predict Behaviour** Construction of choice in social action meant that behaviour can be predicted as it follows a pattern. By observing behaviour patterns, it is possible to identify the norms, codes and social solidarities governing them. For example, in India, younger people bow down to touch feet of elder as a mark of respect and humbleness.

8. What are the basic features of bureaucracy?

Ans. Bureaucracy is a mode of organisation characterised by the separation of the public and domestic domains, where public behaviour is regulated by explicit rules. Key features include the following

- **Functioning of Officials** Officials have fixed areas of jurisdiction governed by rules. Duties are distributed systematically, and only qualified individuals are employed. Official positions are independent of the officeholder.
- **Hierarchical Ordering** Authority is arranged in a hierarchy, allowing supervision and appeals to higher officials.
- **Reliance on Written Documents** Management relies on written records, which are preserved and form part of the public domain.
- **Office Management** Specialised, requiring skilled personnel.
- **Conduct in Office** Governed by strict rules and legal regulations, ensuring accountability and separating public from private behaviour.

9. What is special or different about the kind of objectivity needed in social science?

Ans. The special or different kind of objectivity needed in social science is 'value neutrality'. According to Max Weber, it was important for sociologists to understand the subject matter of sociology in an objective manner as social interactions involved subjective human meanings like, values, feelings, prejudices and ideals. For this, a sociologist had to study and record the views of people and their personal beliefs in a neutral way through empathetic understanding.

Social scientists were themselves a part of society. Therefore, the exercise of such objectivity is considered special and different.

10. Can you identify any ideas or theories which have led to the formation of social movements in India in recent times?

Ans. Many social ideas/theories have been led to formation of social movements in India after independence. These include theories related to socialism, feminism and environmentalism.

- **Socialism** Socialist movements have strived to secure economic justice for backward classes. The ideal of socialism has been recognised in the Preamble of the Constitution of India as well. Dalits and tribals have participated in socio-political movements to acquire political power based on the ideas of social reforms movements of 19th and 20th century. These groups had been exploited from ancient time and are now endeavouring to claim their place in society.

- **Feminism** It seeks to redefine the role of women in society and bring it on equal footing with that of men. Feminist movements have struggled against stereotypes and made efforts to secure the rights of women at home and workplace with some degree of success.
- **Environmentalism** Environmental movements have combined environmental and social concerns of people which have been overshadowed by developmental concerns. The Gandhian ideals of peaceful agitation and simplistic living have their association with most of these movements. Environmentalism has recently acquired a prominent focus among social concerns with problems like climate change and its attendant costs, particularly for developing countries. Major socio-environmental movements in India are the Chipko movement, the Appiko movement, Narmada Bachao Andolan and Silent Valley conservation.

11. Try to find out what Marx and Weber wrote about India.

Ans. **Karl Marx** He referred to the villages of India as 'little communities'. He had opinion that India was a self-sufficient group which had no contact with the outside world. India had its own institutions and beliefs that controlled the human behaviour.

Marx also opposed the British rule in Indian society and was totally against it. He wrote many articles on India under the British Raj, in order to throw light upon his views.

Max Weber He studied India under his works on the 'Sociology of Religion'. Weber understood the Indian society as orthodox and suppressed, under the barriers of the caste system. Throughout his studies, he emphasised the need of the traditional household in an Indian society and also wrote about the position of women in the Indian society.

12. **Can you think of reasons why we should study the work of thinkers who died long ago? What could be some reasons to not study them?**

Ans. The work of thinkers who died long ago needs to be studied because it is important to understand the impact of their ideologies in order to know the present-day societies well.

Reasons to study works of early thinkers

- For understanding the communist model and its failures, one needs to study the theories developed by Karl Marx on capitalism and communism.
- Some theories of scholars are still relevant in the present day societies. The idea of bureaucracy by Max Weber is a very important element of functioning of present day societies.
- Theories of thinkers also provide many answers to social developments of the past. For example, the progress of Western societies compared to Asian societies can be understood through the study of Protestant-Ethic and the Rise of Capitalism by Max Weber.

Reasons for not studying the works of early thinkers

- Some of the old concepts may not be applicable to the present day societies. This can be attributed to unforeseen changes in social, economic, cultural and technological fields which accompany the advent of a new era. For instance, the theory of Karl Marx where he concludes that the working class would protest against the capitalist and a new form of socialist regime would emerge, was eventually proved wrong and later the theory of Max Weber was accepted.
- There are many critics to Karl Marx's theory. For example, the ideology of the Indian villages being self-sufficient entity by the Western scholars, was highly criticised by the Indians.

Exam Pattern Questions

Objective Type Questions

Multiple Choice Questions (MCQs)

1. Observers argued the sociology was the
(a) Science of structures
(b) Science of cultural practices
(c) Science of political systems
(d) Science of new industrial society

2. Referred to as ……… these new philosophies established the human being at the centre of the universe and rational thought as the central feature of the human being.
(a) The Positivism (b) The Rationalism
(c) The Enlightenment (d) The Anarchism

3. Sociology is considered the 'science of the new industrial society' because
(a) it developed in response to changes in agricultural practices.
(b) it analysed social developments caused by industrialisation.
(c) it focused on studying rural community life.
(d) it emerged before the Industrial Revolution.

4. According to Karl Marx, which of the following is the level of alienation in capitalist society?
(a) Humans alienated from nature
(b) Humans alienated from each other or fellow individuals
(c) Working people alienated from fruits of their labour
(d) All of the above

5. Marx's conception of the economy was based on the concept of
(a) Mode of production
(b) Mode of organisation
(c) Capitalism
(d) Political basis

6. Which of the following social thinker advocated an end to oppression and exploitation. He believed that scientific socialism would achieve this goal. To that end he engaged in a critical analysis of capitalist society to expose its weaknesses and bring about its downfall.
(a) Karl Marx (b) Emile Durkheim
(c) Max Weber (d) August Comte

7. Karl Marx placed great emphasis on ……… structures and processes because he believed that they formed the foundations of every social system throughout human history. For Marx, the most important method of classifying people into social groups was with reference to the production process, rather than religion, language, nationality or similar identities.
(a) economic (b) political
(c) power (d) administrative

8. Which of the following revolutions was responsible for the development of sociology in Europe?
(a) Enlightenment (b) French Revolution
(c) Industrial Revolution (d) All of these

9. Who among the following laid the foundations of sociology as a subject?
(a) Karl Marx (b) Emile Durkheim
(c) Max Weber (d) All of these

10. "The French Revolution (1789) announced the arrival of political sovereignty at the level of individuals as well as nation-states. The Declaration of Human Rights asserted the equality of all citizens and questioned the legitimacy of privileges inherited by birth".
Which of the following statements with respect to French Revolutions are correct? **Competency Based Que.**
I. It signaled the emancipation of the individual from the oppressive rule of the religious and feudal institutions.
II. It restored equality and fraternity in the society.
III. It brought radical political and societal change in France.

Codes
(a) II and III (b) I and III
(c) Only II (d) All of these

11. The foundations of modern industry were laid by the Industrial Revolution, which began in Britain in the late 18th and early 19th centuries. It had two major aspects. The first was the systematic application of science and technology to industrial production, particularly the invention of new machines and the harnessing of new sources of power.

What were the implications of Industrial Revolution? **Competency Based Que.**

I. Increased production and efficiency
II. Lower prices and more goods
III. Improved wages
IV. Afforestation

Codes

(a) I and III (b) II and IV
(c) I, II and III (d) IV and I

12. "Production relations refer to all the economic relationships and forms of labour organisation which are involved in production. Production relations are also property relations or relationships based on the ownership or control of the means of production".

Which of the following is not an important factor for Production? **Competency Based Que.**

I. Land II. Labour
III. Capital IV. Automobile

Codes

(a) I and II (b) Only IV
(c) II and III (d) I, III and IV

13. Who is the author of the book 'The Elementary Forms of Religious life'?

(a) Max Weber (b) Karl Marx
(c) Emile Durkheim (d) Friedrich Engels

14. Put the following statements in the correct order regarding Emile Durkheim.

I. Publishes Division of Labour in Society.
II. Enters the Ecole Normale Supérieure in Paris to study philosophy.
III. Publishes Rules of Sociological Method.
IV. Appointed lecturer in social sciences and education at the University of Bordeaux.

Codes

(a) II, IV, I and III (b) IV, II, III and I
(c) II, I, IV and III (d) I, II, IV and III

Assertion-Reason Questions

Direction (Q. Nos. 15-18) Two statements are given in the question below as Assertion (A) and Reason (R). Read the statements and choose the appropriate option.

(a) Both A and R are true and R is the correct explanation of A.
(b) Both A and R are true, but R is not the correct explanation of A.
(c) A is true, but R is false.
(d) A is false, but R is true.

15. **Assertion** (A) Marx argued that human society had progressed through different stages. These were; primitive, communism, slavery, feudalism and capitalism.

Reason (R) Capitalism was the latest phase of human advancement, but Marx believed that it would give way to socialism.

16. **Assertion** (A) A characteristic feature of modern societies is that individuals with similar goals come together voluntarily to from groups and associations.

Reason (R) Modern societies are oriented towards specific goals, they remain distinct from each other and do not seek to take over the entive life of its member.

17. **Assertion** (A) The Industrial Revolution facilitated the mass production of goods for global markets.

Reason (R) New machines like the Spinning Jenny and steam engines improved the productivity of industries.

18. **Assertion** (A) Sociology emerged as a response to the challenges posed by industrial society.

Reason (R) The need for scientific knowledge to address health, sanitation, and governance was a driving factor behind the development of sociology.

Case Based Question

Read the passage given below and answer the questions that follow by choosing the correct option.

19. Marx's conception of the economy was based on the notion of a mode of production, which stood for a broad system of production associated with an epoch or historical period. Primitive communism, slavery, feudalism and capitalism were all modes of production. At this general level, the mode of production defines an entire way of life characteristic of an era.

(i) **What does the concept of 'modes of production' suggest about the evolution of societies over time?**

(a) Societies evolve in a linear fashion without changing their economic systems
(b) Changes in economic systems lead to new ways of life, impacting all aspects of society
(c) Social and cultural aspects of society are unaffected by changes in economic systems
(d) Historical periods follow a random pattern without any connection to economic structures

(ii) **In the context of Marx's view, what does the term 'primitive communism' signify?**

(a) A society focused solely on agriculture
(b) A period before the development of economic systems
(c) A form of economic system where resources are collectively owned
(d) A capitalist society with high levels of technological advancement

20. Emile Durkheim may be considered as the founder of sociology as a formal discipline as he was the first to become a Professor of Sociology in Paris in 1913. Born into an orthodox Jewish family, Durkheim was sent to a rabbinical school (a Jewish religious school) for his early education. By the time he entered the Ecole Normale Superieure in 1876 he broke with his religious orientation and declared himself an agnostic. However, his moral upbringing had an enduring influence on his sociological thinking.

(i) **Which of the following is true about Emile Durkheim?**
(a) He became the first Professor of Sociology in 1913 in Berlin.
(b) He was sent to a rabbinical school for his early education.
(c) He remained deeply religious throughout his life.
(d) He believed society exists only as a collection of individuals.

(ii) **What does Durkheim mean by 'social solidarities'?**
(a) Ties that bind people in groups and exert pressure to conform.
(b) Individual actions that oppose social norms.
(c) Religious values that replace moral codes.
(d) Legal systems that govern individual behaviour.

21. Mechanical solidarity is founded on the similarity of its individual members and is found in societies with small populations. It typically involves a collection of different self-sufficient groups where each person within a particular group is engaged in similar activities or functions. As the solidarity or ties between people are based on similarity and personal relationships, such societies are not very tolerant of differences and any violation of the norms of the community attracts harsh punishment. In other words, mechanical solidarity based societies have repressive laws designed to prevent deviation from community norms.

(i) **Who classified society based on the nature of social solidarity?**
(a) Karl Marx
(b) Émile Durkheim
(c) Max Weber
(d) Auguste Comte

(ii) **Which characteristic is not associated with mechanical solidarity?**
(a) Small population
(b) Similarity among members
(c) Personal relationships
(d) Autonomy for individuals

Answers

1. (d) Science of new industrial society
2. (c) The Enlightenment
3. (c) it analysed social developments caused by industrialisation.
4. (d) All of the above
5. (a) Mode of production
6. (a) Karl Marx
7. (a) economic
8. (d) All of these
9. (b) Emile Durkheim
10. (d) All of these
11. (c) I, II and III
12. (b) Only IV
13. (c) Emile Durkheim
14. (a) II, IV, I and III
15. (b) Both A and R are true, but R is not the correct explanation of A.
16. (a) Both A and R are true and R is the correct explanation of A.
17. (a) Both A and R are true and R is the correct explanation of A.
18. (a) Both A and R are true and R is the correct explanation of A.
19. (i) (b) Changes in economic systems lead to new ways of life, impacting all aspects of society
    (ii) (c) A form of economic system where resources are collectively owned
20. (i) (b) He was sent to a rabbinical school for his early education.
    (ii) (a) Ties that bind people in groups and exert pressure to conform.
21. (i) (b) Emile Durkheim
    (ii) (d) Autonomy for individuals

Subjective Questions

Very Short Answer Type Questions

1. The foundations of modern industry were laid by the Industrial Revolution, which began in Britain in the late 18th and early 19th centuries. It had two major aspects. What were these two major aspects of the Industrial Revolution? Competency Based Que.

Ans. The Industrial Revolution had two main aspects—the application of science and technology to production (inventions like the Spinning Jenny and steam engine) and the organisation of labour and markets on a larger, industrial scale.

2. Capitalist society was marked by an ever intensifying process of alienation operating at several levels.

Ans. According to Marx, alienation is a condition in which men are dominated by the forces of their own creations. It is a process in capitalist society by which human beings are separated from nature, other humans, their self and their work.

3. What do you understand by the term bourgeoisie?

Ans. According to Marx, bourgeoisie is class of people who own the means of production in a capitalist society and enjoy both economic and political power.

4. Marx argued that human society had progressed through different stages. What are these stages?

Ans. Marx argued that human society had progressed through different stages. These were–primitive communism, slavery, feudalism and capitalism.

5. What do you understand by the term 'division of labour'?

Ans. Division of labour basically means that labour will be distributed among the different individuals on the basis of different skills and specialisations. It is based on the fact that a person who is good at something would be given that task according to his expertise.

6. Organic solidarity characterises modern society and is based on the heterogeneity of its members Interdependence is the essence of organic solidarity. Briefly explain the meaning of organic solidarity. Competency Based Que.

Ans. Organic solidarity is the solidarity that originates from people's sense of being different and interdependent. In this type of solidarity, people are specialised in handling tasks and can take care independently. It mainly prevails in modern as well as complex societies.

7. What is the meaning of mechanical solidarity?

Ans. Mechanical solidarity is the solidarity that originates from the people being similar or alike. The level or degree of specialisation is comparatively less in the case of this type of solidarity. It exists in simple societies and the primitive society that is backward and old is the best example of mechanical solidarity.

8. Why is Emile Durkheim referred to as the key classical theorist in sociology?

Ans. Emile Durkheim is referred as the key classical theorist in sociology because he laid down sociology as a scientific discipline and defined the subject matter of sociology. His key theoretical statement claims that social phenomenon are realities that can only be explained by other social facts.

9. What was Weber's interpretation of protestant religion?

Ans. Max Weber interpretated that capitalism originated due to the rules and methods of the protestant religion. This religion further helped to grow capitalism. He had the opinion that there is a strong relation between growth of particular economy and the religion associated with it.

10. Weber used the ideal type of illustrate the three types of authority that he defined as traditional, charismatic and rational-legal.

What is meant by charismatic authority? Competency Based Que.

Ans. Charismatic authority is the authority which is derived from divine sources or the gift of grace. The charisma means a sense of heroism or exemplary character of an individual. It is actually based on normative patterns prescribed by the individual possessing charisma.

11. How does Weber's characterisation of bureaucracy ensure accountability and prevent the abuse of power?

Ans. Weber's bureaucracy ensures accountability by legally defining roles and responsibilities, which limits individual discretion and requires officials to act within a structured framework. It, thereby, prevents arbitrary decision-making and safeguards the public interest.

12. Weber argued that the overall objective of the social sciences was to develop an 'interpretative understanding of social action'.

In this context, briefly explain what is social action? Competency Based Que.

Ans. Social action is a type of action that has certain types of characteristics. It is meaningful. It is something that will either be affected by other's actions or affect one's own actions.

Short Answer Type Questions

1. How did the Enlightenment change the way people viewed humans and society?

Ans. The Enlightenment shifted the focus to human beings as the central figures in understanding the world. It emphasised rational thought and critical reasoning as key to human nature, making humans both creators and users of knowledge. This new worldview placedless importance on religion, nature and divine forces, encouraging a secular and scientific approach to understanding society. The enlightenment also suggested that only those who could think rationally were fully human, often dismissing those who didn't conform to these ideals, such as indigenous peoples, as less evolved.

2. Explain the concept of class antagonism given by Karl Marx.

Ans. Karl Marx gave the concept of class antagonism which actually means class struggle. Marx wrote history of all the existing societies and observed the history of class struggle. He said that antagonism exists between two classes e.g. the oppressor who exploits and the oppressed who becomes the victim in the hands of the oppressor.

He used the terms for these two classes as Bourgeoisie and the Proletariat class. The Bourgeoisie who is generally the oppressor and the owner of the means of production e.g. capital, existing factories, machinery, land etc.

The Proletariat is the one who is oppressed and who has no means of production, has no access to resources but basically forms a part of labour in the society.

3. In the communist manifestio, Marx and Engels presented their views in a clear and concise manner. It's opening lines declare, "The history of all witherto existing societies is the history of class struggle".

Briefly explain the concept of class struggle as given by Karl Marx. **Competency Based Que.**

Ans. Karl Marx was of the view that human society has passed through different stages of development *viz* primitive communism, slavery, feudalism and capitalism. Each of these stages has been defined by a mode of production. The factors of production are in the hands of the oppressors and they control them while the oppressed are completely devoid of them.

There always exists a conflict between the haves and the have nots. Also when the proletariat class becomes conscious and slowly acquires revolutionary character the bourgeoisie is overthrown out of power. This explains the concept of class struggle according to Marx.

4. Distinguish between sub-structure and superstructure.

Ans. The differences between sub-structure and superstructure are

Sub-structure	Superstructure
It is the lower part of the society.	It is the upper part of the society.
It forms the base of the society and includes labourers, production means, experience of production, production relations.	It includes different aspects of social life such as political, intellectual, legal, cultural, etc.
It forms economic structure of the society.	It forms social structure of the society.
The base or sub-structure is pre-dominant in society.	The superstructure often affects the base or sub-structure.

5. Discuss Durkheim's notion of social solidarity.

Ans. Durkheim had the view that in every society there are some values, ideas, beliefs, ways of behaviour, institutions and laws which bind the society into a single unit. Since, these common elements are present in a society, the relations and the unity or solidarity exists in the society. These elements eventually increase acceptance and solidarity in society.

This is the type of solidarity often referred to as social solidarity. If these essential elements start to disintegrate then the society gradually breaks up into many parts. Hence, social solidarity provides a society with a social base of functioning.

6. The laws of modern society are 'restitutive' in nature rather than 'repressive'. What does Durkheim mean by this statement? **Competency Based Que.**

Ans. Durkheim had the view that crimes are an integral part of the society and modern society has laws to deal with those crimes. In traditional societies, laws were made to punish the criminals for their wrongful act. They were repressed and kept in subordination and were revenged for their act.

However in modern societies, the law aims to repair or correct the wrong that is done by a criminal act. Also the individual has been given some autonomy in the modern society. This was completely absent in traditional and primitive societies.

7. The second defining feature of Durkheim's vision of sociology was that, like most of the natural sciences, it was to be an empirical discipline. This was actually a difficult claim to make because social phenomena are by their very nature abstract.

Why does Durkheim consider sociology an empirical discipline, and what challenges does this present?

Ans. Durkheim believed sociology should follow the scientific method, relying on observation and evidence, similar to natural sciences. This makes it an empirical discipline. However, the challenge arises because social phenomena are abstract and cannot be directly observed, unlike physical phenomena. For instance, entities like the Jain community or the Bengali-speaking community are conceptual and not visible objects. Sociologists must infer their existence and study their effects through patterns, behaviours and practices within society.

8. One of Durkheim's most significant achievements is his demonstration that sociology, a discipline that dealt with abstract entities like social facts, could nevertheless be a science founded on observable, empirically verifiable evidence. How did Durkheim demonstrate that sociology, despite studying abstract concepts like social facts, could still be a science based on observable, empirical evidence? Explain this using his study of suicide as an example. Competency Based Que.

Ans. Durkheim showed that sociology could be a science based on observable and verifiable data, even when studying abstract concepts like social facts. In his study of suicide, Durkheim argued that while individual suicides are personal, the overall suicide rate across a large population reveals social patterns. These patterns, although not directly observable in each case, can be studied through aggregated data, such as the number of suicides in different social groups. Durkheim demonstrated that social facts, like the suicide rate, could be understood by analysing these larger, observable social patterns and behaviours.

9. Explain the concept of interpretive sociology given by Max Weber. Competency Based Que.

Ans. Max Weber viewed that sociology is a science which attempts interpretive understanding of social action. This meant that the objective of sociology is to interpret the meaning of social action. Sociology proceeds social action and the effects that it produced over a period of time. This concept of action actually describes all human behaviour to which the actor attaches subjective meaning. A particular action is social when it is oriented or directed towards others in the society.

However, sociology is not concerned with all the meaningful social action or that which takes account of other people. But sociology studies society in detail and it is reflective of the values, norms, religion and thus interprets its validity in a meaningful way thereby interpreting sociology in all respects.

10. Apart from empathetic understanding, Weber also suggested another methodological tool for doing sociology–the 'ideal type'.

What do you understand by the 'ideal type'? Competency Based Que.

Ans. An ideal type is a selection of certain elements, traits or characteristics which are distinctive and relevant to the phenomenon of study. It is a magnified picture of a particular reality. Weber observed society as a complex types of forces.

He developed his own notion of ideal type for making scientific generalisations out of our understanding of the infinitely complex and shifting world. It is a collection of the features of an entity that are logically consistent.

Though the ideal types are constructed from facts existing in reality, they do not represent or describe the total reality. Basically, an ideal type is a mental construct.

Long Answer Type Questions

1. During the late 17th and 18th centuries, Western Europe saw the emergence of radically new ways of thinking about the world. Refered to as 'The Enlightenment', these new philosophies established the human being at the centre of the universe, and rational thought as the central feature of the human being. The ability to think rationally and critically transformed the individual human being into both the producer and the user of all knowledge, the 'knowing subject'.

(a) Explain the central ideas of the enlightenment and their impact on the concept of humanity.

(b) How did the enlightenment challenge traditional ways of understanding the world?

Ans. (a) The enlightenment emphasised rational thought as the defining feature of human beings, placing individuals at the center of knowledge production and utilisation. It viewed reason and critical thinking as essential for being fully human, marginalising those who could not think rationally, such as natives of so-called primitive societies. This era displaced traditional beliefs centered on nature, religion, and divine acts, replacing them with secular, scientific, and humanistic attitudes. These ideas redefined humanity by prioritising reason over faith and tradition, shaping modern perspectives on knowledge and society.

(b) The enlightenment challenged traditional worldviews by rejecting the centrality of nature, religion, and divine acts in understanding the universe. Instead, it promoted secular, scientific, and humanistic attitudes, asserting that society and the human world were products of human creation and thus could be rationally analysed and understood. By emphasising reason, it displaced religious and supernatural explanations, fostering critical thinking and scientific inquiry. This transformation led to a significant shift in how knowledge was produced and how human beings perceived their role in shaping society.

2. The French Revolution (1789) announced the arrival of political sovereignty at the level of individuals as well as nation-states. How did the French Revolution redefine the relationship between the individual, the state and society? Competency Based Que.

Ans. The French Revolution fundamentally transformed the relationship between individuals, the state and society by asserting the sovereignty of the individual and promoting the idea of equal citizenship. The Declaration of the Rights of Man and Citizen proclaimed that all individuals were equal before the law, challenging the old feudal privileges and social hierarchies. Peasants were freed from serfdom and oppressive taxes were abolished. As a result, individuals were granted personal rights and freedoms, including the right to privacy and the state was required to respect these rights. A clear separation between the public and private spheres emerged, with religion and family becoming more private and education becoming a public concern. The nation-state itself was redefined as a sovereign entity with centralised authority. The ideals of liberty, equality and fraternity became the guiding principles of modern democratic states. This shift laid the foundation for modern democratic societies.

3. What are the main features of the theory of alienation?

Ans. Karl Marx argued that the history of mankind is characterised by increasing control of man over nature which led to the increasing alienation of man. Alienation is a condition in which men are dominated by the forces of their own creation and which confronts them with alien powers.

The main features of alienation are as follows

- Out of the different kinds of alienation, Karl Marx thinks economic alienation as the most important one as it is related to everyday activities of human beings.
- Economic alienation alienates the worker from the subject that he produces and from the process of production and from himself and from the community of the fellows. The worker does not at all feel at ease at the working place while he puts his whole life on the production of the product that he produces. This leads to a feeling of apathy and indifference towards the work and the fellow beings.
- Human beings are alienated from each other as capitalism individualises previously collective forms of social organisation. Relationships get more and more market-mediated.
- The large mass of working people is alienated from the fruits of their labour because workers do not own the products they produce and have no connection to the production of a product.
  Also the workers have no control over their product.
- In the theory of alienation, the worker is not only alienated from himself but also from every other person.
- Every person is alienated from the other person and is likewise alienated from humans.

4. Explain in detail the types of authority given by Max Weber.

Ans. Authority is the legal and sanctioned form of power by the state. The term sanction here refers to power which is given approval by the society. Power is generally defined as the capacity of a person to influence the behaviour of the other person against his wish.

There are three types of authority illustrated by Weber.

They are as follows

(i) **Legal Authority** It is the authority which is based on formal rules and laws. This type of authority is commanded by the laws and the rules of the country. An authoritative person uses this type of authority according to the definite rules and a person can be punished if he goes beyond his jurisdiction.

(ii) **Traditional Authority** It is the type of authority which is given on the basis of social values. There are no written laws and rules behind this type of authority. The leader is someone who depends on established tradition or order. While this leader is also a dominant personality, the prevailing order in society gives him the mandate to rule. This type of leadership, however, is reflective of everyday routine and conduct. Example of this type of authority is the head in a joint family in the traditional family system in India.

(iii) **Charismatic Authority** This type of authority points to an individual who possesses certain traits that make a leader extraordinary. This type of leader is not only capable of but actually possesses the superior power of charisma to rally diverse and conflict-prone people behind him. His power comes from the massive trust and almost unbreakable faith people put in him.

SELF ASSESSMENT TEST

Objective Type Questions

1. Which of the following concepts is/are given by Max Weber?

I. Bureaucracy

II. Ideal type

III. Organic solidarity

Codes

(a) Only I and II
(b) Only II and III
(c) Only I and III
(d) All of these

2. **Assertion** (A) Changes in the production system also led to many changes in social life.

Reason (R) Modern industry enabled the rural to dominate over the urban.

(a) Both A and R are true and R is the correct explanation of A.
(b) Both A and R are true, but R is not the correct explanation of A.
(c) A is true, but R is false.
(d) A is false, but R is true.

3. According to Enlightenment thinkers, what was required to be considered fully human?

(a) Wealth and status
(b) The ability to think and reason
(c) Religious devotion
(d) Inherited privilege

4. Which of the following terms best describes the intellectual attitude promoted by the Enlightenment?

(a) Superstitious
(b) Secular, scientific and humanistic
(c) Theocentric and traditional
(d) Mystical and unexplored

Case Based Questions

1. Karl Marx believed that capitalism, though exploitative, was a necessary stage in human history. It created the preconditions for a future egalitarian society. Marx argued that economic structures formed the foundation of every social system, and change in society could be brought through class struggle. He emphasised that material life shaped human ideas and beliefs, contrary to the dominant thinking of his time.

(i) According to Marx, capitalism was

(a) an unnecessary phase in human history
(b) a regressive step in society
(c) a necessary stage for societal progression
(d) independent of class struggle

(ii) Marx believed that ideas and beliefs were shaped by

(a) individual freedom
(b) economic structures
(c) religious practices
(d) supernatural forces

Very Short Answer Type Questions

1. 'The French Revolution (1789) announced the arrival of political sovereignty at the level of individuals as well as nation-states. The Declaration of Human Rights asserted the equality of all citizens and questioned the legitimacy of privileges inherited by birth. It signaled the emancipation of the individual from the oppressive rule of the religious and feudal institutions that dominated France before the Revolution.'

Discuss the key outcomes of the French Revolution.

2. 'The foundations of modern industry were laid by the Industrial Revolution, which began in Britain in the late 18th and early 19th centuries. It had two major aspects. The first was the systematic application of science and technology to industrial production, particularly the invention of new machines and the harnessing of new sources of power.'

   Explain the two major aspects of the Industrial Revolution and their contribution to the growth of modern industry.

3. 'Capitalist society was marked by an ever intensifying process of alienation operating at several levels. First, modern capitalist society is one where humans are more alienated from nature than ever before; second, human beings are alienated from each other as capitalism individualises previously collective forms of social organisation.'

   Analyse Karl Marx's concept of alienation in capitalist society.

4. How is traditional authority difference from charismatic authority?
5. What is 'emergent level' according to Durkheim?

Short Answer Type Questions

1. List any four features of bureaucracy.
2. Explain the importance of enlightenment for the development of sociology?
3. 'Marx's conception of the economy was based on the notion of a mode of production, which stood for a broad system of production associated with an epoch or historical period. Primitive communism, slavery, feudalism and capitalism were all modes of production.'

   Describe Karl Marx's concept of 'modes of production' and explain how it relates to the social and economic systems of different historical periods.

4. 'Being the handwork of humans, society was amenable to rational analysis and thus comprehensible to other humans. For reason to become the defining feature of the human world, it was necessary to displace nature, religion and the divine acts of gods from the central position they had in earlier ways of understanding the world.'

   Why was it important for Enlightenment thinkers to displace nature, religion, and divine acts from the central position in their understanding of the world?

5. Organic solidarity characterises modern society. Discuss.

Long Answer Type Questions

1. Describe the consequences of bureaucracy in social life.
2. Weber was among the first to discuss the special and complex kind of 'objectivity' that the social sciences had to cultivate. The social world was founded on subjective human meanings, values, feelings, prejudices, ideals and so on. In studying this world, the social sciences inevitably had to deal with these subjective meanings. In order to capture these meanings and describe them accurately, social scientists had to constantly practise 'empathetic understanding' by putting themselves (imaginatively) in the place of the people whose actions they were studying.

   (a) How did Weber describe the kind of 'objectivity' needed in social sciences?

   (b) What does 'empathetic understanding' allow sociologists to access in social actors?

03

CHAPTER

Indian Sociologists

Sociology began as a subject mostly studied in the West, but Indian sociologists gave it a new direction. They studied Indian society, its traditions, and problems, adding their ideas to make the subject richer and more meaningful.

▼ **YOUR STUDY GOALS**

3.1 Introduction
3.2 Second Generation of Indian Sociologists
3.3 Sociology in India (1920s-1950s)
3.4 M.N. Srinivas

▼ **YOUR PRACTICE GOAL**

- Objective Type Questions (14 Qs ; MCQs, A-R, Case Based Questions)
- Subjective Questions (7 VSAs, 6 SAs, 4 LAs)

3.1 Introduction

Interest in sociological thinking in India began over a century ago, but formal university teaching of sociology started in 1919 at the University of Bombay.

In the 1920s, the University of Calcutta and the University of Lucknow also began teaching sociology and **anthropology**[1]. Today, sociology is widely taught in most major universities in India.

The first experience of modernity in India was closely tied to colonialism. Furthermore, while Western anthropology was focused on 'primitive' cultures, it was questionable as to what role it would have in India which had ancient as well as modern civilisations but also had primitive societies.

In the begining, many Indians became sociologists and anthropologists by accident. One such pioneer was L.K. Ananthakrishna Iyer (1861-1937).

L.K. Ananthakrishna Iyer

- He started as a clerk and later became a teacher in Cochin (now Kerala). In 1902, he helped the Dewan of Cochin with an **ethnographic**[2] survey, working for free on weekends. His work was praised by British anthropologists, and he later assisted in a similar survey in Mysore.

---

1 **Anthropology** The study of humans, their societies, cultures and evolution.
2 **Ethnography** Related to the systematic study of people and cultures.

- He was a self-taught anthropologist and gained national and international recognition. He helped set up India's first postgraduate anthropology department.
- He worked at Calcutta University from 1917 to 1932. Despite no formal degree, he was elected President of the Ethnology section at the Indian Science Congress.
- A German university gave him an honorary doctorate and Cochin state honoured him with the titles of Rao Bahadur and Dewan Bahadur.

Sarat Chandra Roy

- Sarat Chandra Roy (1871-1942) was trained as a lawyer. He moved to Ranchi in 1898 to teach English at a Christian missionary school. He stayed in Ranchi for 44 years and became an expert on the tribal people of Chhotanagpur (now Jharkhand).
- Roy's interest in anthropology started when he began practicing law. He became an official interpreter in the court, helping with tribal customs and laws. This led him to study tribal society.
- Although not formally trained in anthropology, Roy published over 100 articles in Indian and British journals. He wrote important works on the Oraon, Mundas and Kharias tribes.
- In 1922, he founded **Man in India**, India's first anthropology journal, which is still published today.
- Both Iyer and Roy helped lay the foundations for sociology and anthropology in India in the early 20th century.

3.2 Second Generation of Indian Sociologists

In the second generation of Indian sociologists, figures like G.S. Ghurye, D.P. Mukerji, A.R. Desai and M.N. Srinivas helped shape Indian sociology after independence. They were influenced by Western traditions but also sought to develop a distinct Indian sociology.

G.S. Ghurye

- G.S. Ghurye, in particular, is considered the founder of institutionalised sociology in India. He headed the first postgraduate department of sociology at Bombay University for 35 years.
- He also helped in establishing the Indian Sociological Society and its journal Sociological Bulletin.
- Ghurye played a key role in developing sociology as an Indian discipline, even when there was little financial or institutional support for research.
- At Bombay University, his department became the first to successfully combine teaching and research in one institution. He also merged social anthropology and sociology into a single field.
- Ghurye wrote extensively on topics like caste, race, tribes, kinship, family, religion and urban life.

Ghurye and Tribals of India

- Ghurye's work was influenced by ideas like **diffusionism**[3], **Orientalist**[4] views on Hindu religion, nationalism and Hindu identity. One major theme he focused on was tribal or aboriginal cultures. His debate with Verrier Elwin on this topic made him well-known outside of sociology.
- In the 1930s and 1940s, there was a debate on the place of tribal societies in India.

British Anthropologists and their Views on Tribe

- British anthropologists saw tribes as primitive and distinct from mainstream Hinduism.
- They believed that tribal cultures should be protected from **assimilation**[5] with Hindu society.

---

3 **Diffusionism** It means spread of cultural elements from one society to another.
4 **Orientalist** A scholar or expert in Eastern or Asian cultures.
5 **Assimilation** It is a process by which one culture absorbs another and the assimilated culture disappears or merges completely into the dominant one.

- They thought that contact with Hindu culture would lead to exploitation and cultural loss. Therefore, it was the state's duty to protect the tribes and their culture.

Nationalists Views on Tribe

- They believed in the unity of India and felt that tribes needed to modernise.
- They thought preserving tribal cultures kept them backward. Ghurye supported the nationalist view.
- He argued that tribes were 'backward Hindus', not separate cultures. He used evidence from various tribal cultures to show they had long interacted with Hinduism.
- He believed tribes were just behind in the same process of cultural assimilation that all Indian communities went through.

Ghurye on Caste and Race

- G.S. Ghurye is well-known for his book 'Caste and Race in India' (1932), based on his doctoral dissertation at Cambridge. This book challenged the dominant theories of the relationship between race and caste in India at the time.
- Herbert Risley, a British official, believed that human beings could be divided into distinct races based on physical traits like skull size or nose length.
- Risley argued that India was a unique place to study racial evolution because caste prevents inter-marriage. He suggested that caste originated from race.
- According to him, higher castes had Aryan racial traits, while lower castes belonged to non-Aryan, aboriginal or Mongoloid groups.
- Risley believed the lower castes were the original inhabitants of India, later subjugated by Aryans who came from outside.
- Ghurye did not fully agree with Risley. He pointed out that using average measurements alone was problematic.
- Ghurye accepted that the Aryan/non-Aryan divide was mostly true in northern India, but in other parts of India, there were no clear or systematic differences between groups.
- He argued that 'racial purity' was only preserved in northern India, where inter-marriage was prohibited, while in the rest of India, groups with varied racial backgrounds practiced endogamy (marriage within caste).

Ghurye's Definition of Caste

Ghurye provided a detailed, systematic definition of caste with six main features as follows

(i) **Segmental Division** Caste is divided into separate, closed groups. A person's caste is decided by birth. Children inherit their caste from their parents. There is no way to change or choose a person's caste.

(ii) **Hierarchical Division** Castes are ranked; no two castes are equal. Every caste is either higher or lower than the others.

(iii) **Restrictions on Social Interaction** Caste involves restrictions on social interaction, especially sharing food. There are rules about which groups can share food. These rules are based on ideas of purity and pollution. The same applies to touch. In untouchability, the touch of some castes is seen as polluting.

(iv) **Differential Rights and Duties** Different castes have different rights and duties, both in religious and secular matters. Social interactions follow caste rules.

(v) **Occupation Restrictions** Caste determines the occupation a person can take, with specific castes assigned to specific jobs. Occupation is also hereditary. Thus, there is a strict division of labour.

(vi) **Marriage Restrictions** Caste has strict marriage rules. Caste endogamy means marrying only within your caste. There are also exogamy rules about whom you cannot marry. These rules help maintain the caste system.

Quick Test 1

1. When did the formal teaching of Sociology start in India?
2. Where did LK Ananthakrishna Iyer set up first Post Graduate Anthropology Department?
3. Who was founder of the journal 'Man in India'?
4. Name the sociologist who worked on the theme of 'tribes'.
5. State the reason due to which 'racial purity' is preserved in North India.

3.3 Sociology in India (1920s–1950s)

- Between the 1920s and 1950s, sociology in India was mainly taught at two key departments–Bombay University, led by G.S. Ghurye and Lucknow University.
- Both departments combined sociology with economics. Ghurye's work at Bombay helped establish the discipline of sociology in India.
- In Lucknow, the Sociology Department was led by the famous 'trinity' of Radhakamal Mukerjee, D.P. Mukerji and D.N. Majumdar.

D.P. Mukherji

D.P. Mukerji had a broad intellectual range, with interests in literature, music, film, philosophy and Marxism. Although he was influenced by Marxism, he viewed it more as a tool for social analysis than a political programme. His book **'Introduction to Indian Music'** is considered a classic in it's field.

D.P. Mukerji on Tradition and Change

- D.P. Mukerji turned to sociology because he was dissatisfied with history and economics in India. He believed that India's most distinctive feature was its social system.
- According to D.P., while India's history, politics, and economics were less developed compared to the West, its social dimensions were 'over-developed'.
- For D.P., the primary task of an Indian sociologist was to understand India's social traditions.
- According to him, an Indian sociologist must understand the customs, folkways and traditions of India in order to understand the social system. This study included both 'high' languages (like Sanskrit and Persian) and local dialects.
- D.P. argued that Indian society was not individualistic like Western societies. In India, the average person's desires were shaped by their social and cultural group, such as caste and **deviating**[6] from this pattern was uncommon.
- He believed that Indian society was oriented toward group action, not individual action. Although urban middle classes were beginning to embrace individualism, D.P. thought this shift was worth studying.
- D.P. explained that the word 'tradition' equals the Sanskrit words *parampara* (succession) and *aitihya* it originates from the same root as *Itihas* (history), showing that tradition is deeply connected to the past but evolves over time.
- He believed that change in Indian society comes from both internal and external sources. In Western societies, the economy is seen as a major source of change. However, D.P. Mukerji believed this was less effective in India.

6 **Deviating** It means doing something that is different from the usual or common way of behaving

- He thought class conflict in India was hidden by caste traditions.
- D.P. argued that Indian sociology should focus on non-economic causes of change.

Three Principles of Social Change

- D.P. identified three principles of change in Indian traditions *shruti* (revealed knowledge), *smriti* (remembered tradition) and *anubhava* (personal experience). He viewed *anubhava*, particularly collective experience, as the most revolutionary principle.
- In Indian society, personal experience often led to collective experience, which could challenge and change traditional beliefs. This was evident in movements like the Bhakti movement.
- In Indian Islam, the Sufi tradition emphasised love and experience over strict adherence to texts.
- D.P. believed that change in India often occurred through collective experiences rather than individual reasoning (buddhi-vichar).
- This process, where popular movements challenge but eventually become part of tradition, was typical of caste society, where class formation was inhibited or not allowed.
- D.P. criticised uncritical borrowing from Western intellectual traditions, including in areas like development planning. He argued that tradition should neither be blindly worshipped nor ignored.
- Modernity had shaped his own intellectual perspective, but he saw it as something to be adapted thoughtfully, not adopted blindly.

A.R. Desai

- A.R. Desai was a rare Indian sociologist who was actively involved in politics as a formal member of political parties. He was a lifelong Marxist, joining Marxist politics during his undergraduate years at Baroda.
- After completing his undergraduate studies in Baroda, Desai joined the Bombay sociology department to study under Ghurye. He earned his doctorate in 1946 by writing a dissertation on the social aspects of Indian nationalism.
- In 1948, his thesis was published as The Social Background of Indian Nationalism, which became his most famous work. In this book, Desai used a Marxist approach to analyse Indian nationalism, focusing on economic factors and class divisions while considering the impact of British colonial rule.
- His research covered topics like peasant movements, rural sociology, urban issues, political sociology, state forms and human rights. Desai was honoured and served as President of the Indian Sociological Society but remained an unusual figure in Indian sociology.

A.R. Desai on the State

- A.R. Desai (1915-1994) was a Marxist sociologist who focused on the role of the modern capitalist state. He critiqued the idea of the **'welfare state'**[7] in his essay 'The Myth of the Welfare State'. According to Desai, a welfare state has three main features
  - (i) **Positive state** Unlike classical liberalism, which advocates minimal state intervention or laissez faire, the welfare state actively uses its powers to improve society through social policies.
  - (ii) **Democratic state** A welfare state must be democratic, with multi-party elections and formal democratic institutions.
  - (iii) **Mixed economy** It includes both private capitalist enterprises and public/state-owned enterprises. The state focuses on basic goods and infrastructure, while private industry dominates consumer goods.
- Desai proposed several criteria to evaluate a welfare state
  - Ensuring freedom from poverty, discrimination, and insecurity for all citizens.

7 **Welfare State** It is a way of governing in which the state or an established group of social institutions provide basic economic security for it's citizens.

- Reducing income inequality by redistributing wealth.
- Making the economy serve the needs of the community rather than the capitalist profit motive.
- Ensuring stable economic development, free from cycles of booms and depressions.
- Providing full employment.

- Desai applied these criteria to countries like Britain, the USA and Europe concluded that their welfare state claims were exaggerated. Despite welfare policies, these countries failed to provide social security, reduce inequality or ensure stable economic development. Thus, Desai argued that the welfare state is largely a myth.
- Desai also analysed the Marxist theory of the state. He criticised the shortcomings of communist states, emphasising the importance of democracy, political liberties and rule of law in any genuinely socialist state.

Quick Test 2

1. What are three principles of change?
2. Name the sociologist who joined Bombay Sociology department under Ghurye.
3. Which essay of A.R. Desai provides detailed critique of capitalist state?
4. According to whom it is the first duty of an Indian sociologist to study and to know the social traditions of India.
5. According to whom welfare state is a positive state, democratic state and involves a mix economy?

3.4 M.N. Srinivas

- M.N. Srinivas was a famous Indian sociologist after independence. He earned two doctoral degrees, one from Bombay University and one from Oxford.
- Srinivas studied under G.S. Ghurye at Bombay.
- Srinivas' doctoral dissertation became the book Religion and Society among the Coorgs of South India. The book used the structural-functional approach and made Srinivas internationally known for his detailed ethnographic work.
- Srinivas offered a lectureship in Indian sociology at Oxford but resigned in 1951 to return to India. He became the head of the Sociology Department at Maharaja Sayajirao University in Baroda.
- In 1959, he moved to Delhi to start a new department at the Delhi School of Economics, which became a leading sociology center in India.
- He helped in making Indian sociology known internationally through his connections, especially with British and American anthropology.

M.N. Srinivas on the Village

- M.N. Srinivas focused on the Indian village throughout his career. Although he initially made short visits to villages, his real understanding came after a year of fieldwork near Mysore.
- In the 1950s and 1960s, Srinivas worked with scholars like S.C. Dube and D.N. Majumdar to create detailed ethnographic[8] accounts of village society.
- Srinivas wrote two types of work on villages.
  (i) Ethnographic accounts from his fieldwork.
  (ii) Historical and conceptual discussions about the village as a social unit

8 Ethnographic It is the study of people in their own environment through the methods such as participating observation and face- to-face interviewing.

Views of Louis Dumont vs. Srinivas

- Srinivas debated with social anthropologists like Louis Dumont, who argued that social institutions like caste were more important than the village.
- Dumont believed that villages were merely a collection of people living in a particular place. They were not significant because people moved, but institutions like caste went with them.
- Srinivas disagreed, arguing that the village was an important social entity. He showed that villages had been central to rural identity and had undergone significant changes.
- He also criticised British anthropologists who viewed villages as unchanging and self-sufficient. In reality, villages were interconnected with regional economic, social and political systems.

Conclusion

- These four sociologists—Ghurye, Mukerji, Desai and Srinivas–helped in defining Indian sociology in the post-independence era. They represent different ways in which sociology was made more relevant to India.
- Ghurye used western ideas but added Indian culture and texts. Mukerji, a westernised thinker, valued Indian traditions while noting their problems. Desai, a Marxist, criticised the Indian state at a time when such views were rare. Srinivas applied western anthropology to India and set new directions for sociology.
- Indian sociology grew stronger as new scholars learned from and critiqued these pioneers. This process helped the discipline advance.

Quick Test 3

1. Who was appointed as the head of a newly created department of Sociology at the Maharaja Sayajirao University at Baroda?
2. Name two scholars who worked alongwith MN Srinivas.
3. What is referred to as 'little republics' by Louis Dumont?
4. Name the person credited with the establishment of Delhi School of Economics.

NCERT Folder

1. How did Ananthakrishna Iyer and Sarat Chandra Roy come to practice social anthropology?

Ans. **Practice of Anthropology by Ananthakrishna Iyer** He came to practice social anthropology voluntarily by helping the British administrators in ethnographic surveys of India. He was initially a clerk and then became a college teacher at Ernakulum. In 1902, he was asked by the Dewan of Cochin to assist with an ethnographic survey of the state. Later, he worked for British Government as unpaid Superintendent of Ethnography. His work received appreciation from British anthropologists and administrators.

Iyer became a reader at the University of Madras and set up the post-graduate department of anthropology at the University of Calcutta. Thus, he became the first self-taught anthropologist.

Practice of Anthropdogy by Sarat Chandra Roy He was educated in law and English. He gave up his law practice and became a school teacher in Ranchi. He was appointed as the official interpreter in the court after he resumed his law practice.

Gradually, he became interested in the tribal society, as he had to interpret the tribal customs in the court. He gained considerable knowledge on the culture and society of the tribal people of Chhotanagpur. Roy produced valuable monographs and research articles on this subject. He travelled and did intensive fieldwork pertaining to the tribal community.

Thus, the experiences gained by Iyer and Roy in the course of their work led to their interest in social anthropology.

2. What were the main arguments on either side of the debate about how to relate to tribal communities?

Ans. The main arguments, on either side of the debate about relating to tribal communities, were led by the British administrator-anthropologists and the nationalists.

According to British Thinkers

According to the British, the tribes of India were primitive people and had a different culture from the Hindus. They believed that the simple tribal people would suffer exploitation and cultural degradation at the hands of Hindu people who wanted the assimilation of tribal people with them. Thus, they needed to be protected by the state in order to safeguard their interests.

According to Indian Thinkers

On the other hand, the nationalists, of whom GS Ghurye was the most famous exponent, argued that the tribes of India were not backward, but had been interacting with the rest of Hindu society over a long period. The process of assimilation had been experienced by all the communities in India and the tribes were only a step behind in this process.

According to nationalists, attempts to preserve tribal culture only contributed to their backwardness. They believed tribal society needed as much reform as Hindu society.

Thus, the main difference in both viewpoints was the perception about the impact of mainstream culture on tribes.

3. Outline the positions of Herbert Risley and G.S. Ghurye on the relationship between race and caste in India.

Ans. **Position of Herbert Risley on the Relationship between Race and Caste**

- Herbert Risley believed that human beings could be divided into separate races on the basis of their physical characteristics.
- His main argument was that caste originated in race because different castes belonged to different racial types.
- He believed that the higher castes originated from Indo-Aryans while the lower castes originated from non-Aryan race.
- Risley had the opinion that the conditions in India were suitable for studying racial evolution as inter-caste marriages was strictly prohibited in India.

Position of G.S. Ghurye on the Relationship between Race and Caste

- Ghurye was of a different view. He believed that Risley's argument was partially correct and the argument of upper castes being Aryan and lower castes being non-Aryan was true only for North India.

- He further said that the prohibition of intermixing of different castes was only limited to the Northern India and people in other areas had been mixing for a long time.
- According to him, racial purity was preserved only in North India while other parts adopted the practice of endogamy only after variations had occurred in racial groups.

4. Summarise the social anthropological definition of caste.

Ans. Social anthropologists like L.K. Ananthakrishna Iyer and Sarat Chandra Roy were pioneers who worked during the colonial period, despite limited institutional support. Iyer's ethnographic surveys in Cochin and Mysore and Roy's extensive fieldwork among the tribal communities of Chhotanagpur contributed to a detailed understanding of Indian society. Both scholars worked in unconventional ways and gained national and international recognition.

G.S. Ghurye, considered the founder of institutionalised sociology in India, played a crucial role in advancing the study of caste. He emphasised merging sociology and social anthropology into a unified discipline. His writings on caste explored its social and racial aspects, covering themes such as kinship, family, and tribes. Ghurye's work laid the foundation for analysing caste as a complex system of social stratification deeply embedded in Indian society. His research combined teaching and fieldwork, shaping caste studies as a vital area of Indian sociology and anthropology.

5. What does D.P. Mukerji mean by a 'living tradition'? Why did he insist that Indian sociologists be rooted in this tradition?

Ans. By 'living tradition', D.P. Mukerji means that the traditions were not only formed in the past but also kept on changing with the present and evolved over time. It manages to retain basic elements from the past.

He insisted that Indian sociologists be rooted in this tradition because an Indian sociologist should be an Indian first, which means that he/she should understand his/her social system first.

In Mukerji's words "it is not enough for the Indian sociologist to be a sociologist. He must be an Indian first, that is, he is to share in the folk-ways, mores, customs and traditions, for the purpose of understanding his social system and what lies beneath it and beyond it."

In keeping with this view, he believed that sociologists should learn and be familiar with both 'high' and 'low' languages and cultures, not only Sanskrit, Persian or Arabic but also local dialects.

6. What are the specificities of Indian culture and society and how do they affect the pattern of change?

Ans. The Indian culture and society are not individualistic like the Western society. The behaviour of an Indian individual is fixed by his socio-cultural group. Hence, the Indian social system is oriented towards groups, unlike the Western societies where people are highly individualistic. The actions of individuals in Indian society are mostly involuntary. The traditions are strongly rooted in the past.

Thus, there are fewer changes in Indian societies, as the pattern of desires of an individual are mostly governed by the societal traditions and norms. Changes occur more in the adaptive form than any basic form. The role of economy as an internal source of change is diluted in the Indian society. Conflict due to caste system causes adaptive changes without overriding the institution of caste.

7. What is a welfare state? Why is A.R. Desai critical of the claims made on its behalf?

Ans. **Meaning of Welfare State** A.R. Desai explained welfare state with the help of three features which are mentioned below

- A welfare state is a positive state that uses its power in order to implement social policies for the betterment of society. It is interventionist in nature.
- Democracy and democratic institutions are considered the most important factors for the emergence of the welfare state.
- A welfare state includes a mixed economy. It means the co-existence of both the private and state owned enterprises.

Critical Claims of A.R. Desai on Welfare State

- Desai is critical of welfare states like Britain, USA and countries in Europe.
- He argues that the claims of these states are not real.
- They are not even able to provide basic social and economic security to their citizens. They are unable to reduce economic inequality.
- The process of development in these states is not independent of market fluctuations.
- A high level of unemployment alongside excess economic capacity indicates the failure of welfare state.
- Therefore, AR Desai is critical of the claims made on behalf of welfare state and concludes that its existence is a myth.

8. What arguments were given for and against the village as a subject of sociological research by M.N. Srinivas and Louis Dumont?

Ans. M.N. Srinivas and Louis Dumont had contrasting views on the relevance of the village as a subject of sociological research. Srinivas argued that the village was a significant social entity with historical and sociological importance. He believed villages played a unifying role in rural social life and highlighted their relevance in understanding social change in India.
Through his ethnographic research, Srinivas showed that villages were not static or self-sufficient "little republics," as described by British administrators, but were connected to broader economic, social, and political networks. He emphasised the dynamic nature of villages and their role in India's modernisation and nation-building efforts.

In contrast, Louis Dumont argued against the centrality of the village as a unit of social analysis. He contended that social institutions like caste and religion were more enduring and significant than villages, which he saw as temporary and interchangeable collections of people. Dumont believed that focusing on caste and other overarching institutions provided a deeper understanding of Indian society, as these institutions followed individuals regardless of their location.

9. What is the significance of village studies in the history of Indian sociology? What role did M.N. Srinivas play in promoting village studies?

Ans. Significance of Village Studies in Indian Sociology

The study of Indian villages has always been important in the history of Indian sociology because of the following reasons

- It provided with an opportunity to emphasis the importance of ethnographic research methods.
- It provided examples of rapid social change that took place in the country after independence and implementation of planned development.
- The village studies provided sociology with a new role in the context of independent nation as it enabled urban Indians and policy makers to form their opinions about developments in the villages of India.

Role of Srinivas in Promoting Village Studies

- MN Srinivas played a very important role in promoting village studies by concentrating his research on village areas.
- He conducted field work in villages and coordinated efforts at producing detailed ethnographic accounts of villages.
- His writings featured ethnographic accounts and historical and conceptual discussions about villages. He was critical of the arguments presented by the British anthropologists.
- He concluded that the village was as important as any other social institution.
- He also presented the links of the village community to the economy of the outside world.

Exam Pattern Questions

Objective Type Questions

Multiple Choice Questions (MCQs)

1. Which of the following statements is correct about L.K. Ananthakrishna Iyer?

(a) He was the first formally trained anthropologist in India.
(b) He was conferred the titles of Rao Bahadur and Dewan Bahadur by Mysore state.
(c) He set up the first post-graduate anthropology department in India.
(d) He began his career as a lawyer in Ranchi courts.

2. Which of the following statements correctly describes Sarat Chandra Roy's contribution to anthropology?

(a) He founded the Indian Sociological Society.
(b) He extensively studied tribal communities in the Chhotanagpur region.
(c) He was the first to study caste in India.
(d) He established the first journal of anthropology in Britain.

3. Who was the founder of the Indian Sociological Society as well as its journal 'Sociological Bulletin'?

(a) Sarat Chandra Roy
(b) Govind Sadashiv Ghurye
(c) D.P. Mukerji
(d) A.R. Desai

4. Who among the following was the head of India's first post-graduate teaching department of Sociology at Bombay University for 35 years?

(a) Govind Sadashiv Ghurye (b) Sarat Chandra Roy
(c) D.P. Mukerji (d) A.R. Desai

5. According to Ghurye Risley's thesis of the upper castes being Aryan and the lower castes being non-Aryan was broadly true for which part of India? **Competency Based Que.**

(a) Central part (b) Northern part
(c) Southern part (d) Eastern part

6. Which of the following is the feature of caste defined by Ghurye?

(a) Segmental division
(b) Restriction on social interaction
(c) Restrictions on choice of occupation
(d) All of the above

7. Who is considered the founder of institutionalised sociology in India?

(a) G.S. Ghurye (b) Sarat Chandra Roy
(c) A.R. Desai (d) M.N. Srinivas

8. The institution of caste necessarily involves restrictions on social interaction, specially the sharing of food. There are elaborate rules prescribing what kind of food may be shared between which groups.

The idea of casteism is based on the concept of which of the following?

(a) Intellect (b) Purity and pollution
(c) Big house (d) Education

9. Which among the following sociologists played a key role in Indian Sociology?

(a) L.K. Ananthakrishna Iyer (b) Sarat Chandra Roy
(c) Govind Sadashiv Ghurye (d) All of these

10. He was strongly influenced by Marxism, though he had more faith in it as a method of social analysis than as a political programme for action. DP wrote many books in English and Bengali. His introduction to Indian Music is a pioneering work, considered a classic in its genre. Who is the sociologist being referred to in their paragraph? **Competency Based Que.**

(a) Ananthakrishna Iyer (b) D.P. Mukerji
(c) Sarat Chandra Roy (d) G.S. Ghurye

11. "The welfare state is a democratic state. Democracy was considered an essential condition for the emergence of the welfare state. Formal democratic institutions, specially multi-party elections, were thought to be a defining feature of the welfare state".

What do you mean by a welfare state? **Competency Based Que.**

(a) Institution working for the interest of society
(b) Panchayati raj institution
(c) Union of state
(d) None of the above

12. Risley and others believed that India was a unique 'laboratory' for studying the evolution of racial types because caste strictly prohibits inter-marriage among different groups and had done so for centuries.

Which of the following factors prohibits the inter-caste marriages in Indian Society? **Competency Based Que.**

I. Health II. Education
III. Casteism IV. Prejudice

Codes

(a) I and II (b) Only III
(c) II and III (d) All of these

Assertion-Reason Questions

Direction (Q. Nos. 15-18) Two statements are given in the question below as Assertion (A) and Reason (R). Read the statements and choose the appropriate option.

(a) Both A and R are true and R is the correct explanation of A.
(b) Both A and R are true, but R is not the correct explanation of A.
(c) A is true, but R is false.
(d) A is false, but R is true.

13. **Assertion** (A) Caste is an institution based on segmental division.

Reason (R) Caste does not restrict the choice of occupation.

14. **Assertion** (A) The welfare state is a democratic state.

Reason (R) A welfare state involves a mixed economy.

15. **Assertion** (A) Desai wrote his doctoral dissertation on the social aspects of Indian nationalism and was awarded the degree in 1946.

Reason (R) A.R. Desai is one of the rare Indian sociologists who was directly involved in politics as a formal member of political parties.

16. **Assertion** (A) In 1979 M.N Srinivas moved to Delhi to set up another department at the Delhi School of Economics.

Reason (R) M.N. Srinivas was born on 16 November 1916 in an Iyengar brahmin family in Mysore.

Case Based Questions

Read the passage given below and answer the questions that follow by choosing the correct option.

17. A.R. Desai is one of the rare Indian sociologists who was directly involved in politics as a formal member of political parties. Desai was a life-long Marxist and became involved in Marxist politics during his undergraduate days at Baroda, though he later resigned his membership of the Communist Party of India. For most of his career he was associated with various kinds of non mainstream Marxist political groups.

(i) What was the title of A.R. Desai's doctoral dissertation?

(a) The Social Background of Indian Nationalism
(b) Marxist Thought and Indian Society
(c) The Impact of Colonialism on Indian Nationalism
(d) Economic Divisions in India

(ii) Which of the following statements is true about A.R. Desai's political career?

(a) He was a lifelong member of the Communist Party of India.
(b) He was directly involved in politics and associated with non-mainstream Marxist political groups.
(c) He was never involved in any political groups.
(d) He was associated with mainstream political parties throughout his career.

18. Probably the best known Indian sociologist of the post-independence era, M.N. Srinivas earned two doctoral degrees, one from Bombay University and one from Oxford. Srinivas was a student of Ghurye at Bombay. Srinivas' intellectual orientation was transformed during the years he spent at the department of social anthropology in Oxford. British social anthropology was at that time the dominant force in western anthropology, and Srinivas also shared in the excitement of being at the 'centre' of the discipline.

(i) Which of the following books established M.N. Srinivas' international reputation?

(a) The Coorgs of South India
(b) Religion and Society among the Coorgs of South India
(c) The Hindu Caste System
(d) Social Structure in India

(ii) In which of the following city did M.N. Srinivas set up a new department of sociology in 1959?

(a) Mumbai
(b) Baroda
(c) Delhi
(d) Bangalore

Answers

1. (c) He set up the first post-graduate anthropology department in India.
2. (b) He extensively studied tribal communities in the Chhotanagpur region.
3. (b) Govind Sadashiv Ghurye
4. (a) Govind Sadashiv Ghurye
5. (b) Northern part
6. (d) All of the above
7. (a) G.S. Ghurye
8. (b) purity and pollution
9. (d) All of these
10. (b) D.P. Mukerji
11. (a) Institution working for the interest of society
12. (b) Only III
13. (c) A is true, but R is false.
14. (b) Both A and R are true, but R is not the correct explanation of A.
15. (b) Both A and R are true, but R is not the correct explanation of A.
16. (d) A is false, but R is true.
17. (i) (a) The Social Background of Indian Nationalism
    (ii) (b) He was directly involved in politics and associated with non-mainstream Marxist political groups.
18. (i) (b) Religion and Society among the Corrgs of South India.
    (ii) (b) Delhi

Subjective Questions

Very Short Answer Type Questions

1. State any two achievements of Ananthakrishna Iyer.

Ans. Two achievements of Ananthakrishna Iyer are as follows

(i) He was elected president of the Ethnology section of the Indian Science Congress despite having no formal qualifications.

(ii) He was awarded with an honorary doctorate by German University during his lecture tour of European Universities.

2. The British felt that the state had a duty to protect the tribes and to help them sustain their way of life and culture, which were facing constant pressure to assimilate with mainstream Hindu cultures.

What do you understand by the term 'assimilation'? **Competency Based Que.**

Ans. Assimilation is a process by which one culture (usually the larger or more dominant one) gradually absorbs another. The assimilated culture (or the one that has mixed) merges into the assimilating culture, so that it is no longer alive or visible at the end of the process.

3. Herbert Risley, a British colonial official who was deeply interested in anthropological matters, was the main proponent of the dominant view. This view held that human beings can be divided into distinct and reparate races.

Define Risley's concept of race. **Competency Based Que.**

Ans. Risley was of the view that humans could be divided on the basis of physical features like the circumference of the skull, length of the nose and the size of the cranium or the the region of the skull, where the brain is located. On such grounds, Risley divided the humans into different races.

4. What was Ghurye's contribution to sociology?

Ans. Ghurye created a generation of first class sociologists through his guidance. He had been deeply interested in castes and races and contributed immensely in the field of caste, races, marriages, family and kinship system. He also laid emphasis in the study of rural urbanisation, demography, sociology of religion.

5. What do you understand by living tradition?

Ans. D.P. Mukerji defined living tradition as a tradition which maintained links with the past by retaining something from it and at the same time trying to incorporate many new things.

6. D.P. Mukherji believed that there were three principles of change reconised in Indian traditions. Identify these principles. **Competency Based Que.**

Ans. The three principles of change that are evident in the Indian tradition according to D.P. Mukerji are *shruti*, *smriti* and *anubhava*. *Anubhava* is the revolutionary principle and it means the most important principle of change in Indian society.

7. A welfare state is a positive state. This means that, unlike the 'Laissez-faire' of classical liberal political theory, the welfare state does not seek to do only the minimum necessary to maintain law and order.

Briefly explain the Laissez-faire state and its features. **Competency Based Que.**

Ans. Laissez-faire stands for a political and economic doctrine that advocates minimum state intervention in the economy and economic relations. It is usually associated with belief in the regulative powers and efficiency of the free market and interferes to minimum extent with the market.

Short Answer Type Questions

1. What was the contribution of Sarat Chandra Roy to tribal society?

Ans. Sarat Chandra was a lawyer and an anthropologist who pioneered the discipline of sociology in India. He was deeply interested in tribal society which was a by product of his professional need to interpret tribal customs and laws to the court.

He published more than one hundred articles in leading Indian and British academic journals in addition to his famous monographs on the Oraon, the Mundas and the Kharias. He founded the journal 'Man in India' in 1922, which is still published.

2. How did Ghurye and the nationalists view the impact of mainstream culture on tribal communities compared to the 'protectionists'?

Ans. Ghurye and the nationalists believed that the negative impacts of mainstream culture, such as exploitation and cultural extinction, were not unique to tribal communities but were a broader issue affecting all marginalised groups in Indian society. They argued that these challenges were part of the natural process of societal development. In contrast, the 'protectionists' feared that assimilation into mainstream culture would result in the severe loss of tribal identity and culture. They ,thus, emphasised the need to protect tribal communities from external influences.

3. D.P.'s views on tradition and change led him to criticise all instances of unthinking borrowing from Western intellectual traditions. How did D.P. Mukerji critique the unthinking adoption of Western intellectual traditions in India? **Competency Based Que.**

Ans. D.P. Mukerji criticised the uncritical borrowing of Western intellectual traditions, particularly in contexts like development planning. He argued that tradition should not be blindly worshipped or ignored, just as modernity should be embraced but not adopted without critical reflection.

Mukerji positioned himself as both a proud inheritor of Indian tradition and a critical admirer of modernity. He believed that a balanced approach, one that acknowledged the value of both tradition and modernity while adapting them thoughtfully to the Indian context, was essential for meaningful social change and development.

4. Using these criteria, Desai examines the performance of those states that are most often described as welfare states, such as Britain, the USA and much of Europe, and finds their claims to be greatly exaggerated. Briefly explain how can the performance of a 'welfare state' be measured , according to A.R. Desai? **Competency Based Que.**

Ans. According to A.R. Desai, the test criteria against which the performance of the 'Welfare State' can be measured are as follows

- Welfare state should ensure freedom from poverty, social discrimination and security for all its citizens.
- Welfare state should remove inequalities of income through measures to redistribute income from the rich to the poor and by preventing the concentration of wealth.
- Welfare state should transform the economy in such a way that the capitalist profit motive is made subservient to the real needs of the community.
- Welfare state should ensure stable development free from the cycle of economic booms and depressions.
- Welfare state should provide employment for all.

5. Srinivas' writings on the village were of two broad types. There was first of all ethnographic accounts of fieldwork done in villages or discussions of such accounts. A second kind of writing included historical and conceptual discussions about the Indian village as a unit of social analysis. In the latter kind of writing, Srinivas was involved in a debate about the usefulness of the village as a concept.

How did Srinivas challenge the British administrators' view of the Indian village as an unchanging, self-sufficient entity? **Competency Based Que.**

Ans. Srinivas challenged the British administrators' portrayal of the Indian village as a self-sufficient, unchanging 'little republic' by presenting historical and sociological evidence that highlighted the dynamic nature of village life. He argued that villages were never self-sufficient and were part of broader economic, social and political networks at the regional level. Furthermore, Srinivas emphasised that villages experienced significant change over time, contrary to the British view of them as static entities. This critique underscored the importance of considering the village as a relevant social unit in understanding rural life.

6. What were the two broad types of writings by Srinivas on the Indian village?

Ans. Srinivas' writings on the Indian village can be broadly categorised into two types. The first type consisted of ethnographic accounts based on his fieldwork in villages or discussions of such fieldwork. These writings provided detailed insights into the social dynamics of rural life. The second type involved historical and conceptual analyses, where Srinivas engaged in debates about the village as a unit of social analysis. In these writings, he defended the relevance of the village as an important social entity, challenging views that downplayed its significance in understanding Indian society.

Long Answer Type Questions

1. What are the structural features of caste as given by Ghurye?

Ans. Ghurye defined caste as a complex social institution with several structural features. These are

- **Segmental Division** Caste is divided into closed, mutually exclusive groups. Membership is determined by birth, and a person cannot change their caste.
- **Hierarchical Division** Caste operates on a hierarchical system where every caste is ranked either higher or lower than others. This ranking is rigid, and equality among castes does not exist.
- **Restrictions on Social Interaction** Caste involves rules on social interactions, particularly concerning the sharing of food.
- **Differential Rights and Duties** Each caste has specific rights and duties that govern both religious and secular activities. These duties differ based on caste rank and are enforced in daily life.
- **Occupational Restrictions** Caste determines the occupations one can engage in, often hereditary. Specific castes are assigned particular professions, forming a division of labor.
- **Marriage Restrictions** Caste mandates endogamy, meaning individuals can only marry within their caste. This rule is coupled with exogamy restrictions, defining who one cannot marry.

2. Given the centrality of society in India, it became the first duty of an Indian sociologist to study and to know the social traditions of India. For D.P. this study of tradition was not oriented only towards the past, but also included sensitivity to change.
How did D.P. Mukerji view the role of tradition in understanding Indian society and what did he identify as the key source of change in Indian social structures? **Competency Based Que.**

Ans. D.P. Mukerji viewed the role of tradition as important in understanding Indian society. He emphasised that Indian sociologists must be deeply familiar with both high and low cultures, including local dialects. He argued that tradition in India is not just a link to the past, but a living, evolving force that adapts to contemporary changes. According to Mukerji, the Indian social system is predominantly group-oriented, shaped by caste, sect and community, rather than individualistic or voluntaristic action seen in the West. While Western societies often cite the economy as a source of change, Mukerji believed that class conflict in India had been muted by caste traditions. He identified non-economic internal sources, such as caste-based social practices and cultural traditions, as central drivers of social change in India. Mukerji's approach called for a dynamic sociology that could account for these unique, non-economic forces shaping Indian society.

3. The most important principle of change in Indian society was generalised *anubhava* or the collective experience of groups .How did D.P. Mukerji view the role of personal and collective experience in driving social change in India? **Competency Based Que.**

Ans. D.P. Mukerji believed that in India, personal experience, or *anubhava*, was a powerful force for social change. He argued that anubhava was not just about individual feelings, but could also become a collective experience, shared by groups and communities. This collective experience played a major role in challenging traditional beliefs and bringing about change. Mukerji pointed to the Bhakti movement as an example, where personal devotion and shared love for God went beyond the strict rules of religious texts. He also applied this idea to Indian Islam, especially Sufism, which focused on love and personal spiritual experience rather than strict following of religious scriptures. For Mukerji, *anubhava* (experience) and *prem* (love) were more important than logical reasoning (buddhi-vichar) in driving social and cultural change in India.

4. Read the following passage and answer the question that follow.

Conflict and rebellion in the Indian context have tended to work through collective experiences. But the resilience of tradition ensures that the pressure of conflict produces change in the tradition without breaking it. So, we have repeated cycles of dominant orthodoxy being challenged by popular revolts which succeed in transforming orthodoxy, but are eventually reabsorbed into this transformed tradition.

(i) What do you understand by conflict and rebellion in Indian context?

(ii) What is tradition?

(iii) Why does a society challenge dominant orthodoxy?

Ans. (i) Conflict and rebellion have actually worked through collective experiences but it has ensured that the pressure of conflict produces change in the tradition without breaking it. Many orthodox ideas have been challenged by way of revolutionary conflicts that have eventually transformed the orthodox ideas.

(ii) Tradition refers to the transfer of beliefs and customs from one generation to another. It shapes social behaviour of human beings and some traditions are orally passed on from one generation to the successive generation.

(iii) Society challenges the dominant orthodoxy as there is inacceptance of orthodoxy ideas in the society. Hence, through rebellion and conflict, these ideas are challenged and orthodoxy is transformed.

SELF ASSESSMENT TEST

Objective Type Questions

1. Which of the following is not the feature of caste defined by Ghurye?

(a) Segmental division (b) Equal opportunity (c) Restrictions on marriage (d) Hierarchical division

2. Who believed that there were three principles of change recognised in Indian tradition namely Shruti, Smriti and Anubhava?

(a) D.P. Mukerji (b) Sarat Chandra Roy (c) AR Desai (d) Ghurye

3. **Assertion** (A) Notion of the welfare state is something of a myth.

Reason (R) So called welfare states are unable to reduce economic inequalities.

(a) Both A and R are true and R is the correct explanation of A.
(b) Both A and R are true, but R is not the correct explanation of A.
(c) A is true, but R is false.
(d) A is false, but R is true.

Case Based Questions

1. Ghurye argued that the tribes of India should not be seen as isolated or primitive communities but rather as backward Hindus. He believed that tribes had long been interacting with Hinduism and were simply at an earlier stage of the assimilation process. This view contrasted with protectionists who believed that preserving tribal culture was essential to prevent their exploitation and cultural extinction.

(i) According to Ghurye, tribes in India should be regarded as

(a) primitive communities (b) distinct racial groups (c) backward Hindus (d) culturally extinct groups

(ii) The protectionists believed that tribal assimilation into mainstream society would result in

(a) greater cultural development (b) severe exploitation and cultural extinction
(c) economic independence (d) strengthening of tribal identity

Very Short Answer Type Questions

1. 'Sociology in India has evolved as a discipline deeply influenced by colonialism and the complexities of post-colonial identity.' Explain the statement.

2. What were Louis Dumont's views regarding Indian villages?

Short Answer Type Questions

1. Examine the role of sociologists in understanding the challenges of nation-building in India, particularly in relation to its diverse social and cultural landscape.

2. Describe the position of Herbert Risley and G.S. Ghurye on the relationship between caste and race in India.

Long Answer Type Questions

1. Analyse the arguments given for and against the village as a subject of sociological research.

2. It was through his dissatisfaction with Indian history and economics that D.P. turned to sociology. he felt very strongly that the curcial distinctive feature of India was its social system and that therefore, it was important for each social science to be rooted in this context. the decisive aspect of the Indian context was the social aspect–history, Politics and economics in India were less developed in comparison with the west; however, the social dimensions were 'over developed'. As D.P. wrote "... my conviction grew that India had society and very little else. In fact, she had too much of it."

(a) What did D.P. believe was the most distinctive feature of India?

(b) How did D.P. describe the development of history, politics and economics in India comarison to the West?

PROJECT WORK

Project Work

Meaning of Project

The word project comes from the Latin word 'Projectum' which means "before an action". At school level, a project is a research assignment given to a student which generally requires a larger amount of effort and more independent work that is involved in a normal assignment. It requires students to undertake their own fact finding endeavours, either from library, or from the internet or by means of primary data collection. A project report should

- be handwritten
- be concise and clear
- have diagrammatic presentation
- have a length of 25 to 30 pages
- have topics with suitable headings
- end up with conclusion

Utilities of Making a Project

Following points state the uses/utility of project work

(*i*) To provide information about the development and growth of institutions, business products, and government activities.

(*ii*) To provide information to the consumers about the price of commodities, quality and uses, etc of a product as per their interest.

(*iii*) It is helpful in estimating the preference of consumers for petrol car or diesel car, telephone or mobile phone, etc.

(*iv*) Project report is helpful for the shareholders, who may be interested in knowing the earning of an enterprise and possibility of getting dividend.

(*v*) To help in the policy formulation about the economic and social development of any country.

Thus, we can say that project work may help marketers, shareholders, economists, consumers and government in effective and efficient decision-making.

Elements of Project Report

A good project report should contain the following elements.

Title Page

This should include the project title, name of the company on which you are conducting your research and name of the student. You can also list the name of your school, class and subject teacher.

Acknowledgement

It is usual to thank those individuals, who have provided particularly useful assistance, technical or otherwise, during your project.

Content Page

This should list the main sections and sub-sections of your report. Choose self-explanatory titles with their respective pages and use double spacing for clarity.

Introduction

This is one of the most important component of the project report. It should begin with a clear statement of what the project is about, so that the nature and scope of the project can be understood by a reader. It should summarise everything which you set out to achieve and provide a clear summary of the project's background, relevance and main contributions. The introduction should set the context for the project and should provide the reader with a summary of the key things to look out for in, the remainder of the report.

Background

The background section of the report should set the project into action, it specifies the problem of the company, what remedial actions were taken by the company and what are its effects.

Body of Report

The central part of the report usually consists of three or four sections detailing the technical work undertaken during the project. The structure of these sections is highly project dependent.They can reflect the chronological development of the project. It includes the detailed description regarding the matter of the project.

Evaluation

This might involve quantitative and qualitative evaluation such as expressibility, functionality, ease-of-use, etc of a product. At some point, you should also evaluate the strengths and weaknesses of what you have done. It includes certain questionnaires, sampling test which help in evaluating the result on the basis of truths and facts.

Conclusion

The conclusion should list the things, which have been learnt as a result of the work you have done. It shows the ultimate response of the project undertaken by a student. It should be expressive and impressive so that a reader would clearly evaluate the result and rated you on the basis of your presentation.

Bibliography

In this section, you should mention the details of all the secondary sources, *i.e.*, magazines, newspapers, reports, internet links, etc. used for developing the project.

Methodology/ Technique Used in the Project

Various methodology or techniques like social surveys, experiments, interviews, participant observation etc are used in project work but social survey is probably the best known sociological method.

Purpose of the Project

Project Work is a learning experience which aims to provide students with the opportunity to synthesise knowledge from various areas of learning, and critically and creatively apply it to real life situations. This process, which enhances students' knowledge and enables them to acquire skills like collaboration, communication and independent learning, prepares them for lifelong learning and the challenges ahead. The learning outcomes identify the key areas of learning of the subject.

Sample Project

CHANGING ASPIRATIONS OF DIFFERENT AGE GROUPS

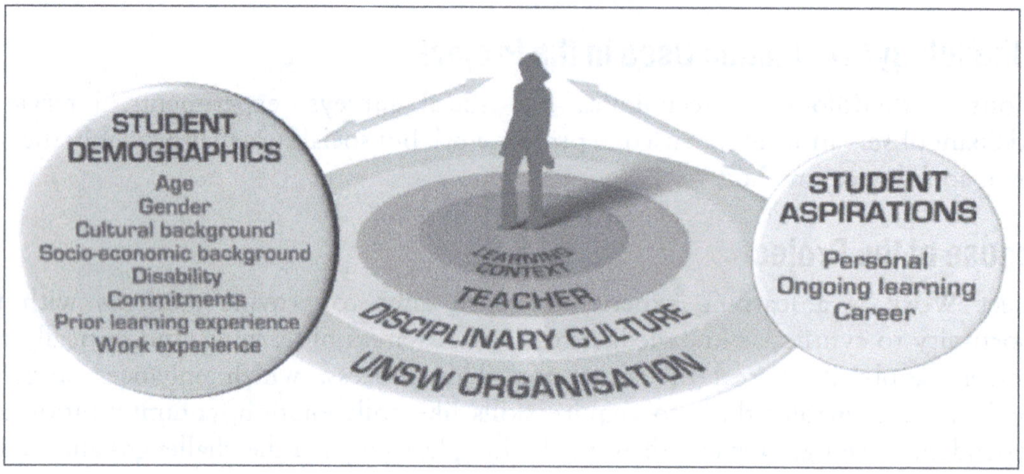

Name : ....

Class : ....

Roll No. : ....

Subject : ....

School : ....

Submitted by .... *Submitted to* ....

Acknowledgement

I would like to extend my sincere and heartfelt obligation towards all those who have helped me in making this project. Without their active guidance, help, cooperation and encouragement, I would not have been able to present the project on time.

I am extremely thankful and pay my gratitude to my teacher Mr/Ms .... for his/her valuable guidance and support for completion of this project.

I extend my gratitude to my Principal Mr/Ms .... for the moral support extended during the tenure of the project.

I also acknowledge with a deep sense of reverence, my gratitude towards my parents, other faculty members of the school and friends for their valuable suggestions given to me in completing this project.

Date...........   ....

Name of Student

Certificate

This is to Certify that the project work

.... is the bonafide

work of .... (Name of the student) who

carried out the work under my supervision

....

Name and Signature of
Teacher/Supervisor

Contents

S.No.	Particulars
1.	Statement of Purpose
2.	Introduction
3.	General Scenario of Changing Aspiration in Children
4.	Changing Aspiration of Rural and Urban Youth
5.	Methodology (Survey Research Method)
6.	Different Forms of Survey
7.	Detailed Procedure for Implementation of Survey Method
8.	Research Questions (Questionnaire)
9.	Advantages of the Survey Method
10.	Limitations of Survey Method
11.	Conclusion

Changing Aspirations of Different Age Groups

Introduction

Aspiration is a personal goal that changes over time. For children, it starts as a dream and later becomes a life ambition, helping them grow and improve.

Many factors shape a person's aspirations, such as parental support, mentoring, extra curricular activities, and peer influence.

Teachers play an important role in guiding students toward subjects that can help them succeed.

Providing career counselling, real world exposure, and learning resources also helps students set and achieve their goals.

Statement of Purpose

The Purpose of this project is to find how aspirations of different age groups change. It also focus on studying why people change their goals, specially at young age. This research topic tries to discover what these changes are and whether there are some similar pattern in changes among different groups.

General Scenario of Changing Aspirations in Children

Children most commonly aspired to be art professionals, followed by school teachers, veterinarians, architects and science professionals. These were the top five jobs that usually needed a university degree.

The next most popular careers were Engineering Professionals, Medical Professionals, Social and Welfare Professionals, Legal Professionals and Registered Nurses/Midwives.

Why do Children Change Their Aspirations?

The process of forming aspirations can have a profound influence on the life prospects of a child. Using both qualitative and quantitative data, this report examines the changing educational and occupational aspirations and educational achievements of children. The children have high aspirations at an earlier age but that these changed later. Sometimes poverty also influence their earlier aspirations.

Children with high educational achievement, mostly urban children and some rural girls, maintained their high ambitions. Education policy imposed constraints and provided varied opportunities for rural and urban children that affected their educational achievement and aspirations. Educational achievement was influenced by age of entry to school and continued attendance.

Government development programmes and agricultural livelihoods attracts rural children's labour and thereby negatively affected their education and realisation of their ambitions. Some children consider out-of-school transitions (e.g. girls' early marriage and full-time work for girls and boys) and, as a consequence, very few poor children will be able to realise their ambitions.

Changing Aspirations of Rural Youth

India is a land of villages where 70% of youth live in villages. Thier role is very important in bringing change in rural social structure. Their aspirations towards education, occupation, family, recreational activities change accordingly. Now, attitudes of rural youth are changing towards modern outlook.

Indian rural societies are changing and coming under the impact of urban life. This is marked by opportunities, risks, individual freedom, complex social demands and framework of support.

Changing Aspirations of Urban Youth

Young people in urban places often develop sense of self identity from their surroundings. These surroundings usually offer far greater social, cultural and ethnic diversity than rural environments. Thus, their aspirations change rapidly. They have more exposure to extra-curricular activities and professional courses. So, their scope of aspiration is wide and dynamic.

Methodology (Survey Research Method)

The survey is probably the best known sociological method. It is now so much a part of modern public life. Today it is used all over the world in all sorts of contexts going well beyond the concerns of sociology alone. In India, too, we have seen the increasing use of surveys for various non-academic purposes, including the prediction of election results, the devising of marketing strategies for selling products, and for eliciting popular opinions on a wide variety of subjects.

Different Forms of Survey

Interviews

An interview is different from a survey in that it is always conducted in person and usually involves much fewer persons (as few as 5, 20, or 40, usually not much more than that). Interviews may be structured, that is, follow a pre-determined pattern of questions or unstructured, where only a set of topics is pre-decided, and the actual questions emerge as part of a conversation. Interviews may be more or less intensive, in the sense that one may interview a person for a long time (2-3 hours) or in repeated visits to get a really detailed version of their story. Interviews have the advantage of being flexible in that promising topics may be pursued in greater detail, questions may be refined or modified along the way, and clarifications may be sought. The disadvantage of the interview method is that it cannot cover a large number of people and is limited to presenting the views of a selected group of individuals.

Observation

Observation is a method where the researcher must systematically watch and record what is happening in whatever context or situation that has been chosen for the research. This sounds simple but may not always be easy to do in practice. Careful attention has to be paid to what is happening without pre-judging what is relevant to the study and what is not. Sometimes, what is not happening is as important or interesting as what does actually happen. For example, if your research question is about how different classes of people use specific open spaces, then it is significant that a given class or group of people (say poor people, or middle class people for example) never enter the space, or are never seen in it.

Detailed Procedure for Implementation of Survey Method

- As the word itself suggests, a survey is an attempt to provide an overview. It is a comprehensive or wide-ranging perspective on some subject based on information obtained from a carefully chosen representative set of people. Such people are usually referred to as 'respondents' — they respond to the questions asked by the researchers. Survey research is usually done by large teams consisting of those who plan and design the study (the researchers) and their associates and assistants (the latter are called 'investigators' or 'research assistants').
- The survey questions may be asked and answered in various forms. Often, they are asked orally during personal visits by the investigator, and sometimes through telephone conversations. Responses may also be sought in writing, to 'questionnaires' brought by investigators or sent through the post.
- Finally, with the increasing presence of computers and telecommunication technology, these days it is also possible for surveys to be conducted electronically. In this format, the respondent receives and responds to questions by e-mail, the internet, or similar electronic medium.
- The survey's main advantage as a social scientific method is that it allows us to generalise results for a large population while actually studying only a small portion of this population. Thus a survey makes it possible to study large populations with a manageable investment of time, effort and money. That is why it is such a popular method in the social sciences and other fields.
- The sample survey is able to provide a generalisable result despite being selective by taking advantage of the discoveries of a branch of statistics called sampling theory. The key element enabling this 'shortcut' is the representativeness of the sample.
- The first principle is that all the relevant sub-groups in the population should be recognised and represented in the sample. Most large populations are not homogenous — they belong to distinct sub-categories. This is called stratification.
- The second principle of sample selection is that the actual unit — i.e., person or village or household — should be based purely on chance. This is referred to as randomisation, which itself depends on the concept of probability.

Research Questions (Questionnaire)

The following questionnaire was conducted among the school going and school passed out students of different age groups (4-5, 6-8, 9-12, 13-18, 19-21) years. It helped to know the changing aspirations of different age groups.

Name : ....

Age : ....

Gender : ....

Profession : ....

1. Why are you studying?
   - (i) For job ☐
   - (ii) For knowledge ☐
   - (iii) For status ☐
   - (iv) Don't know ☐
2. What do you aspire to become in future? ....
3. Does your aspiration changes time to time?
   - (i) Yes ☐
   - (ii) No ☐
   - (iii) Sometimes ☐
4. Who influences your aspirations?
   - (i) Parents ☐
   - (ii) Teachers ☐
   - (iii) Friends ☐
   - (iv) Ideal ☐
   - (v) No one ☐
5. According to you which occupational aspiration is best?
   - (i) Teaching ☐
   - (ii) Government Job ☐
   - (iii) Social Service and Politics ☐
   - (iv) Agriculture ☐
   - (v) None ☐
6. What extra effort you have done to fulfil aspiration?
   - (i) Take extra class ☐
   - (ii) Practice at Home ☐
   - (iii) No effort ☐
   - (iv) Will do effort in future ☐

7. What is the role of schooling in shaping your aspiration?
   (i) Big role ☐
   (ii) No role ☐
   (iii) Can't say ☐
8. What is the role of higher education in fulfilling your aspiration?
   (i) Big role ☐
   (ii) No role ☐
   (iii) Don't know ☐
9. Would you like to opt higher studies abroad if got opportunity?
   (i) Yes ☐
   (ii) No ☐
   (iii) Can't say ☐
10. Are you sure that your aspiration will get fulfilled?
   (i) Yes ☐
   (ii) Don't know ☐
   (iii) Might be ☐
   (iv) Will change aspiration if not get fulfilled ☐

Data Analysis

Sample Answers of Different Age Groups

Groups--> #Q. No. |	(4-5) yrs	(6-8) yrs	(9-12) yrs	(13-18) yrs	(19-21 yrs)
1.	Don't know	For Job	For knowledge	For status	For Job
2.	Teacher	Dancer	Doctor	Government Servant	Anything that gives good status and money
3.	No	Yes	Yes	Sometimes	Sometimes
4.	Parents	Ideal	Teachers	Friends	No one
5.	Teaching	Agriculture	None	Government Job	Social Service and Politics
6.	No effort	Will do effort in future	Take extra class	Take extra class	Practice at Home
7.	Big role	Big role	No role	Can't say	Big role
8.	Don't know	No role	Don't know	Big role	Big role
9.	No	Can't say	Can't say	Yes	Yes
10.	Yes	Yes	Don't konw	Will change aspiration if not get fulfilled	Might be

Advantages of the Survey method

- Survey research is relatively inexpensive.
- Survey research is useful in describing the characteristics of a large population, population structure based on age, and its emerging trends and patterns.
- Survey research can be administered from remote locations using mail, e-mail or telephone. Consequently, very large samples are feasible, making the results statistically significant even when analysing multiple variables.
- In survey research one can ask many questions about a given topic, which gives considerable flexibility to the analysis.
- We can choose different ways of administering a survey. From face- to-face interviews to telephones and emails one can use any mode of collecting data depending on one's requirements and limitations.
- Unlike the qualitative methods, survey research is carried out through standardised questions, which makes measurement more precise by enforcing uniform definitions upon the participants. Standardisation ensures that similar kinds of data are collected from groups and then interpreted comparatively (between-group study),implying more objectivity and higher reliability.

Limitations of Survey Method

- A pre-occupation with standardisation results in designing questions in very general terms to make them minimally appropriate for all respondents. This could lead to simplification and one may end up missing what may be most appropriate to many respondents.
- Survey research is inflexible in the sense that it requires a precise study design. Everything must be worked out in advance, the tools to be used and the method of administering the tools. In order to make a survey methodologically sound, it should remain unchanged throughout the period of data collection.
- In order to make a survey viable and meaningful the researcher has to make sure that a large proportion of selected respondents agree to respond. This, however, may not always be an easy task to achieve. In such situations carrying out a survey becomes difficult.
- Surveys also demand a great deal of attention and honesty on the part of respondents, particularly when a questionnaire is being used and the survey is self-administered. Respondents may not always be willing to give such attention to filling the questionnaire. Sometimes, it may be hard for participants to recall certain information or to take a clear position on controversial issues.
- Another problem with survey research is that it is invariably context- blind. However, in the social world, context and the environment in which questions are being asked and answers are given is very important. For example,the responses of a

female respondent being asked questions about gender equality in her home, in the presence of her husband and other family members, may be very different from the same questions asked at her work place where she is employed. Survey research can rarely see the questions of "context".

Conclusion

We found that interest in some occupations – arts, architecture and veterinary, science – declines in the later years of schooling, while interest in others – engineering, nursing, and social and welfare work – grows.

Interest in teaching, medicine, legal and science careers is more stable across the school years.

In some occupational categories, interest appears to rise or fall towards the very end of high school. For example, students are less likely to aspire to be an artist as they mature, but more likely to aspire to architecture, engineering, medicine, social work or law. Furthermore, significant interest in these careers is often expressed in the age group of 5-8 years. In other careers, such as teaching and science, student interest is more consistent across year levels.

Based on the answers given by different age groups, it is concluded that more males than females are interested in educating themselves for economic benefit. Female aspire to education for status and getting suitable match for mairrage.

It can be also concluded that aspiration of rural youth about education is increasing. They are aspiring for higher education as an instrument of seeking job.

Viva Voce Questions

1. *What is a aspiration?*

Ans. Aspiration is a dream or goal that children have, which later turns into their life ambition.

2. *At what level, an aspiration can be interpreted?*

Ans. An aspiration can be interpreted at individual level.

3. *Who plays key role in changing one's aspiration?*

Ans. Parents, mentors, extra-curricular activities, peer, etc play key role in changing one's aspiration.

4. *Give examples of some careers that are popular among small children.*

Ans. School teachers, musician, artist, veterinarians, science professionals are some popular careers among small children.

5. *State a few factors due to which only few poor rural children are able to realise and fulfill their ambition.*

Ans. Government development programmes and agricultural livelihood attracts poor rural children's labour. This negatively affects their education and realisation of their ambition.

6. *How does youth of urban places develop a sense of self identity?*

Ans. Youth of urban places develop a sense of self identity from their surroundings.

7. *Name two advantages of survey method.*

Ans. Survey method is inexpensive and makes it possible to study large populations with a manageable investment of time, effort and money.

8. *Name two other research methodologies.*

Ans. Participant observation and archival analysis are other research methodologies that can be used in sociological research.

SAMPLE
QUESTION PAPERS (1-3)

SAMPLE QUESTION PAPER 1

A Highly Simulated Sample Question Paper for CBSE Class XI

(Solved)

SOCIOLOGY

General Instructions

- The question paper is divided into four sections.
- There are 35 questions in all. All questions are compulsory.
- Section A includes question No. 1-16. These are MCQ type questions. As per the question, there can be one answer.
- Section B includes questions 17-25. These are very short answer type questions carrying 2 marks each. Answer to each question should not exceed 30 words.
- Section C includes question No. 26-32. These are short answer type questions carrying 4 marks each. Answer to each question should not exceed 80 words.
- Section D includes question No. 33-35. They are long answer type questions carrying 6 marks each. Answer to each question should not exceed 200 words.

Time : 3 hours **Max. Marks : 80**

Section-A

1 In everyday language, the word .... means unbiased, neutral, or based on facts alone. In order to be neutral about something, we must ignore our own feelings or attitudes about that thing. On the other hand, the word .... means something that is based on individual values and preferences. As you will have learnt already, every science is expected to be neutral, to produce unbiased knowledge based solely on facts. (1)

(a) objective, subjective
(b) subjective, objective
(c) qualitative, quantitative
(d) quantitative, qualitative

2 **Assertion** (A) Colonialism was an essential part of modern Capitalism and Industrialisation.
Reason (R) The invaders wanted to make their colony developed and prosperous. (1)

(a) Both A and R are true and R is the correct explanation of A.
(b) Both A and R are true, but R is not the correct explanation of A.
(c) A is true, but R is false.
(d) A is false, but R is true.

3 The human relationships that are highly personal, intimate and enduring, those where a person's involvement is considerable if not total, as in the family, with real friends or a close-knit group. The phenomenon is known as .... (1)

(a) Association
(b) Community
(c) Society
(d) Agreement

4 **Assertion** (A) Women have started doing jobs and have become self sufficient that led to women empowerment.
Reason (R) They live in Patriarchal society. (1)

(a) Both A and R are true and R is the correct explanation of A.
(b) Both A and R are true, but R is not the correct explanation of A.
(c) A is true, but R is false.
(d) A is false, but R is true.

5 **Assertion** (A) The writings of Western sociologists on capitalism and other aspects of modern society are therefore relevant for understanding social change in India.
Reason (R) Sociology in India also had to deal with Western writings and ideas about Indian society that were not always correct. (1)

Codes
(a) Both A and R are true and R is the correct explanation of A.
(b) Both A and R are true, but R is not the correct explanation of A.
(c) A is true, but R is false.
(d) A is false, but R is true.

6 As a result of .... processes, family and kinship are subject to change and transition, but the course of change does not have to be the same in all countries and regions. Furthermore, transition does not imply that previous standards and structures are fully obliterated. Continuity and change coexist. (1)
(a) sustainability (b) patrilocal
(c) microeconomic (d) macroeconomic

7 **Assertion** (A) Water pollution is a very serious issue affecting surface as well as groundwater.
Reason (R) Major sources include not only domestic sewage and factory effluents but also the runoff from farms that are responsible for it. (1)
(a) Both A and R are true and R is the correct explanation of A.
(b) Both A and R are true, but R is not the correct explanation of A.
(c) A is true, but R is false
(d) A is false, but R is true

8 **Assertion** (A) Sovereignty refers to the undisputed political rule of a state over a given territorial area.
Reason (R) These states were achieved largely through struggles, which limited the power of monarchs, or actively overthrow them. (1)
Codes
(a) Both A and R are true and R is the correct explanation of A.
(b) Both A and R are true, but R is not the correct explanation of A.
(c) A is true, but R is false.
(d) A is false, but R is true.

9 **Assertion** (A) Persons with disability face attitudinal barrier including prejudice, low expectations and even fear.
Reason (R) Social behavior impacts the vulnerable section both positively and negatively. (1)
(a) Both A and R are true and R is the correct explanation of A.
(b) Both A and R are true, but R is not the correct explanation of A.
(c) A is true, but R is false.
(d) A is false, but R is true.

10 Which of the following statements correctly describes the gendered nature of the family in India? (1)
I. Male children are often believed to provide support in old age, leading to greater investment in them.
II. The infant mortality rate for male children is higher than that for female children in India.
III. Prosperous states like Punjab and Haryana show a sharp decline in the child sex ratio.
Codes
(a) I and II (b) II and III
(c) I and III (d) I, II and III

11 Which of the following statements is correct about modern forms of work? (1)
I. Modern economies exhibit a complex division of labour where people specialise in different jobs.
II. Industrialisation separated work from home, leading to the establishment of factories.
III. Most people in modern societies produce their own food and goods to sustain their needs.
Codes
(a) I and II (b) II and III
(c) I and III (d) I, II and III

12 Which of the following is true about education in society? (1)
I. Education is a process that includes both formal and informal learning.
II. In simple societies, formal schooling is necessary for children to learn life skills.
III. Functionalists believe education maintains social structure and places individuals in roles based on their abilities.
Codes
(a) I and II
(b) II and III
(c) I and III
(d) I, II and III

FULLY SOLVED

Read the passage given below and answer the questions that follow.

Social change is influenced by many factors—internal or external, deliberate or accidental. Economic and technological changes can have cultural effects, and politics may be influenced by the environment. Understanding social change is important, especially since it is happening faster in modern times. While social change is often better understood after it happens, we also need to recognise and adapt to it as it occurs.

13 Which of the following statements is incorrect? (1)

(a) Social change is always deliberate and planned.
(b) Social change can be internal or external.
(c) Political changes can also be influenced by environmental factors.
(d) Understanding social change is crucial in modern times.

14 Based on the passage, which of the following best explains the impact of technological changes on society? (1)

(a) Technological changes have only short-term effects.
(b) They have immediate and long-lasting effects on society.
(c) They rarely influence political systems.
(d) Technological changes are irrelevant to social structures.

Read the passage given below and answer the questions that follow.

Edward Tylor defines culture as 'a complex whole' that includes knowledge, beliefs, art, morals, laws, customs, and other habits learned by people in society. He focuses on non-material aspects like beliefs and values and studied culture through artifacts in museums, without much interaction with people.

Bronislaw Malinowski defines culture as a mix of material and non-material things, like tools, goods, ideas, and values. He emphasises how culture helps meet people's needs and studied it by living with communities to understand their way of life directly.

15 Which of the following statements correctly distinguishes Tylor's and Malinowski's views on culture? (1)

(a) Tylor focused on the material aspects of culture, whereas Malinowski emphasised non-material aspects.
(b) Tylor studied culture in interaction with communities, whereas Malinowski studied it through museum artifacts.
(c) Tylor focused on non-material aspects like beliefs and values, whereas Malinowski emphasised both material and non-material aspects of culture.
(d) Both focused only on the non-material dimensions of culture, ignoring the material ones.

16 Which of the following statements about Malinowski's approach to studying culture is incorrect? (1)

(a) He emphasised studying culture in isolation from communities.
(b) He considered culture as a mix of material and non-material elements.
(c) His fieldwork approach involved living among the people to understand their way of life.
(d) He focused on how culture fulfills human needs.

Section B

17 Discuss the significance of religion according to Ghurye. (2)

18 How do sociologists anticipate culture in various societies? (2)

19 "The groups to which we belong are not all of equal importance to us. Some groups tend to influence many aspects of our lives and bring us into personal association with others. The term primary group is used to refer to a small group of people connected by intimate and face-to-face association and co-operation. The members of primary groups have a sense of belonging. Family, village and groups of friends are examples of primary groups."
What is the role of a primary group in a person's life? (2)

Or "Secondary groups are relatively large in size, maintain formal and impersonal relationships. The primary groups are person-oriented, whereas the secondary groups are goal oriented. Schools, government offices, hospitals, students' associations etc. are examples of secondary groups."

How does the Secondary group impact individual life? Explain.

FULLY SOLVED

20 "Endogamy requires an individual to marry within a culturally defined group of which he or she is already a member, as for example, caste".
What are the implications of endogamy in India? (2)

21 How is conflicts made visible or recognisable in the society? (2)

22 How does sociology study religion? (2)

23 What is material dimension of culture? (2)

24 Does socialisation give birth to individual freedom? (2)

25 "The political institution determines and enforces the laws and punished those who disobey them." In context to the statement, what is political institutions? (2)

Or The Industrial Revolution was based upon a new, dynamic form of economic activity — capitalism. This system of capitalism became the driving force behind the growth of industrial manufacturing. Capitalism involved new attitudes and institutions. Entrepreneurs now engaged in the sustained, systematic pursuit of profit. The markets acted as the key instrument of productive life. And goods, services and labour became commodities whose use was determined by rational calculation. The new economy was completely different from what it replaced. England was the centre of the Industrial Revolution.

Read the passage and show any two features of English society which changed after the advent of Industrial Revolution.

FULLY SOLVED

Section C

26 What was the main feature of sociology in pre-modern period? (4)

Or What do you mean by patriarchal society? Explain with example.

27 What are the citizenship rights in the modern state or welfare state? (4)

28 How are the capitalism and colonialism associated with each other? (4)

29 According to Weber, what is the overall objective of social sciences? (4)

30 The cultural identity can often be done through the recognition of the particular language. How? (4)

31 Define social facts. Mention the theory proposed by Durkheim for social facts. (4)

Or The cultural identity can often be done through the recognition of the particular language. How?

32 Peer groups are extremely important agents of socialisation. Discuss. (4)

Section D

33 Study the table and answer the following question accordingly. (6)

Sex-Ratio in India between 1901-2011
(Age : 0-6 years)

Year	*Sex-Ratio*	*Year*	*Sex-Ratio*
1901	972	1961	941
1911	964	1971	930
1921	955	1981	934
1931	950	1991	926
1941	945	2001	933
1951	946	2011	940

(i) What are the reasons for the declining sex ratio in India?

(ii) In your opinion what steps should be taken to deal the female infanticide? Explain with example.

(iii) What do you understand by gendered family?

34 "As late as the 19th century for example, it was considered good and proper that children start to work as soon as they were able to. Children were often helping their families at work from the age of five or six; the early factory system depended on the labor of children. It was during the 19th and early 20th centuries that ideas about childhood as a special stage of life gained influence."

What is the relevance of child labour in present Indian society? Which actions should be supported to stop the same? (6)

35 Discuss the revolutionary changes in 19th century Europe that led to the emergence of sociology. (6)

Answers

1 (a) objective, subjective

2 (c) A is true, but R is false.

3 (b) Community

4 (b) Both A and R are true, but R is not the correct explanation of A.

5 (b) Both A and R are true, but R is not the correct explanation of A.

6 (d) macroeconomic

7 (a) Both A and R are true and R is the correct explanation of A.

8 (a) Both A and R are true and R is the correct explanation of A.

9 (a) Both A and R are true and R is the correct explanation of A.

10 (c) I and III 11 (a) I and II 12 (c) I and III

13 (a) Social change is always deliberate and planned.

14 (b) They have immediate and long-lasting effects on society.

15 (c) Tylor focused on non-material aspects like beliefs and values, whereas Malinowski emphasised both material and non-material aspects of culture.

16 (a) He emphasised studying culture in isolation from communities.

17 Ghurye made original contribution to the study of Indian religions, beliefs and practices. He wrote six books viz Gods and Men (1962), Indian Sadhus (1953), Religious Consciousness (1965), Indian Acculturation, Vedic India (1979), The Legacy of Ramayana (1979). It is to certify the role in the society. Ghurye has delineated (trace the outline of) five foundations of culture that are religion, consciousness, justice, free pursuit of knowledge and toleration. He believed religious consciousness as a value that is manifested itself at the dawn of history.

18 The sociologists look at culture not as something that distinguishes individuals, but as a way of life in which all members of society participate. According to Edward Tylor, "The culture or civilisation taken in its wide ethnographic sense, is that complex whole which includes knowledge, belief, art, morals, law, custom and any other capabilities and habits acquired by man as a member of society." According to Bronislaw Malinowski, (founder of functional school), the culture comprises inherited artefacts, goods, technical process, ideas, habits and values. Leslie White had placed a comparable emphasis on culture as a means of adding meaning to objective reality, using the example of people regarding water from the particular source as holy.

19 Primary groups are important in several senses. They are equally important for individual as well as society. It helps in socialisation process and development of personal identity by learning and using culture. The primary group is so great that individuals cling to primary ideals in more complex associations and even create new primary groupings within formal organisations.

Or A secondary group increases efficiency of its members. To fulfill their self interest and specific goals all the members work efficiently. A formal authority is set up and a set of rules are formulated to manage and regulate the secondary group efficiently. These groups serve an instrumental function rather than an expressive one, meaning that their role is more goal- or task-oriented than emotional. One's fellow students or coworkers can be examples of a secondary group.

20 Endogamy is a form of segregation that helps groups or communities resist integrating or merging with other groups or cultures who do not share the same beliefs or resources. This type of practice can help smaller or minority cultures survive over a long period of time. But it may also led to some social evils such as caste practice, class domination, etc.

21 Social change and greater assertion of democratic rights by disadvantaged and discriminated groups make the conflicts visible in the society. It leads to disharmony among the various sections of the society and harm the 'Unity in Diversity' stance of India.

22 Sociologists measure religiosity by asking people about their religious beliefs, their membership in religious organisations, and attendance at religious services. It studies the functioning of the religion in society and its relationship with other Institutions in society. It uses comparative method to study religion because it brings all societies at one level with each other and helps to study without bias and prejudice.

23 The material dimension of culture includes any activity which is made possible by the means of materials which is said to be a part of the culture. For example, using internet as chatting, etc.

24 Yes, socialisation gives birth to individual freedom. In modern societies, one's biological gender no longer determines the functions that an individual can perform. It allows greater freedoms and opportunities to all people to explore the desired things.

25 A political institution is a system of politics and government. It is usually compared to the law system, economic system, cultural system and other social system. It is different from them and can be generally defined on a spectrum from left to right. On the other side, a political institution is concerned with the distribution of power in society on the basis of two concepts i.e. power and authority.

Or Following are the features of its society which changed after the advent of Industrial Revolution.

(i) Population of England shifted from rural areas to urban areas to work in industries.

(ii) Capitalism led to degradation of labour and loss of work from the protective contexts of guild, village and family.

26 In the pre-modern period, there were contrary and contesting understandings of society. For instance, Karl Marx understood society through class and conflicts. Whereas, social solidarity and collective conscience were the key terms for Emile Durkheim.

Or Patriarchal society by definition means a society controlled by men in which they use their power to their own advantage. An example of a patriarchy is when the family name comes from the man in the family. The dominance of men in social or cultural system. Some of the examples are discrimination against women, exclusion of women from decision-making, institutional discrimination against women, and the relegation of women to the domestic sphere.

FULLY SOLVED

27 Citizenship rights include civil, political and social rights. Civil rights involve the freedom of individuals to live where they choose, freedom to speech and religion, the right to own property and the right to equal justice before law. Political rights include the right to participate in elections and to stand for public office. In most countries, government were reluctant to admit the principle of universal franchise. For instance, women had to wait longer for the vote. As regards social rights, these concern the prerogative of every individual to enjoy a certain minimum standard of economic welfare and security. They include such rights as health benefits, unemployment allowance, setting of minimum level of wages. The broadening of social or welfare rights led to the welfare state, which was established in Western societies.

28 The term Capitalism refers to the economic system established just to make a maximum profit through trade and industry whereas the term colonialism refers to the establishing political control over the area or state in order to rule and exploit it economically. Thus, human tries to extend its political control to acquire one's territory with the mindset to generate wealth through trade and by exploiting its natural resources. Thus, Capitalism and Colonialism are linked to each other.

29 Weber argued that the overall objective of the social sciences was to develop an 'interpretive understanding of social action'. He believed that these sciences were very different from the natural sciences, which aimed to discover the objective 'laws of nature' governing the physical world. His view was that the methods of enquiry of social science also had to be different from the methods of natural science. 'Social action' included all human behaviour that was meaningful, i.e, action to which actors attached a meaning.

30 Identities are not inherited but fashioned both by the individual and the group through their relationship with others. The language becomes an identity for an individual. Therefore, language becomes another important aspects to understand culture. The social identity is to appreciate how language and culture are intricately interwined, mutually dependent and socially constructed. Recognisation and acknowledgment can often be done through the recognition of the particular language that is used among role players, like

(i) Students in schools have their own way of referring to their teacher, other students, class performances.

(ii) Women are known to create their own language and thought it their own private space beyond the control of men.

31 Durkheim defined a social fact as: "Those shared ways of acting, thinking and feeling which are capable of exercising external constraint on the individual, are generally diffused in society, and which have a life of their own." For Durkheim this 'subject' of sociology is the social fact, and that social facts must be regarded as 'things'. The main characteristics of social facts are (i) externality, (ii) constraint, (iii) independence, and (iv) generality. Social facts, according to Durkheim, exist outside individual consciences.

Or Identities are not inherited but fashioned both by the individual and the group through their relationship with others. The language becomes an identity for an individual. Therefore, language becomes another important aspects to understand culture. The social identity is to appreciate how language and culture are intricately interwined, mutually dependent and socially constructed. Recognisation and acknowledgment can often be done through the recognition of the particular language that is used among role players, like:

(i) Students in schools have their own way of referring to their teacher, other students, class performances.

(ii) Women are known to create their own language and thought it their own private space beyond the control of men.

32 Peer groups are friendship groups of children of a similar age. In some cultures particularly small traditional societies peer groups are formalised as age grades. Even without formal age grades, children over four or five usually spend a great deal of time in the company of friends of the same age. A forceful or physically strong child may to some extent try to dominate others.

Yet there is a greater amount of give and take compared to the dependence inherent in the family situation. Because of their power parents are able to enforce codes of conduct upon their children. In peer groups, by contrast a child discovers a different kind of interaction within which rules of behaviour can be tested out and explored. Peer relationships often remain important throughout a person's life.

Informal groups of people of similar ages at work and in other context usually of enduring importance in shaping individual's attitudes and behaviour.

33 (i) There are multiple trends in declining the sex ratio. Some of the factors are Pre Natal-Sex Determination, Patriarchal societies, Dowry, Extreme poverty, Son preference and Daughter aversion, Social attitude and perceptions, Lack of education and awareness etc.

(ii) By reducing the financial burden on families, the eradication of the dowry system could therefore potentially reduce the apparent preference of male children as well as female infanticide rates. Another way of decreasing female infanticide rates is by providing families with incentives to give birth to females.

(iii) Gendered family is a family in society which believe that the male child will support the parents in the old age and the female child will leave on marriage. Such family invest more in a male child.

34 The term 'child labour' is often defined as work that deprives children of their childhood, their potential and their dignity, and that is harmful to physical and mental development.some steps like educating people, social awareness, mass campaign about the ill effects can help prevent child labour. Talk to them about the impact of child labour on children's mental and physical health and how it can affect their future. Also, informing them about the laws and their penalties.

35 The revolutionary changes in 19th century Europe that led to the emergence of sociology are discussed below

(i) Sociology was born in 19th century Europe as a result of the revolutionary changes brought about by Enlightenment the French Revolution and the Industrial Revolution.

(ii) Medieval Europe was a feudal society. The church dominated all spheres of society including matters of state and the king was regarded to be divinely ordained to rule over his people as he deemed fit. Gradually, people began to question every aspect of life including the authority of the church and the monarchy.

(iii) This led to the Age of Enlightenment which laid great stress on reason and rationality. There was a growing conviction that the methods of natural sciences could be extended to study affairs of human society e.g., Poverty began to be seen not as a natural phenomenon but as a social problem caused by exploitation and human ignorance. Hence, poverty could be redressed and revolved.

(iv) Enlightenment values of intellectual and political freedom found expression in the French Revolution of 1789. The revolution popularised the notion that all individuals possessed the right to liberty, equality and fraternity. The revolution ended monarchy and ushered in democracy. The age of feudalism ended and the birth based privileges were abolished.

(v) The Industrial Revolution began with the advancement of science and technology. It brought in capitalism as industry became economically very important. Farmers left their holding to work in factories in the industrialcities of Britain. The features of society changed and the working class became important once again society was transformed as the new social order emerged.

(vi) People like Comte, Marx and Durkheim tried to make sense of these revolutionary changes and restore order to chaos. Their efforts helped the emergence of sociology as they believed that the scientific study of sociology would help in the reconstruction and reorganisation of a strong and healthy society.

SAMPLE QUESTION PAPER 2

A Highly Simulated Sample Question Paper for CBSE Class XI

(Unsolved)

SOCIOLOGY

General Instructions

- The question paper is divided into four sections.
- There are 35 questions in all. All questions are compulsory.
- Section A includes question No. 1-16. These are MCQ type questions. As per the question, there can be one answer.
- Section B includes questions 17-25. These are very short answer type questions carrying 2 marks each. Answer to each question should not exceed 30 words.
- Section C includes question No. 26-32. These are short answer type questions carrying 4 marks each. Answer to each question should not exceed 80 words.
- Section D includes question No. 33-35. They are long answer type questions carrying 6 marks each. Answer to each question should not exceed 200 words.

Time : 3 hours **Max. Marks : 80**

Section-A

1 .... makes an unusual but effective comparison to make the point. In any political or military conflict, it is of advantage to capture the information used by the intelligence organs of the opposing side. But this is so only because good intelligence consists of information free of bias. (1)

(a) MN Srinivas
(b) Peter Berger
(c) RK Lakshman
(d) Herbert Spencer

2 **Assertion** (A) Education is a life–long process, involving both formal and informal institutions of learning.

Reason (R) Both Primary and Secondary groups play a significant role in providing education and new skills to an individual. (1)

(a) Both A and R are true and R is the correct explanation of A.
(b) Both A and R are true, but R is not the correct explanation of A.
(c) A is true, but R is false.
(d) A is false, but R is true.

3 .... is such a general term that it can be and often is, used to refer to almost any kind of change not qualified by some other term, such as economic or political change. Sociologists have to work hard to limit this broad meaning in order to mark the term more specific and hence useful for social theory. (1)

(a) Social change (b) Political change
(c) Cultural change (d) Economic change

4 **Assertion** (A) Endogamy requires an individual to marry within a culturally defined group of which he or she is already a member.

Reason (R) Endogamy promotes casteism in Society. (1)

(a) Both A and R are true and R is the correct explanation of A.
(b) Both A and R are true, but R is not the correct explanation of A.
(c) A is true, but R is false.
(d) A is false, but R is true.

5 **Assertion** (A) The Industrial Revolution was based upon a new dynamic form of economic activity-capitalism.

Reason (R) Capitalism involved new attitudes and institutions. (1)

Codes

(a) Both A and R are true and R is the correct explanation of A.

(b) Both A and R are true, but R is not the correct explanation of A.

(c) A is true, but R is false.

(d) A is false, but R is true.

6 **Assertion** (A) Aggregates are simply collection of people who are in this same place at the same time, but share no definite connection will one another.

Reason (R) Passengers waiting at a railway station or airport or bus stop or a cinema audience are examples of aggregates. (1)

Codes

(a) Both A and R are true and R is the correct explanation of A.

(b) Both A and R are true, but R is not the correct explanation of A.

(c) A is true, but R is false.

(d) A is false, but R is true.

7 **Assertion (A)** Social reform movements changed the fate of women.

Reason (R) Women played a significant role in reform movement. (1)

(a) Both A and R are true, and R is the correct explanation of A.

(b) Both A and R are true, but R is not the correct explanation of A.

(c) A is true, but R is false.

(d) A is false, but R is true.

8 "Culture is the common understanding, which is learnt and developed through social interaction with others in society. A common understanding within a group demarcates it from others and gives it an identity. But cultures are never finished products. They are always changing and evolving."

Which of the following factors strengthens the culture of a particular group? (1)

(a) Unified purpose

(b) Belief

(c) Both (a) and (b)

(d) None of these

9 **Assertion** (A) In pre-modern forms of society most people worked in the field or cared for the livestock.

Reasoning (R) As there was a primitive society and lack of technology, people preferred subsistence farming. (1)

(a) Both A and R are true and R is the correct explanation of A.

(b) Both A and R are true, but R is not the correct explanation of A.

(c) A is true, but R is false.

(d) A is false, but R is true.

10 Which of the following statements is correct about political institutions? (1)

I. Power is the ability to enforce one's will, even against opposition.

II. Authority is a form of power that is institutionalised and considered legitimate.

III. Modern states are characterised by sovereignty, citizenship, and nationalism.

Codes

(a) I and II (b) II and III

(c) I and III (d) I, II and III

11 Which of the following statements is correct about caste and class systems? (1)

I. In caste systems, a person's status is determined by birth and is rigidly fixed.

II. In class systems, social hierarchy is based on achievement and is more open.

III. Urbanisation has completely eradicated caste discrimination in India.

Codes

(a) I and II (b) II and III

(c) I and III (d) I, II and III

12 Which of the following statements about family structures in India is correct? (1)

I. Joint families have been decreasing steadily in post-independent India.

II. Rising life expectancy has contributed to an increase in joint households.

III. Nuclear families have always existed, especially among poorer castes and classes in India.

Codes

(a) I and II (b) II and III

(c) I and III (d) I, II and III

Read the passage given below and answer the questions that follow.

Domination essentially refers to the power of an individual to exercise a certain degree of influence on another individual. This power works through egitimacy, which is the degree of acceptance involved in power relations. Legitimate power ensures conformity to existing norms and is often formalised in roles like those of police officers or judges. However, not all power is legitimate. Domination can be resisted, leading to contestation or outright defiance, challenging social norms and structures.

13 Which of the following is true about legitimacy in domination? (1)
(a) Legitimacy is irrelevant in power relations.
(b) Legitimacy always guarantees obedience in society.
(c) Legitimacy is the degree of acceptance that justifies power.
(d) Informal authority is always less significant than formal authority.

14 Contestation is best described as (1)
(a) following all social norms and rules.
(b) broad disagreement or protest against societal norms.
(c) an act of crime against the law.
(d) acceptance of domination without any resistance.

Read the passage given below and answer the questions that follow.

Culture has material and non-material aspects, each playing a crucial role in society. Material culture involves tangible objects like tools, technologies, and infrastructure. Non-material culture includes cognitive and normative dimensions, such as beliefs, values, and social norms. While material culture evolves rapidly, non-material aspects like values often take longer to adapt, creating a gap known as 'Culture Lag'. For instance, while mobile phones have advanced, societal norms regarding their use in public settings may lag. This interplay of material and non-material culture defines the pace of social and technological progress.

UNSOLVED

15 Which of the following best describes 'Culture Lag'? (1)
(a) The rapid advancement of material culture.
(b) The inability of non-material culture to adapt to technological changes.
(c) The conflict between cultural values and social norms.
(d) The evolution of tools and technologies in society.

16 Which of the following statements about material and non-material culture is correct? (1)
I. Material culture includes tangible objects like tools and technologies.
II. Non-material culture involves social norms, values, and beliefs.
III. Material culture adapts more slowly than non-material culture.
IV. Culture Lag is caused by the delayed adaptation of material culture.

Codes
(a) I and II
(b) I, II and III
(c) II, III and IV
(d) I, II and IV

Section B

17 What was the main feature of sociology in pre-modern period? (2)

18 Who was appointed as the head of a newly created department of Sociology at the Maharaja Sayajirao University at Baroda? (2)

19 What does Karl Marx mean by Ancient mode of production? (2)

Or "Economics is the study of production and distribution of goods and services. The classical economic approach dealt almost exclusively with the inter- relations of pure economic variables: the relations of price, demand and supply; money flows; output and input ratios, and the like. The focus of traditional economics has been on a narrow understanding of 'economic activity', namely the allocation of scarce goods and services within a society. Economists who are influenced by a political economy approach seek to understand economic activity in a broader framework of ownership of and relationship to means of production."

How economic activities influences social relation in broad?

20 "The Industrial Revolution was based upon a new, dynamic form of economic activity — capitalism. This system of capitalism became the driving force behind the growth of industrial manufacturing. Capitalism involved new attitudes and institutions. Entrepreneurs now engaged in the sustained, systematic pursuit of profit."

Based upon the given passage answer the following question.

How did the Industrial Revolution impact society? What changes were observed as a result? (2)

Or "Women's struggles have also been helped or hindred by other historical circumstances.

For example, during the Second World War, woman in Western countries started to work in factories doing jobs that they had never done before."

Based upon above passage, answer the following question.

Why women were forced to go out for work?

21 What do you mean by norm in Sociology? (2)

22 Give any two perceptions of any sociologists about the social groups. (2)

23 Why is culture said to be dynamic as a functioning unit? (2)

24 What do you understand by concept of a city? (2)

25 What do you understand by living tradition? (2)

Section C

26 Peer groups are extremely important agents of socialisation. Disuss. (4)

Or "Universal Adult Franchise brought about a major political change in India." Justify the statement.

27 Explain human intervention of nature and to what extent have human beings modified the natural environment. (4)

28 Discuss the different aspects of the term 'society'. How is it different from your common sense understanding? (4)

29 How the success of Industrial Revolution caused changes in social life of people universally? (4)

30 What were the philosophical views that went to the making of sociology? (4)

Or Define social control? Enlist different perspective about the concept and meaning of social control?

31 What do you understand by choice of method? (4)

32 Why social facts should be broken into problems? Explain with the view of Emile Durkheim. (4)

Section D

33 What are the main features of the theory of alienation? (6)

34 Darwin's ideas about organic evolution were a dominant influence on early sociological thought. Society was often compared with living organisms and efforts were made to trace its growth through stages comparable to those of organic life. This way of looking at society as a system of parts, each part playing a given function influenced the study of social institutions like the family or the school and structures such as stratification. We mentions this here because the intellectual ideas that went into the making of sociology have a direct bearing on how sociology studies empirical reality.

How did Darwin's ideas influence the sociologists in the beginning? What the social institutions mentioned in the passage that values of any societies? Why it is mentioned in the passage? (6)

35 What are political institutions? Also differentiation between power and authority. (6)

UNSOLVED

Answers

1 (b) Peter Berger

2 (b) Both A and R are true, but R is not the correct explanation of A.

3 (a) Social change

4 (b) Both A and R are true, but R is not the correct explanation of A.

5 (b) Both A and R are true, but R is not the correct explanation of A.

6 (a) Both A and R are true and R is the correct explanation of A.

7 (a) Both A and R are true and R is the correct explanation of A.

8 (c) Both (a) and (b)

9 (a) Both A and R are true and R is the correct explanation of A.

10 (d) I, II and III **11** (a) I and II **12** (b) II and III

13 (c) Legitimacy is the degree of acceptance that justifies power.

14 (b) broad disagreement or protest against societal norms.

15 (b) The inability of non-material culture to adapt to technological changes.

16 (d) I, II and IV

SAMPLE QUESTION PAPER 3

A Highly Simulated Sample Question Paper for CBSE Class XI

(Unsolved)

SOCIOLOGY

General Instructions

- The question paper is divided into four sections.
- There are 35 questions in all. All questions are compulsory.
- Section A includes question No. 1-16. These are MCQ type questions. As per the question, there can be one answer.
- Section B includes questions 17-25. These are very short answer type questions carrying 2 marks each. Answer to each question should not exceed 30 words.
- Section C includes question No. 26-32. These are short answer type questions carrying 4 marks each. Answer to each question should not exceed 80 words.
- Section D includes question No. 33-35. They are long answer type questions carrying 6 marks each. Answer to each question should not exceed 200 words.

Time : 3 hours **Max. Marks : 80**

Section-A

1 The social survey that was based on the belief that human phenomena can be classified and measured.Thinkers of the early modern era were convinced that progress in knowledge promised the solution to all social ills.......... , the French scholar (1789–1857), considered to be the founder of sociology, believed that sociology would contribute to the welfare of humanity. (1)

(a) C Wright Mills
(b) Peter Berger
(c) Auguste Comte
(d) RK Lakshman

2 **Assertion** (A) India is facing major issues of increasing population, poverty and unemployment.

Reason (R) Illiteracy restricts growth of nation. (1)

(a) Both A and R are true and R is the correct explanation of A.
(b) Both A and R are true, but R is not the correct explanation of A.
(c) A is true, but R is false.
(d) A is false, but R is true.

3 **Assertion** (A) Legitimacy implies conformity to existing norms of right, propriety and justice.

Reason (R) Legitimacy refers to the degree of acceptance that is involved in power relations. (1)

Codes

(a) Both A and R are true and R is the correct explanation of A.
(b) Both A and R are true, but R is not the correct explanation of A.
(c) A is true, but R is false.
(d) A is false, but R is true.

4 **Assertion** (A) Marx argued that human society had progressed through different stages. These were; primitive, communism, slavery, feudalism and capitalism.

Reason (R) Capitalism was the latest phase of human advancement, but Marx believed that it would give way to socialism. (1)

Codes

(a) Both A and R are true and R is the correct explanation of A.
(b) Both A and R are true, but R is not the correct explanation of A.
(c) A is true, but R is false.
(d) A is false, but R is true.

5 **Assertion** (A) A characteristic feature of modern societies is that individuals with similar goals come together voluntarily to from groups and associations.

Reason (R) Modern societies are oriented towards specific goals, they remain distinct from each other and do not seek to take over the entive life of its member. (1)

Codes

(a) Both A and R are true and R is the correct explanation of A.
(b) Both A and R are true, but R is not the correct explanation of A.
(c) A is true, but R is false.
(d) A is false, but R is true.

6 **Assertion** (A) Large women participation in agricultural activity leads to feminisation of agriculture.

Reason (R) Men tend to migrate from their villages in the search of better opportunities and employment. (1)

(a) Both A and R are true, and R is the correct explanation of A.
(b) Both A and R are true, but R is not the correct explanation of A.
(c) A is true, but R is false.
(d) A is false, but R is true.

7 "The French Revolution (1789) announced the arrival of political sovereignty at the level of individuals as well as nation-states. The Declaration of Human Rights asserted the equality of all citizens and questioned the legitimacy of privileges inherited by birth."

Which of the following changes were brought in the society with the emergence of French Revolution? (1)

(a) Civil rights restored
(b) Serfdom abolished
(c) Democracy established
(d) All of the above

8 The implementation of one's own cultural principles in judging the actions and beliefs of people from other cultures is known as .... (1)

(a) Cosmopolitan (b) Ethnocentrism
(c) Normative (d) None of these

9 **Assertion** (A) During the late 17th and 18th centuries, Western Europe saw the emergence of radically new ways of thinking about the world.

Reason (R) It was popularly referred as 'The Enlightenment' or Renaissance (1)

(a) Both A and R are true and R is the correct explanation of A.
(b) Both A and R are true, but R is not the correct explanation of A.
(c) A is true, but R is false.
(d) A is false, but R is true.

10 Which of the following statements is correct about primary and secondary social groups? (1)

I. Primary groups are small, intimate, and face-to-face associations where members feel a strong sense of belonging.
II. Secondary groups are goal-oriented and have formal, impersonal relationships.
III. Secondary groups are more person -oriented compared to primary groups.

Codes

(a) I and II (b) II and III
(c) I and III (d) I, II and III

11 Which of the following statements is correct about family forms in India? (1)

I. Nuclear families have always existed in India, especially among poorer castes and classes.
II. A.M. Shah observed that joint families have been decreasing in post-independent India.
III. Research indicates that joint families are increasing due to higher life expectancy.

Codes

(a) I and II (b) II and III
(c) I and III (d) I, II and III

12 Which of the following statements is correct about ethnocentrism? (1)

I. Ethnocentrism is judging the beliefs and behaviours of other cultures based on one's own cultural values.
II. Ethnocentrism promotes sharing and borrowing of cultural elements to enrich one's own culture.
III. Ethnocentrism often leads to a belief that one's culture is superior to others.

Codes

(a) I and II (b) I and III
(c) II and III (d) I, II and III

Read the passage given below and answer the questions that follow.

Universal suffrage refers to the right of all adults to vote in elections, a significant political change in

UNSOLVED

history. Earlier, voting was restricted to wealthy men or high-status groups, excluding women and the underprivileged. Over time, universal suffrage was achieved through struggles, making democracy a powerful norm. It redistributes power across social groups and compels governments to seek approval from people, creating significant societal changes.

13 Which of the following statements is false about universal suffrage? (1)

(a) It allows only wealthy men to vote in modern democracies.
(b) It was achieved through historical struggles for equality.
(c) It is a hallmark of modern democratic systems.
(d) It ensures governments are answerable to the people.

14 What is one major impact of universal suffrage on society? (1)

(a) It restricts the power of certain groups to participate in governance.
(b) It redistributes power across social groups and enhances equality.
(c) It prioritises the wealthiest groups in decision-making.
(d) It eliminates the need for democratic governance.

Read the passage given below and answer the questions that follow.

The introduction of modernity in Indian society, shaped by colonialism, had distinct effects compared to its Western counterpart. Colonial officials and scholars often portrayed Indian society inaccurately, seeing it as static and archaic. Industrialisation, promoted by the East India Company, disrupted traditional industries, particularly in sectors like cotton production. At the same time, Indian sociology developed as a discipline to counter the inaccurate comparisons drawn by Western scholars between Indian and Western societies.

15 Which of the following statements is correct? (1)

(a) Indian sociology entirely borrows its methods and concepts from Western sociology.
(b) Colonialism did not influence the growth of sociology in India.
(c) Indian sociology arose partly to counter the portrayal of Indian society as static by Western scholars.
(d) Industrialisation in India had the same effects as in the West.

UNSOLVED

16 Which of the following best explains the impact of industrialisation under the East India Company in India? (1)

I. Indian cotton industries faced bans and heavy taxation in England.
II. English cotton goods were heavily taxed when sold in India.
III. Industrialisation disrupted local industries, particularly cotton production in India.
IV. The East India Company sought to promote Indian traditional industries globally.

(a) I and III (b) II and IV
(c) I, II and III (d) I, III and IV

Section B

17 Why there is a need of terminology in sociology? (2)

18 State the knowledge which is based purely on the opinions of the individuals. (2)

19 What are the major causes of environment degradation? How can it impact the future generation in a long run? (2)

Or "Environmental management is, however, a very difficult task. Not enough is known about biophysical processes to predict and control them. In addition, human relations with the environment have become increasingly complex. With the spread of industrialisation, resource extraction has expanded and accelerated, affecting ecosystems in unprecedented ways."

Read the passage and show which solutions will you suggest to reduce the impact of industrialisation on environment?

20 "Ecology has been modified by human action. What appears to be a natural feature of the environment — aridity or flood proneness, for example, is often produced by human intervention."

Based upon above passage, answer the following question.

How is the unsustainable development caused by humans impact the society? (2)

Or The foundations of modern industry were laid by the Industrial Revolution, which began in Britain in the late 18th and early 19th centuries. It had two major aspects.